ART MUSIC IN THE AMERICAN SOCIETY

the condition of art music in the late twentieth century

by

Nicholas E. Tawa

The Scarecrow Press, Inc.
Metuchen, N.J., & London
1987

Library of Congress Cataloging-in-Publication Data

Tawa, Nicholas E.
   Art music in the American society.

   Bibliography: p.
   Includes index.
   1. Music--United States--20th century--History and
criticism.   2. Music and society.   I. Title.
ML200.5.T34 1987   780'.43'0973   86-31486
ISBN 0-8108-1976-7

CONTENTS

iii

PREFACE

This book is not about late 20th-century composers, nor about musical styles and compositions. I have dealt with these subjects in another book: <u>A Most Wondrous Babble: American Art Music in American Life, 1950-1985</u>. Here instead, I attempt to accomplish the far more difficult task of examining the relationships between the ideals of American democracy, the realities of late-20th-century American society, and the condition of art music. I mean by the term "art music," music of artistic intent, written by trained composers, and normally meant for performance in concerts or through musico-dramatic presentations.

Of paramount interest to me are the forces that shaped American society and the art-music scene after World War II-- the tensions produced by the emergence of the United States as one of the most powerful and affluent nations in the world, by the willingness to use power militaristically, by the faith in technological progress, and by the continuing adherence to an economic system characterized through private ownership and the maximizing of monetary profit.

After 1950, the United States increasingly harbored a footloose society with pluralistic values and a yen for the "good life." To help realize the possibility of the "good life" for everyone, young men and women from families that previously had slight hope of improving their condition were given the opportunity for higher education. Education became the gateway to better jobs, higher wages, and improved status.

The benefits of a higher standard of living spilled over into the arts. Private and governmental funds, ostensibly in the spirit of democracy, helped build arts centers, set up composers, musicologists, and musicians as educators, gave support to artistic endeavors, and introduced the public to culture beyond the popular. Yet, the effort, though a determinedly serious one, was often guided by people who did not consider all the ramifications of their actions. Little of lasting consequence resulted.

Extra-musical factors affected public taste. The strengthening of the star system and the exploitation of musical personalities for their popular appeal weakened the entire support structure of the art world. Talented young musicians found it more and more difficult to make a living in their profession. In addition, cultural leaders with narrow imaginations determined the policies of music associations. They limited the repertoire, leaving unperformed those works that had a small following, or were unknown, or might cause controversy. In short, they chose not to lead, especially where American music was concerned. The amount of native artistic compositions performed in the United States was a shockingly small percentage of the total music heard each year in America.

Further depressants to the full articulation of art music were the many educational administrators and intellectuals who felt that music was not a serious area of academic activity, nor one justifiable in relation to the needs of the American society and to the demands of diverse cultural groups within the confines of the United States, all of whose interests deserved equal attention. Even as musical offerings in higher education expanded, the nature of the teaching was modified to meet these demands.

The postwar period saw the growth of a mass-music entertainment industry, dedicated to creating a vast and uniform market for its goods and unresponsive to the desires of the art-music minority. Indeed, mass media sometimes pilloried its tastes as snobbish and outmoded. To sell as many copies of a book or recording as possible, to attract as many viewers for motion pictures and television as possible, to fill vast auditoriums with as many warm bodies as possible--these were major imperatives of prominent publishers, large record manufacturers, broadcasting systems, and music impresarios. It was fortunate that this push toward music of high profitability was counteracted by public and private funding for the arts and by the activities of cultural enterprises (many of them non-profit and subsidized with public and corporate grants) that were oriented toward art music. Among these enterprises were record companies and broadcasting stations.

From what has just been suggested and will be demonstrated, the ideals of cultural democracy may have been compromised by the limiting of choice, by the valuation of material improvement over qualitative improvement, and by the re-
lentless judgments of the marketplace. Yet, the ideals do
exist. They have made more than a few Americans aware of
the cultural deficiencies in their nation. And they provide
a yardstick to measure what the people of the United States
are becoming, against what they should be as a civilized society.

All of this said, it is sad to note that as the history
of art music lengthens, studies of its relation to human beings and societal concepts fail to increase. On the one hand,
the raw evidence that can add up to meaningful understanding
accumulates; on the other hand, too many scholars place narrow limits on what they will investigate and write about. As
a result, some of the most significant events that influence
the course of music are neglected. To scholars, for example,
music scores, composers' letters, and watermarks on music
paper are palpable truths. Concentration on such matters
may give them no broad insights but does assure accuracy
of reportage after careful investigation. The dangerous im-
precision attendant on too widely viewed a subject is avoided.
Honesty of sorts is preserved through painstaking analyses
of verifiable documents and a shunning of speculation.

Unfortunately, as is evident in several published oral
histories, by thus limiting one's scope and demoting other
testimony that is less concrete, one may reach no conclusions
at all or conclusions of slight import in comprehending the nature and function of American art music and the world in
which it must operate. Why not try to enter peoples' minds
and try to understand peoples' motivations? How does the
generality of American music lovers apprehend sound? What
do they, not the isolated musical modernists of the day, mean
by the term "music"? More music historians must take the
responsibility for making intelligible what actually has occurred
and is occurring in American music and why.

I know that any synthesis of possibly intractable facts
into a coherent whole, which is significant to the world beyond
the narrow circle of scholars, is an act fraught with peril.
But it is imperative to make the attempt in a United States
where the acceptance of art music remains at a low level. I

begin my narration knowing what perils lie ahead. Unavoidable deductions by inference and theorizing from conjectures will be necessities for a social historian like myself, who wants to extract meaning from his data. I beg indulgence for my temerity.

Chapter 1

MUSICAL CULTURE IN AMERICAN SOCIETY

American democracy has always existed both in the dimension of the ideal and of the actual, the latter often seeming to deny the precepts of the former. This opposition of concept and reality has given rise to the dramatic and often discordant activities that characterize America's most ambitious cultural efforts. The tug-of-war between what should be and what frequently is in the world of American art music and the effect of this contest on the quality of democratic culture form the subject of this study. The music-making in concert hall, recital chamber, and opera house, and on recordings, radio, and television--met with in the years after 1950--is the main concern; the relationship of this music-making to the interests and beliefs of American society, the main focus.

An essential premise of our democracy as applied to music stresses the idea that the greatest and ultimate control over cultural processes should pertain to the general music public, not to a dictator of musical taste, nor to an aristocracy presumed to be most gratified by, sensitive to, or fervent about aesthetic matters. Carried into practice, as will be seen, this premise can prove both bane and boon to art music in the United States.

From the democratic standpoint, composer and musician propose cultural agendas, through composition and performance; the listeners dispose of these subjects up for consideration by determining the particular level of acceptability of either the composition or the performance. Unless a powerful private patronage or a governmental one (contradicting the decision of the government's main constituency) intervenes, the unpleasing musical work disappears from the repertoire and the unpleasing musician finds nobody to support the performances.

Furthermore, as a corollary to the democratic premise

just stated, the citizenry entrusts composer and performer
to exercise the authority of artist and cultural representative
of their society so long as that authority, at least to some extent, responds to and presents in sublimated form those human values shared by significant segments of the music public. The public may view the composer who cultivates an exclusive creative vision and the performer who pursues an ec-
centric interpretation as unrepresentative and disfavored.
Unless championed by a well-fixed supporter resolved to dis-
regard the public will, the disfavored musician disappears
from sight.

Rule by the majority unfortunately carries the danger
of cultural conformity and tyranny over men and women with
divergent tastes. At least in theory, a significant counter-
poise balances this danger: the conviction that generosity
toward the preferences of minority groups distinguishes the
quality of a society's democracy. The liberty that a society
grants to express one's self in different ways and the special
care it takes regarding the fundamental right of every individual to realize his or her maximum potential as participator
in the cultural experience further distinguish a democracy.
Any abrogation of this freedom of expression and this right
of the individual diminishes the democratic impulse.

Crucial, therefore, for the proper operation of a democracy is the delicate adjustment of majority rule to accommodate
divergent interests. Majority preference today usually takes
the form of popular music suitable to the swift understanding
of the masses and having wide acceptance. The minority
preference we are committed to exploring takes the form of
art music, which may require a greater effort at understanding and will probably never have more than limited acceptance.

It is not being argued that all art music is necessarily
better than all popular music. Excellence and reprehensive-
ness are found in each camp. Each music arises from different premises and has a different function in the American society. What is being said is that in a country which acknowledges its diversity and believes in a system of checks and
balances, some allowance should be given to artistic expression that fails to have overwhelmingly widespread support.

Crucial also to the excellence of a democracy is the need
to offer every individual a vision transcending the limitations

imposed by social inequality and class distinctions, and the need to provide the possibility of achieving that vision, whether social, economic, or cultural. In short, the democratic individual should be allowed to know all the possibilities open in music, whether folk, popular, or artistic. While it is true, that compositions exhibiting superior quality can be found in each of the three categories, it unfortunately is also true that, of the three, art music is given the shortest shrift in the actual democratic process. In the latter part of the twentieth century it has been battered by the contending forces of know-nothingism, status-seeking, iconoclastic avant-gardism, mercenary professionalism, and, not least, an economic system which all too often rewards artistic talent and sustains artistic effort only reluctantly.

The divergence of art music from popular music began in earnest in the United States during the 1840s and 1850s. It was then that American writers first insisted on making distinctions between music intended for the educated and cultured elite and music intended for the masses. Compositions meant for the concert hall or opera house and for well-trained professional performers were seen as truly inhabiting a world completely separate from the one inhabited by the simpler songs and dances. Composer and publisher intended these songs and dances for performance before an indiscriminate public, by anybody with only modest musical training.[1]

For the remaining decades of the nineteenth century, art song, opera, string quartet, and symphony were the province of foreign-born musicians--whether composers, instrumentalists, or vocalists. They attracted audiences consisting largely of affluent and Europhile Americans and of European immigrants recently arrived in the United States. Nothing democratic or native seemed to attach to any of this music-making and music-attendance.

With rapid industrialization, wealth accumulated in the hands of the fortunate few and urban centers added millions of new inhabitants to the thousands that had been there before. The sponsorship of permanent performing-art groups, symphony orchestras and opera companies by private patrons became a reality. The expectation that a large body of urban music lovers would regularly come to listen grew. Musical establishments of high quality, like the Boston Symphony Orchestra, the Metropolitan Opera Company, and the Kneisel

String Quartet, were born. Individual supporters, who appeared both rich and culturally enlightened, assumed the responsibility for whatever deficits resulted from their operation. Local, state, and federal governments--in contradistinc-
tion to their European counterparts--took no interest in and
offered no financial assistance to any of these enterprises.
Nor was interest and assistance expected or wanted.

With the twentieth century came world wars and severe
economic depressions which destabilized society, weakened the
old certainties about the noblesse of the wellborn, well-bred,
and well-disposed, and diminished the wealth of quite a few
prominent cultural figures. At the same time orchestras and
opera companies became more and more expensive to maintain.
Soon, more than just a handful of patrons were required in
order to bear the burden of deficits. The Great Depression
of the thirties threatened to topple some of the most respected
performing ensembles. Attendance at musical events decreased.
Thousands of musicians, music teachers, and musical-instrument
craftsmen and women found themselves jobless. The outlook
for the continuation of art music in the United States grew
more and more dubious.

Appeals for contributions, however modest, from the
generality of music lovers increased. Often, the response was
gratifying, though rarely enough to meet needs. With the onset of the Roosevelt administration, all levels of government
were showing concern for the large number of unemployed
musicians, music teachers, and composers. At the same time
the notion grew that art music should somehow be democra-
tized and made the possession of the ordinary citizenry. Then
began the exciting experiment to provide employment for the
one, and musical education and performances, either gratis
or at a nominal price, for the other--the Federal Music Project. Success seemed assured. Thousands of performances a
month, which aired a great many contemporary American works,
became the norm. Countless men and women newly converted
to music flocked to concerts and musical-theater productions.
Composers felt wanted and needed; instrumentalists and singers no longer worried about economic survival; the audience
for art music, including that written by Americans, expanded
rapidly.

Regrettably, also increasing were the criticisms of right-
wing politicians and those who were prosaic-minded. They

heard a communist message in every musical note or found no
merit in any sort of high culture. Spokespeople for the established private musical organizations and for private music
teachers feared the competition from publicly supported musicians and music groups; they added their weight to the opposition. World War II began. The Federal government's
thoroughgoing effort to aid the arts perforce had to end.
The many federally supported performing groups had either
to convert into privately run associations or disband. American music's share of musical programming shrank. Those
Americans who were economically disadvantaged, culturally
inexperienced, and wavering between affection for or rejection of art music could no longer attend musical presentations
at affordable prices.[2] The tenuous tie of art music to the
larger American public was severed.

POSTWAR ATTITUDES TOWARD ARTISTIC MUSIC

In the years after World War II, the promising union of
composer, performer, and audience once fostered by the Roosevelt administration and by the democratic attitudes, which
caused each copartner in the art-music world to consider the
other's good, came apart. The United States again seemed a
battleground for conflicting and irreconcilable cultural interests. More and more composers refused to compromise their
art for what they saw as mere entertainment of an ignorant
society. Grants and university positions sheltered them from
the public that they repudiated. They became unreachable
strangers to the common run of people and communicated only
with themselves.

Most performers limited their repertoire, and most music
teachers educated their students, to a few old, well-tested,
and European compositions. Knowledge and curiosity about
the new or different in music was stifled. Music lovers, that
is to say those who could afford the price of entry to concerts
and opera productions, came to dislike most contemporary-
music offerings and sometimes seemed to value as much the
personalities of the instrumentalists and singers as the conservative music they preferred. No Federal agency was any
longer completely funding public performing groups, composer's workshops encouraging artist-listener dialogue, and teachers for the masses. Nor was any openness in repertoire fostered, including a more than token representation for American
compositions.

Oftentimes highly cultivated musicians felt as if an in-
sensitive and materialistic majority waited outside the environs
of the arts, whose will stood ready to submerge all culture
in what they saw as mediocrity. Artistic music, to its advocates, appeared particularly undervalued by American society
and without importance in people's lives. By no means infre-
quent was the sort of accusation made by a bitter pianist, in
a letter to Musical America. He wrote of how he had "struggled for years" to prevent his "talent from being buried completely." But nobody seemed to care. To him, the United
States stood for "anti-fine art, anti-intellectual, anti-sensory,
anti-body, anti-expressive from the very start." The country
was inhabited and ruled by "the culturally ignorant." The
pianist then quotes an Albert Einstein statement about America uttered in 1921, which he claims was still true: "The visual arts and music have little place in the life of the nation
as compared with Europe."[3]

The writer sounds hysterical. His words are laced with
exaggeration. Nevertheless, other instrumentalists, as well
as singers and composers, were making similar accusations.
Whatever money, private or public, was spent on the arts,
whatever efforts were made to win over a larger public,
seemed to avail nothing. As always had been true, only a
minority wanted to listen to any art music, and scarcely anybody paid attention to contemporary American works. Was
American society hopelessly inane or brutish, as these musicians claimed? Or was all art-music becoming passé? What
was the case for an America lacking or rejecting a high level
of cultural development?

What follows may seem somewhat one-sided and simplistic. However, it is intended to set forth a relative position
from which the question of high culture and its relation to
the American public may be considered, and also to prepare
the stage for the pages coming after.

From the 1950s on, members of the young professional
classes, from whom had come the new audiences for art music,
were busy leaving the cities and moving to suburbia. Nuclear middle-income families with weaker societal roots began
living in transient communities, where conspicuous consumption and the "good life" of television watching, club activities,
card playing, backyard entertaining around the swimming pool,
and other forms of "artificial togetherness" increasingly took

precedence over other ways of experiencing and thinking.[4]
Yet, this was only a part of the problem for music.

At the same time that cities were becoming only work
places for many suburbanites, women ceased to be home dwel-
lers and joined the work force by the millions. The threat
grew that fewer women, from whose ranks came the thousands
of willing workers for cultural causes, would have the leisure
time or energy to devote to the promotion of symphony and
opera. Furthermore, added many commentators, before the
movement for women's liberation, boredom, a yearning for
some distinction in their otherwise humdrum existence, and an
acceptance of the woman's role as the civilizing and gentling
sex, not personal conviction about or love for music, had motivated the volunteerism of women on cultural committees and
the attendance at cultural functions. This sort of motivation,
they claimed, was becoming a thing of the past.

Artistic music competed and attempted to survive in a
pluralistic society, where values were not only many and conflicting, but also often declared of equal worth. Some years
ago, for example, a sociologist, then teaching in the Boston
area, found it reasonable to assert that the then popular
"Ballad of the Green Berets" had equal merit with Aaron Copland's Third Symphony. His was not a solitary opinion. Indeed, Samuel Lipman, in Music After Modernism, claims a
growing preferment for popular culture was making deep in-
roads "on an increasingly disorganized and doubt-ridden elite."
Their offspring, "the privileged young," had a goal "of down-
ward mobility," of embracing "a pop culture based on musics
at once vulgar, temporary, and corrosive."[5]

The movement toward "a pop culture" may possibly be
true, but whether the music was always "vulgar, temporary,
and corrosive" is, of course, open to debate. What should
be noted, however, is the absolute cleavage between art and
popular that Lipman assumes, whether rightly or wrongly.

Political leaders and well-to-do Americans, according to
Edward Shils, gave the preponderant impression of indifference to works of "superior" culture, unless forced to consider
them for nonaesthetic reasons. As World War II receded in
the distance, self-interest and the craving for materialistic
acquisitions, not the common good, guided citizens from every
walk of life. "Why should my money go to the symphony, or

to the library, or to the public schools?" an irate insurance
salesman once asked me. "I'm bored with that music stuff.
I never use the library. And my kids go to parochial school."
Pointing to such thinking, the British philosopher Quentin
Skinner declared it to be a "dangerous privatization" of the
democratic ideals that threatened the total "cultural fabric"
of American society.[6]

    This privatization, in the form of self-fulfillment, states
Daniel Yankelovich, was an idea whose force grew in the sixties, seventies, and early eighties. It was sought in activities hitherto less explored by the majority--for example, the
pursuit of physical love free of inhibitions, the craving for
instant sensation and gratification, and the breaking away
from everything that stood in the way of self-regard, whether
marriage or any other sort of pledging of the individual to
other people and values.[7]

    The pictures painted by Shils, Skinner, and Yankelo-
vich is somewhat one-sided. To fill it out, one must also include the increased American largesse, public and private,
to education, the needy, and all of the arts. Nevertheless,
after all is said and done, art music is not always immediately
gratifying. Moreover, its understanding requires an ongoing
relationship between listener and musical works, in short a
degree of commitment; the more complex the idiom, the deeper
the commitment. Few people in the past had willingly made
such a commitment; few people in the present were making it.
Brought to mind is a comment of Frank Boaz, in Primitive
Art (1955), that though the enjoyment of artistic beauty exists in every society, it is always "intense among a few, slight
among the many."

    In America, despite the lip-service paid to the arts,
most men and women continued to consider them as luxuries,
occupying "unimportant positions ... in primary and secondary
educational programs," and maintaining "a relatively minor role
in a society dedicated to the deification of science and technology." Several attentive students of the native scene
reached this conclusion.[8]

    From the point-of-view of many Americans, writes Chris-
topher Small, music was an unessential commodity, the composer a mere producer of goods for others to consume. Inter-
mediaries had to promote, perform, and sell their products in

order to make their living. If an intermediary could make
no living from the composer's products, they were dropped.

The techniques of advertising and marketing were therefore relevant to the propagation of art music. Articles and
advertisements in newspapers and periodicals praised certain
works, often at the expense of rival works, all of which were
"vying for the attention of the public." Critics advised the
public on what works were worthy of attention, and the performers on what works should figure in their repertoires.

Continuing his discussion of music as a commodity,
Small states that for the listener, "all that is at risk is the
price of a concert ticket or an LP record, plus the outlay of
an evening, but for the would-be vendor an unfavorable critical verdict" could be economically devastating, since "music
is in the main a buyer's market."[9] This boded no good for
venturesome programming.

At any moment, the buyer could get out of the market.
The attendance at urban concerts and opera productions, to
be sure, often fluctuated. Television or high-fidelity recordings might keep large portions of the music public at home.
Young men and women gave convincing evidence of preferring
to listen to rock music. Moreover, parking problems, high
ticket prices, and unsafe streets deterred even the ardent
music lovers.

As the years went by, fewer newspapers existed and
fewer writers on music were employed to call attention to art
music. Seldom did advertisements of more than modest proportions alert the public to coming concerts. Editors reluctantly gave free space to cultural events, especially if no
prominent musicians or innovational presentations were involved.
Most of their readership, they decided, was little interested
in such matters.

To add to the difficulties of selling art music, its traditional audience had always contained a large portion of
ethnic-Americans, who had received their cultural bearings
in Europe. The dying out of this group prompted the concert-
manager Sol Hurok to state, in 1968: "Every day I look at
the obituaries, and every time I see a Russian or Jewish name,
I say there goes another customer."[10]

Men and women prominent in cultural affairs kept on warning that the world's concept of the United States included not only its military, economic, and political aspects, but also its cultural attitudes and achievements. If the world assessed the country as encouraging its commonest denominator in taste and life preferences, then it would perceive America as harboring a shallow civilization not worthy of any other nation's respect. As the Rockefeller Report on the future of the arts stressed, in 1965, the United States had emphasized progress in commerce and technology and forgotten "that in history's final analysis a nation would be judged by the quality of the civilization it achieved, not by its material well-being." Worrisome to the compilers of the Report was the conclusion that the people of the United States historically had little urge for art music and dance, believing instead that any profession of affection for these arts was effete and unessential, and making no contribution to the nation's health. The Report went on to state that the habit of liking and wanting these arts, now so slightly evidenced, had to be "based on a strong sense of need--and without a sense of urgent necessity on the part of people, the performing arts will always remain peripheral, exotic, and without any true significance."[11]

The arts, insisted some observers of American life, could not help but be affected by the social and cultural values demonstrating the changing attitudes of society. As Fred Schroeder saw it, after World War II American society began, as never before, to regard the works of high art as "fixed perfections" consignable to museums or to performing groups acting as museums [devoted almost exclusively to an unchanging repertoire drawn from the past]--separate from contemporary living, separate from the contemporary "marketplace." Americans dedicated to the marketplace, Schroeder continues, assumed the museum meant death and the marketplace meant life, despite the existence of those few others who assumed the museum meant art, and the market implied a dispensable commodity. Echoing Schroeder's duality of museum and marketplace, Jon Roush, a poet, warned of high culture's trend to self-aggrandizement and a separation leading to death. He wanted all the arts to leave the shelter of museums and enter the arena of the marketplace, to remain not isolated but a part of America's "processes and events."[12] A number of reputable painters and sculptors did engage in the arena of the marketplace. Unfortunately, it was something easier said than done for composers.

Were the arts demeaned by competing for acceptance in the marketplace, as so many American composers of art music maintained? Even more important, were the values contained in art compositions capable of being identified and appraised, whether by the majority, or even by that part of society comprising the general public for art music? No, came the reply of several critics. What they perceived as the postwar public's tendency towards standardization, timidity about new experiences, and drab sameness was giving the kiss of death to serious musical life.

On the other hand, Alvin Toffler, although recognizing the dangers inherent in the marketplace concept, thought the possibility fo antidotes to the public's conformity existed. When a person attended a concert or purchased a recording, the act could be considered as an expression of individuality, Toffler said, whether the preference was Baroque, Classical, Romantic, or recent experimental music. In the midst of chaos, uprootedness, and transiency, the individual's urge, thus expressed, toward cultural objects was not necessarily death-dealing but possibly life-giving. It seemed to buoy the inner self by imparting a sense of stability and order. The lovers of art did want their hunger for stimuli assuaged. They did seek engagement with a symbolism which affected the "psyche on multiple levels simultaneously.... It is the symbolic content of art that arouses those ineffable emotional states that almost nothing else seems able to produce." Seen from this standpoint, the marketplace tested all sorts of intangible artistic values contained in countless numbers of works, discarding those works least capable of arousing human response. People elevated and demanded the repeated experiencing of certain compositions, in part because they were the most efficacious in arousing human response and held the greatest meaning for the greatest number of listeners. Toffler therefore advised caution when assessing the reasons for standardization in leisure-area pursuits and cultural consumption. [13]

Composers, musicians, and music critics who persisted in seeing the worst in people, particularly those who professed a liking for art music, could leave art music still more isolated from American society (even though millions of men and women did attend performances and purchase recordings). The isolation was furthered by contemporary composers, especially the avant-gardists and their advocates, who persisted in a

possible fiction: that their refusal to conform to traditional
values and practices is a principal distinguishing feature
which separates them from the plebian public.

This assumption, although containing a grain of truth,
could also become self-fulfilling. Anger, not sympathy, might
quite understandably infuse the public at large. Intimidating
of audiences prevented the formation of coalitions to advance
what surely was a common cause. Insisting on the separation
of art from the greater community vitiated any ability to compete in the marketplace. In 1974, Harlan Hoffa expressed
concern about how the separation poisoned efforts at educating and winning over those who were different. "The art
world," he said, "is, in sociologists' terms, a micro-culture
embedded within the culture at large, dependent upon it in
some ways but also isolated and distinctive in many of its
values and behaviors. Political scientists would probably call
it an anarchy. Economists could call it underprivileged. And
historians might see it as an inevitable product of its own
traditions. To the artist, however, the art world is 'where
it's at'--disorderly, remote, and narrow though it may seem
to the outsider. Yet, those very qualities of the art world
which make it a special place for the artist also prevent it
from being an effective social or political force, even in its
own behalf."[14]

Although, beginning with the sixties, a limited amount
of governmental money commenced flowing to high culture's
composers and performing groups, Americans as a whole had
little to do with either. Different musics were associated in
many minds with class distinctions. The least affluent and
educated men and women and most youths, if they thought
about it at all, considered art music as barred to them, sis-
sified, or manifestations of snobbery.[15]

Members of the middle class, even when they liked art
music, were often aware of the special place artists reserved
for themselves and of the criticisms directed at them by intellectuals and aesthetes. They felt like outsiders allowed no
direct participation in aesthetic matters. Distrust of their
own personal aesthetic experiences was sometimes the result.
Some decided they had no business indulging in the arts. A
few feared something corrupting might ensue (here was a new
and paradoxical equation influencing middle-class thinking).
"Traditionally, the idea of art has had too many untoward

associations--with High Culture, with ... snob appeal, with
pleasure, wickedness, finesse," writes Leo Steinberg. "To
American minds, the word 'art' is the guilty root from which
derive 'artful,' 'arty,' and 'artificial.'"[16]

The average American could not help but hold to the
opinion that art music belonged to a limited group, one that
fostered social exclusivity. In part, owing to an aristocratic
origin, such music could scarcely take on democratic trap-
pings, writes Mel Scott. As illustration, he claims, at least
fifty percent of all the publicity given arts organizations appeared on the "society" pages of newspapers. In 1969, for
example, when the Texas Fine Arts Commission worried over
the narrow support given it, coming from the upper crust
and the economically privileged alone, it engaged the services of a public relations consultant. The consultant advised
the commission: "If you are really concerned with broadening
the audience of the arts or if you are concerned truly with
communicating what you really are to a broader segment of
the public, then that high society image, that mink coat image is very destructive to you."[17]

In all the ways just enumerated, cultural development
was inhibited, if not arrested. Art music was fortunate if it
could just hold its own. Scarcely any contemporary works,
however the momentary enthusiasm for one or two of them,
entered the permanent repertory. The same few compositions
from the past dominated concert and opera life. On occasion
a style or a composer, like minimalism and Philip Glass, won
a large cult following. Yet, the general audience continued
to listen primarily to its Beethoven, Brahms, and Tchaikovsky.
It remained, at best, stable in its membership, even as the
population of the United States increased. Thus, it was a
minority audience that could become more minor with each
passing day.

THE CULTURAL EXPLOSION

Not everyone agreed with the negativism about the relation of the American public to high culture. For a decade
or so after the conclusion of World War II, it was the conviction of several reporters on the cultural scene that the arts
were proving attractive to increasing numbers of Americans.
For example, at the end of the year 1960, Max Kaplan wrote,

in the Music Journal, of the emergence of a large middle-class
audience for music and a sizeable group of competent amateur
performers. Music making and listening, he said, were spread-
ing to communities and college campuses throughout the country. Community orchestras, combining amateur and professional players, numbered over a thousand. Women especially
were volunteering their services for every kind of artistic
enterprise. The public school's commitment to training students in intelligent listening and in participation in music ensembles was expanding rapidly. Truly, he stated, what he
and others were witnessing was an American cultural explosion.[18]

    Audiences no longer contained a preponderance of women
was an additional claim. More men, somewhere around fifty
percent of the total, now attended concerts. Also, the portion of the audience less than thirty five years of age was
growing rapidly, these writers stated. More money, shorter
working hours, and better education all contributed to the
burgeoning number of listeners. Regrettably, they also noted,
black Americans and bluecollar workers rarely entered symphony halls or opera houses. Most of the audiences were
white, middle class, and with at least some college education.[19]

    Seeking an all-encompassing reason for the increase in
attendance at museums, theaters, concert halls, and opera
houses, and for the increase in the purchase of books and
recordings, Alvin Toffler said he had discovered broad sec-
tors of the public shifting their attitude towards the arts,
owing to growing concern with the texture of life (thus contradicting the Lipman and Yankelovich views given earlier).
He said further that, after political leaders (including the
President and the Congress of the United States) were convinced the number of people drawn to the arts was increasing,
they sensed a mandate to begin funding artistic endeavors.[20]
(A culminating consequence of this altered political thinking
would be the National Foundation on the Arts and Humanities.)

    To observers like Toffler, Americans now found no
shame in openly asserting their love for music and painting.
The former repressive awe and mystery fencing off art from
ordinary men and women had gone. "Culture is now, for
many people, an altogether everyday affair, capable of yield-
ing intense joy, but no longer awesome. Perhaps something
has been lost in the process, some sense of the majesty of

accomplishment of truly great art. Yet this loss, if indeed
it has occurred, need not be permanent, and there are ample
reasons to be optimistic. We are busy freeing the arts in our
society from their dependence upon a tiny, cult-like following.
We are converting, as it were, from cult to culture."[21]

On the heels of the announcements of a cultural explosion came unfavorable criticisms to counter the glowing reports on the arts-addiction of the public. Statistics, the
contrarians insisted, were often inaccurate or deceptive.
Statistics gave no qualitative assessment of the new interest
in the arts. Reasons other than aesthetic pleasure had encouraged the growth of the arts-public. To some extent,
their argument could hold up. For example, on 27 July 1966,
a New York Times news item reported that a record in attendance had been set in a concert given in Central Park by the
New York Philharmonic Orchestra under Leonard Bernstein.
The figures cited ranged from 75,000 to 90,000, representing
a cross-section of the city: families, students, babies, representatives of every ethnic strain.[22] Not clear, however, was
to what extent the large turnout was owing to the beautiful
weather, a chance to enjoy the outdoors at minimum expense,
the liquid refreshments offered, and, most of all, the great
popular esteem accorded to the personality of Bernstein.

Evaluating the increase in concert attendance around
1960, Marya Mannes concluded that the practice of cultural
democracy, and the bringing of music to the millions necessitated some trivializing of high culture. Exposure did not
mean acceptance, she warned. Quantitative evaluations were
profoundly untrustworthy. If millions of people watched a
concert or opera performance on television, she gives as an
instance, how many of them really paid attention; how many
conversed; how many slept? When the American Symphony
Orchestra League estimated that around three and a half million people regularly attended concerts, how many of them
went as "a civic duty," or "to lose themselves in vague emotions?" She knew people who attended concerts every week
and said they loved music, but they could not tell Bach from
Haydn.[23]

We must, however, keep in mind that any measurement
of an aesthetic experience is fraught with subjective predilec-
tions and distortions of judgment. Cultural democracy does
not of necessity bring on the trivialization that Mannes

assumes. To raise the question about home listening and
concert attendance proves nothing. And one cannot univer-
salize from one or two examples of people who attended concerts. Moreover, what precisely is meant by people who
"could not tell Bach from Haydn"?

Warnings also came designating what was taking place
as anything but an explosion in culture. A Gallup Poll taken
in 1962 showed only fourteen million people, or 7.5 percent of
the population, had attended one or more concerts during the
previous twelve months. William Baumol and William Bowen,
economists who gave the arts world of the sixties a thorough
going-over, insisted the cultural explosion was more "media
hype" than anything else. After carefully studying the evidence, they found only "a modest expansion in performing art
activity, one which, though by no means negligible, is far
from universal and can hardly be called a cultural explosion."
Another commentator stated that the explosion was only wish-
ful thinking on the part of some people interested in shoring
up serious music. For every person who enjoyed art music,
"there are several hundred who have never even heard the
names of Sutherland, Serkin or Szell--not necessarily illiterate
day-laborers or farm folk from the backwoods districts, but
many of them college graduates regarded as highly cultured
members of metropolitan communities."[24]

While all of the above may be true, not considered were
the millions who purchased recordings for private listening
and felt no need (or had little opportunity) to attend concerts. In addition, Baumol and Bowen apparently did not
consider the crowds involved with community, college, and
amateur music making, both as performers and listeners.

Unfortunately, most musical performances by professionals had to charge an entry fee sufficiently high to exclude
the poor and dissuade the borderline music lover. Since musical enterprises were labor intensive, frequently operated
with less than proper financial management, and were bur-
dened by a star system necessitating the payment of excessive fees to admired conductors and soloists, prices for admission continued rising. Not merely the poor, but also the
lower end of the middle class gradually was affected. Whatever cultural expansion there was might soon find itself
checked or in recession.

As early as 1965, some writers warned of a direction
away from the concert hall. By the beginning of the seventies, they were declaring rising ticket prices to be a serious
problem. At the start of the eighties, Beverly Sills spoke
for most directors of artistic activities when she worried over
the fate of the New York City Opera: "A continual rise in
prices may destroy the art form. We need a big base of new
subscribers now, and we have to attract young people."[25]
How to get them to come with ticket prices what they are
seemed an unsolvable problem without massive governmental
intervention.

In 1983 and 1984, surveys published by the American
Symphony Orchestra League showed concert attendance drop-
ping more and more. Such a shrinkage, however, had been
going on for a while. By the end of the sixties, an increasing number of writers were finding the cultural explosion,
however large it might have been, ended. A major shrinkage
in the size of music audiences was taking place throughout
the country. In 1969, to give one instance, New York City's
concert attendance had dropped at least ten percent lower than
that of 1967.

One writer, Philip Hart, grew disgusted at the indifference of music managers to investigating the reasons why people did or did not attend musical performances. Guessing
took the place of certainty regarding every aspect of musical
life. Nothing was really known about the "symphonic nonaudience, what it consists of, what it wants, or how in practical
terms it can be attracted," he said.

He singled out a failing of considerable moment to the
survival of art music: "One can attend countless meetings
of symphony management, at ASOL [American Symphony Orchestra League] conferences or elsewhere, and hear the same
tired talk of audience building--special promotions, ethnic
programming, popularization of repertory, employment of Madison Avenue techniques--without hearing one comment that
concerns itself either with hard facts about the nonaudience
or with any understanding of the psychological process involved in artistic communication. Such failure would still be
deplorable if symphony audiences were keeping pace with population growth; it becomes critical when there is good reason
to believe they are not."[26]

Also unthought-out was the continuing impulse toward
the building of arts centers. By the early sixties, an aston-
ishing number of them were either constructed or planned.
Thus, the perceived cultural explosion was concurrent with
a proliferation of new and rehabilitated edifices to house
music, dance, and dramatic performing groups, epitomized
in the building of the Lincoln Center, in New York City.

In 1954, Robert Moses had decided to set aside fourteen acres of land, part of the West Side urban renewal area,
for a possible arts complex. The Metropolitan Opera Association soon became interested. John D. Rockefeller, the 3rd,
then chaired a committee to make a feasibility study. Corporate heads, community leaders, and other influential people
put pressure on the state and federal governments to provide
funds in order to help realize the project. When, in 1959,
the tearing down of Carnegie Hall seemed imminent, the New
York Philharmonic Society also stated its interest in relocating
at the site. Construction began in 1959; Avery Fisher Hall,
the first building, stood complete in 1962. The entire Center
was in place by 1969. Among the groups housed in the complex were the Philharmonic Orchestra, the Metropolitan Opera,
the New York City Opera, the Juilliard School, and the New
York City Ballet.[27]

Within ten years after the completion of Avery Fisher
Hall, other ambitious arts centers opened their doors. To
give two instances, in 1966, the Saratoga Performing Arts
Center commenced functioning as the summer residence of the
Philadelphia Orchestra and the New York City Ballet. Five
years later, the Kennedy Center for the Performing Arts began its first season in Washington, D.C., principally as the
temporary home of visiting performing groups.

The year 1962 was nominated as "the great watershed
year" for the arts by Milton Goldin, in The Music Merchants.
Not only did the Philharmonic Orchestra move into its new
quarters at Lincoln Center, but also the Ford Foundation
started up its ambitious arts-funding program, and President
John F. Kennedy carried into action the cultural phase of his
New Frontier, with the appointment of August Heckscher to
coordinate the government's cultural exertions.

These happenings activated a rapid expansion in the
construction of cultural edifices in various communities and

on university campuses outside of the New York City metrop-
olis. Music lovers, "accustomed to performances in high school
auditoriums," felt "overwhelmed" by the alterations in the arts
landscape. "By June 1962, some form of building connected
with the arts was planned or underway in sixty-nine cities,
involving $375 million of public and private funds. Arts cen-
ters ranged from Lincoln Center to a $10,000 building in Key
West. Arts centers were created in an old canning factory
in Yakima, a pumping station in Statesville, North Carolina,
and a city jail in Tacoma. Thirteen states either set up arts
councils or planned to establish them." Goldin then sounds
an ominous note when he states that the expenditures for arts
centers were occasioned as much for the providing of jobs as
for the encouragement of cultural activities.[28]

Quickly, some of the building committees' lack of planning for using the centers and their lack of strong commitment to the arts grew apparent. The year after the opening
of Avery Fisher Hall, Winthrop Sargeant expressed his alarm
at the absence of forethought about what was to be done inside the many centers being built. He feared the demise of
their arts function and the conversion of the centers into
skating rinks, bowling alleys, and "rock palaces."[29]

Fashion seemed the motivating force behind a great deal
of the new construction. Widely accepted was the concept
that any urban area worthy of being considered as possessing
an urbane and advanced state of cultural development had to
have a center of some sort. Whether a clear need existed for
such an addition was not always investigated. How to cope
with the yearly deficits that invariably accompanied ambitious
and expensive arts presentations, like grand opera and ballet,
formed no part of the planning.

"All this compulsive construction," wrote Herbert Hecsh,
"would seem to have a good bit more to do with the pompous,
ego-puffing business of committees, socialite fund drives with
their attendant, splendid parties, and a brass plaque on the
back of a seat. It doesn't seem to have much to do with the
arts." Many of the edifices were used perhaps four or five
times a year, and some had no staff to keep them operating.
Of three centers within a hundred miles of New York City,
one of them, costing eight-million dollars, opened to a symphony concert, then remained unused "except for a few tes-
timonial dinners and the like." A second, just completed,

had no resident companies and only four performances were
projected in the first year.[30]

In the late sixties, an increasing number of people
saw arts centers as less valuable than they had previously
thought. R. Philips Hanes, Jr., President of the National
Arts Councils of America, commented that most civic leaders
wanted to build centers, but none were aware that they had
to fill them with quality productions or else face failure. Significantly, Hanes admitted: "I don't know anything about
opera," but he felt it a civic responsibility to advance high
culture in his state (he was from Winston-Salem, North Carolina). However, he was now realizing that getting people interested in cultural matters was a problem. Especially when
prices to events went up to cover deficits, arts centers sold
less and less tickets.[31]

"Quality" productions, regrettably, did not insure success. For example, Roger L. Stevens, board chairman of the
Kennedy Center for the Performing Arts, reported a loss of
$1,878,000 for the 1983-1984 fiscal year, even though private
subsidies totalling $1,700,000 came in to help support quality
productions. A two-week engagement of the Metropolitan
Opera had ended with a million-dollar deficit. Other big
losers were the New York City Ballet, and the production of
two operas by Leonard Bernstein, Trouble in Tahiti and A
Quiet Place. No federal assistance for its productions had
reached the center. The drive for increased private support
was not achieving its aim. People were resisting higher ticket
prices and waiting for favorable reviews before attending anything at all. Thus solitary or brief engagements (the usual
state of affairs for music) had only tiny audiences and longer
engagements remained underattended until newspaper critics
showed enthusiasm. As a result, the Kennedy Center could
no longer take chances on new or costly productions. In the
future, "safe hits" and "big names" would influence the
scheduling.[32] In short, the hope had been that the arts
would mostly pay for themselves. They weren't doing so.

Soon after the Garden State Arts Center was completed,
in Holmdel, New Jersey, the advocates of art music complained
of discrimination against them. This center, for example, allowed the New Jersey Symphony only five concerts there,
though the orchestra wanted more, and the concerts were
widely separated, not concentrated within a brief period, as

requested. A speaker for the Symphony said that confirmation of even the five dates took so long to come through (July
dates confirmed in late March), that the director was unable
to engage soloists for the concerts. He accused the center
of giving precedence to the scheduling of pop groups.

John P. Gallagher, chairman of the New Jersey High-
way Authority, which ran the center, rebutted: "We lose
money on the New Jersey Symphony. The orchestra receives
$9,300 a performance and soloists are extra. Our daily over-
head runs up to $8,000, so the net tops $17,000. Receipts
at a typical New Jersey Symphony performance are $10,000
to $12,000. We can absorb the deficit, but we can't have too
much of a loss, and that has to be offset by profit from more
popular programs. Some of these have drawn up to $33,000
a performance. Besides, the bulk of the audiences seem to
prefer them [!]." Gallagher said his main obligation was not
to high culture but "to the people of the whole state;" he
gave them what they wanted. A Symphony official replied:
if the programming was to be geared to popular and money-
making events, then why call it an arts center?[33] An argument could be made in support of each side of the equation.

Evidence of arts centers doing as much harm as good
to the arts accumulated. Too many social leaders prominent
in the erection of these structures held a hodgepodge of cultural values. They displayed indifference or ignorance about
what constituted imaginative programming and about how to
cope with shortfalls in receipts. "From an economic standpoint," states Milton Goldin, "the results were often ludicrous.
Businessmen promised that inherently money-losing institutions
would henceforth not be run by strict box-office principles;
then they interfered in choices of artists and repertory to
insure maximum income at the box office."[34]

Twenty years after Avery Fisher Hall opened its doors,
around 2,000 arts centers existed, according to an estimate
made public by the National Endowment for the Arts. Looking
at thier positive side, many centers did provide adequate
housing, frequently for the first time, for arts programs,
whether presented by local or touring ensembles, and did
provide Americans with easier access to high culture. De-
centralization resulted; New York City and other large cities
no longer concentrated most artistic activities within their
boundaries. Performers, composers, and writers on music

might be found in scattered communities and university campuses, at all points of the compass. Certainly all of this acted to the benefit of art music.

The music soloist, ensemble, and composer "in residence" began settling in what were once "the provinces," in part encouraged to do so because the centers created a demand for their services. Restaurants, book and music stores, galleries, art-music houses, and upgraded housing clustered around the successful centers. Large municipal centers, like Minneapolis's Walker Arts Center and New Orleans's Contemporary Arts Center, tended toward conservativism and relied on the tried and true, said Harold C. Schonberg, in 1983. But university centers, like the Hopkins Center at Dartmouth, the Iowa Center at the University of Iowa, and the Krannert Center at the University of Illinois, because they worried less about deficits, did air new, experimental, and untested examples of art music and did give exposure to lesser known professional musicians.[35]

When planners thoroughly explored and acted upon the cultural needs of a community, a university, or both together, when knowledgeable and concerned people carefully designed the center to accommodate these needs, and when public or private sources provided funds on an ongoing basis to moderate prices and meet deficits, then the arts center did truly contribute to the enrichment of community life.

Unforeseen events of the seventies helped squelch the ebullience of the fifties and sixties that sparked audience growth and motivated the push toward erecting arts centers. The prolonged effects of the Vietnam War, continuing social and racial turmoil, the oil embargo, the realization that the economy of the United States no longer had the natural resources or the entrepreneurial talents of former years to sustain it, inflation, national deficits, and rising interest rates had their effect in limiting the financial means, and dampening the curiosity and enthusiasm necessary, for cultural expansion.

That general interest in the arts increased during the fifties and sixties seems obvious. That growing public attention to, and liberal expenditures on, arts projects took place is not debatable. Add to these the strengthening of arts education and sales of art-music recordings, and one must conclude some sort of cultural explosion did indeed take place.

IDENTIFYING THE AUDIENCE

Most commentaries by writers on the composition of the audience for art music consist of surmises based on personal observation, therefore limited to specific locales; or they are bare, unsupported statements. Earlier, a complaint of Philip Hart was mentioned on the lack of research by symphony managers into the makeup of their audience. The same complaint could be levied against newspaper writers on music, who freely opined about the music public without divulging the basis for their remarks, or, at best, with the backing of rickety evidence.

Just before the century's midpoint, Howard Taubman, critic of the New York Times, said that an important segment of the audience consisted of musical and social snobs who would appear only at those concerts currently in fashion and approved by the "best circles." They attended not so much to enjoy the music as to see and be seen. Fortunately, the great majority of the audience came to hear the music. Some were experienced listeners who carefully selected programs and performers. Others were uninitiated listeners, unable to discriminate between various compositions, and attracted by big names, whether they were really worth listening to or not. On the whole, Taubman concluded, listeners were the same the world over. Usually, they loved the big names, were taken in by clever advertising, and were otherwise cautious and conservative.[36] Many critics, writing in every decade of the twentieth century, have made similar comments.

However, other reasons for attending concerts are not mentioned. Moreover, the comments if applicable at all, apply mainly to attendees in the larger cities. What of the men, women, and children who crowded into the auditorium of their local high school to cheer on a town's civic symphony, whose program was not bolstered by the commendations of the "best circles," and whose conductor and concerto soloists were not prominent in the music world? Pride in a community's cultural achievement and in a family member or friend playing in the ensemble offer only a partial answer.

A little over thirty years after the Taubman observation, another critic of the New York Times, John Rockwell, also wrote about the audience. Symphony-goers, he said, were mostly middle-class and white, with some admixture of

large. Assuming that concert attenders also were included
in the media audience, then the total figure comes to around
18 million adults.

When totaling up the number of Americans involved with
art music, one further consideration should be set forth.
Most Americans have heard and will continue to hear art music in connection with important national events, commemora-
tions, deaths, and celebrations or ceremonies of moment in
any area of the country. The music of European composers
like Handel, Bach, Haydn, and Beethoven, and that of American composers like Billings, Ives, Copland, and Barber, have
marked such noteworthy happenings. In at least this technical
sense, all inhabitants of the United States form an audience
for art music.

When describing the Americans who actually attend concerts and opera performances, some writers have given attention to the difference between subscription and non-subscription
audiences, occasionally critical of the former and laudatory of
the latter. A neutral Edward Shils, in 1971, summed up both
audiences as consisting of people having occupations requiring
intellectual preparation and practising higher intellectual skills:
university teachers and students, scientists, writers, artists,
secondary-school teachers, lawyers, medical doctors, the
clergy, etc. Yet, in contrast to other Western countries,
Shils says, the political elite in the United States showed the
greatest indifference to "works of superior culture" and was
"definitely unintellectual in the impression it" gave. Moreover, representatives of big business, even those who were
patrons of the arts, also as individuals exhibited a "dominant
indifference and inhospitality" to the arts.[41] General agreement with Shils's conclusions exists amongst observers of the
arts scene.

An objective statement of the differences between subscription and non-subscription audiences was attempted by
David Cwi, after studying the data on audiences, which had
been collected by 44 performing groups during 1978-1979.
Cwi starts by making observations similar to those made by
Shils. Then he goes on to say that more than half of the
subscription audience was over 45 years of age; more of the
single-ticket buyers under 35 years of age. At least 40 percent of the subscribers had graduate and professional degrees,
while less than 30 percent of the single-ticket buyers did.

Not surprisingly, subscribers tended to be wealthier than the single-ticket buyers. [42]

A lack of objectivity affected Harris Green, music critic of Commonwealth, when he wrote about subscription audiences (he had the audiences of New York City particularly in mind). Subscription audiences, he said, were a curse and had to go. Subscribers showed up at concerts out of habit alone, not to listen. They mainly consisted of imbecile women who prattled, "hissed," and "croaked" their way through every musical performance, interrupting every piece save the last with premature applause, and the last with a dash for the exits before it was over. An even more abominable audience attended performances of the New York City Opera, Green said. "The City Opera pulls in a mob that either wonders out loud what in God's name is going on or exclaims about what a bargain it all is, when not relaying orders for candy or gum down the row to the relative serving as quartermaster for that performance. Being a cheaper house [than the Metropolitan], it attracts whole families." As for the New York Philharmonic, it boasted "the usual gabbers, gluttons, and deserters." On the whole, Green found the single-ticket buyers to be more serious about their music and anxious to hush up the noisy subscribers. [How Green could tell the difference between subscriber and non-subscriber in the auditorium is not revealed.] He suggested that agencies granting federal subsidies to music groups require that recipients banish all subscription sales. [43]

To this incredible suggestion Norman Singer, general administrator of New York's City Center, reacted in a letter to the New York Times, which denounced Green as "snobbish and supercilious toward our audiences." All performing groups, Singer said, were fortunate to have on-going audiences, or else they would have gone under a long time ago. Subscriptions were the life blood of art music and not to be taken lightly. They freed music programmers to plan a more adventurous season than otherwise would have been possible. As for the non-subscribing public, it could be fickle and capricious in its ticket-buying habits. When tickets over and beyond those needed for subscribers were put on sale, this public did not readily buy them up. Both Singer and others responding to Green's remarks with letters to the Times asserted that non-subscribers were the noise makers, contrary to what Green claimed. [44]

On the other hand, Richard Barri, director of the Opera Theater of New York (who had his own bone to pick with the more established opera associations), agreed with Green about the subscription audience, but for different reasons. He said that though some producers of opera sense no cause for alarm if their subscription list is large, they forget that this audience "is largely a closed circle of fans of certain operas or certain stars, connoisseurs who deplore the slightest variation from what they think is the time honored custom or authenticity, the socialite and publicity seeker, the peripatetic patron of the arts who wants to be in the charmed inner circle, and of course," so Barri claimed, "the real estate interests to whose great financial interest it is to build ... opera houses." None of these, Barri maintained, represented "the real public," and invariably they opposed anything new or different. [45]

While it is true that the average opera devotee tends to be conservative in taste, disliking most operatic music composed in any of the twentieth-century post-tertian styles, much of what Barri asserts is subjective, smacks of scurrility, and seems motivated by personal frustrations in art-music production.

Symphony subscribers have not escaped adverse criticism, either. George Solti, music director of the Chicago Symphony, has admitted an enthusiasm for non-subscription audiences and chariness about subscription audiences. The former, he states, buy tickets because they want to go to a concert; the latter buy tickets beforehand and have to go. The former receive music more warmly and give generous applause; the latter, he regretted to say, however lukewarm their reception of music, are necessary for financial security. Since, presumably, there are no all-subscription or all-non-subscription concerts, his conclusion lacks reliability. The best of the sucribers, Solti also asserts, are those who attend on Saturday evening, well rested, facing a relaxing Sunday, and free to enjoy musical compositions. The worst are those attending on Thursday nights, who come straight from work or after rushing home to change their clothes. They are tired, present because they have to be there, and capable of feeling nothing at all. As for the Friday afternoon subscribers, historically they are rich, old ladies, who applaud daintily and leave before the concert is over in order to have tea or catch a train.[46] Certainly Solti's is an unflattering picture of most of the attenders of the Chicago Symphony's concerts. Unexplained is why so many continue to subscribe, if they care so little for the musical experience.

Harry Ellis Dickson describes Boston Symphony Orchestra subscribers similarly. Friday afternoon seats, he writes, have been held for years by the same family. Many of their occupants, usually women, habitually leave before the last piece is over, however brief the concert. The audience is quite sedate, often applauding so weakly that it ends before the conductor or soloist gets off the stage. Saturday night attenders are more "earthy," "outspoken," and "bourgeois." They dislike modern dissonant music and tell the musicians so. He says in conclusion: "Our most vital, live, and swinging audience is our informal, 'open rehearsal' audience," consisting of a lot of young bright people.[47]

Like Solti's statement, that of Dickson must be questioned. I have been a part of this open-rehearsal audience for years and have seen little evidence of this vitality and "swingingness." Indeed, I have seen numbers of senior citizens brought in by the busload and met many novitiate attendees with negligible musical sophistication.

The writings about audiences came out mostly in the late sixties and early seventies. In the eighties, change was taking place. Friday afternoons had less of the "old lady" types in attendance, more of the young--even Solti admitted that this change was occurring. Saturday evenings have had an increasingly disloyal group of subscribers, one year's subscribers not necessarily those of the previous year--Dickson admitted to this. As for Thursday night, less and less people subscribed. Theoretically, it should make Solti and Dickson happy, because more of the enthusiastic single-ticket buyers would find it possible to attend. Unfortunately, as a Boston Symphony Orchestra official told me, in 1984, it has caused worry, not jubilation, for non-subscribers have not rushed forward to make up the difference. The subscriber would therefore seem to be the golden goose that musicians and music critics are in haste to kill.

THE PROBLEMATICAL MUSIC PUBLIC

When times are uncertain and stability is imperiled, even

a society strongly oriented towards democracy tends to will
some part of its power to figures of authority who can command attention, clarify attitudes and behavior, and enhance
orderliness. When the same uncertainty holds true in any
dimension of one's personal life, the same tendency comes to
the fore. Quite a few members of the general music public
have experienced a plethora of uncertainty and instability in
matters of taste and in their capacity to discern the difference
between excellence and mediocrity in musical compositions and
performers.

Given the modicum of arts education and the recently
acquired inclination to art music on the part of many concertgoers, the criticisms accusing them of Babbittry, the miasma
of conflicting twentieth-century aesthetic views about music's
meaning, the lack of an American tradition of listening to art
music, and the endless contemporary innovations in musical
styles from regimented serialism to anarchistic Cagianism, the
audience yearns for reassurance and guidance in its pursuit
of the listening experience. At the same time, it has an ever
present propensity to put on pedestals its artistic heroes,
usually a charismatic two or three musicians elevated, sometimes for no strong reason, from the generality of operatic
soloists, instrumental virtuosic soloists, and orchestral conductors.

Herein lies the heart of the problem, whose lack of
resolution could help fossilize art music. Quite a few members
of the music public, though they may take pleasure in their
musical experiences, also seize upon a number of means to
stabilize their felt insecurity: the guaranteed masterpiece,
the idolized soloist or conductor, the ruling newspaper reviewer, and the edifices memorializing continuity from an
ordered past, to a steadfast present, to a confirmable future:
the arts center, opera house, and symphony hall. Each of
these legitimized authority symbols, which so many music lovers have voluntarily accepted as secure beacons in art music,
has force only as long as listeners believe in their efficacy
to heighten the musical experience in its entireness. [48]

When a newspaper reviewer, for example, fails to report
on a concert, that concert has not existed for most music lovers. As Richard Schickel once pointed out: "There is a
basic law of mass communication that holds that what the audience does not see, has never seen, it cannot possibly miss."

(By the same token, when favorite novelists, literary figures,
politicians, painters, scholars, etc. pay no attention to art
music, or praise rock or jazz only--as is often the case--then
art music does not exist or takes on an inferior status in the
minds of a vastly larger public than the one comprehended
by art music.) An influential reviewer urging attendance at
an event or praising a work, can assure a bigger turnout,
provided that the music to be heard is in a style that has provided enjoyment to the reviewer's readers. Assuredly, when
Pablo Casals, most certainly an authority figure for his time,
appeared on television, in 1960, and denounced all modern
music, including that of Stravinsky, as not music at all, many
viewers took heed of his criticism.[49]

The psychologists Hans and Shulamith Kreitler write that
the public is prepared to enjoy an artistic composition if the
"prestige and popularity of an artist or of a supporting critic
reflect" the attitudes shared by many members of a circle of
society. They add that such a condition has been "promul-
gated, even created, by the mass media and often takes the
form of a star cult." This comment on the mass media bears
out Schickel's assertion that the history of celebrity and of
communications technology are inseparable. Though in one
sense they uphold the democratic ideal of building a better
informed public, the policy directors of radio, television,
magazine, and newspaper reporting may produce an opposite
effect.[50]

The highly publicized musician elevated to preeminency
by the media and public is a source of distress for those who
want to fashion art music into a vital, going concern. The
mass media fosters "the cult of celebrity," surrounded with
glamour and excitement, writes Christopher Lasch, thus sec-
onding the conclusion of the Kreitlers. It has helped create
"a nation of fans," by intensifying people's "narcissistic dreams
of fame and glory," and encouraging identification "with the
stars" and hatred of "the 'herd.'" Luciano Pavarotti, the
darling of the popular press, provided an excellent example
of the cult of celebrity, in November 1984, when he presented
a concert--audible mostly by means of loudspeakers--in Madison Square Garden. Excited aficionados gave him vociferous
applause, despite his not always being in good voice that
night and despite his singing for the nth time mostly selections from his limited repertoire of Italian arias and Neapolitan
songs. Presumably, the concert enhanced the sale of his

recordings of these selfsame numbers and lessened the sale
of recordings of other vocalists, which were competing for
attention.

The "star system," especially as applied to singers, occasioned numerous complaints. Since so many in the opera
audience demanded to hear the most prominent singers, the
price of these soloists did rise exorbitantly. Their hire could
mean the cutting back on rehearsals and on the quality and
quantity of the assisting instrumental and vocal performers.
Tickets had to be sold at higher and higher levels. The
operas performed were those the celebrities could and wanted
to sing or those most certain of appealing to the audience,
for the opera association had to ensure a full house to recoup
its expenses. Many other operas, new and old, had to remain unperformed because the celebrities did not sing them
or because mounting them involved financial risk.

Troubled by the artistic suffocation in the production
of operas that such a system entails, Speight Jenkins, who
was host of the television broadcasts Live from the Met, and
who became general director of the Seattle Opera, in September 1983, bravely declared: "I don't believe in opera with
the lion's share of the money concentrated on one artist. Ensemble and theatricality are the goals I seek."[52]

Achieving such goals are never easy. In all periods
of history and in all countries, a significant portion of the
public has insisted on lionizing its stars and has attended
only those performances featuring them. Every music lover,
however sophisticated he or she believes himself or herself
to be, treats a select number of musicians as individuals of
the greatest importance. These ties to them are both emotional and intellectual, and only in part owing to aesthetic
reasons. Recognizing this all-too-human tendency and making
room for other considerations is the issue here.

The cult of personality extends also to instrumentalists
and orchestra conductors. About the "jet-setting star conductor," a bothered John Rockwell writes as follows: "When one
is dashing about, it simplifies matters to carry along a narrow
repertory that can be repeated from city to city. To please
both musicians and budget-conscious boards, it is wise to
concentrate on familiar or simple pieces that do not require
excessive rehearsal. In this, the conductors are happily

abetted by the unions, whose contractual stipulations often preclude the allotment of extra rehearsal time for complex new pieces."[53] The consequences to music are obvious.

The pressure on the celebrity to maintain his or her popular image and on administrative officials of musical associations to sell out every last seat introduces a real, not fictional, danger. Celebrity and officials both are driven to forming conclusions, whether rightly or (as often as not) wrongly, about their audience's tastes and then letting their conclusions have considerable impact on programming. They are tempted to downgrade or abandon tests of variety and quality in the works they select to perform. At the same time, they may abandon their role of honest and concerned cultural brokers ready to assist the public to a fuller knowledge of music. It could lead to their becoming entrepreneurs managing a business and fearful of risks.

When cultural leadership disappears, as some claim it has during the course of the last few decades, the richness of the arts experience inevitably suffers. Nobody seems certain of what to believe in, save for culture narrowly defined as consisting of a handful of compositions approved by all. Musicians are less inclined to present the many facets, old and new, of art music that any person with pretensions to musical culture should know. Rather, each of their musical programs turns into a pieced-together conglomeration of safe works meant to appease the assumed unadventurous and utterly incurious tastes of the public and to increase box-office receipts. The leaders forget a psychological truism--that an audience will either learn to enjoy or fail to value a catholicity of styles and compositions depending on the expectations of their mentors.

Whether cultural leadership has really lessened is unproven. The weaknesses detected in the postwar years were also evident in the earlier part of the century. They are nothing new. How to cope with them remains the problem.

The next issue, one involving musical amateurism, has drawn forth conflicting opinions. One group of writers worries about the failure to encourage greater amateurism in art music, its premise being that the more the amateur performers are heard from, the more solid the bedrock upon which all art music can stand. Discouraging to amateurs, these

commentators state, is their comparison with the stars, who
are backed by a great deal of money, romantic attractiveness,
and high technical skills. They add that the music public is
encouraged, by fawning articles and reviews in newspapers
and popular magazines that exaggeratedly laud the stars, to
have no patience with the less than perfect efforts of non-
professionals. Therefore, the virtuosic performance-for-pay
of the star becomes irreconcilable with the playing-for-pleasure
of the amateur. The latter must always suffer by the comparison, and since the starry-eyed public does tend to com-
pare, the amateur is either reluctant to perform before anyone or abandons music making altogether.[54]

Like most one-sided arguments, this one may be true for
some amateurs and some elements of the music public, but it
cannot apply to all. As many amateurs see their playing as a
matter of self-expression and enjoyment first, with less concern over rank in the hierarchy of prestige. As many music
lovers make allowances for their neighbors' music making and
appreciate their efforts.

Members of the art-music world frequently misunder-
stand the role of the amateur, says Alvin Toffler, in reaction
to a statement by Harold Schonberg, writer for the New York
Times, who complained about amateur groups causing performance standards to deteriorate whenever they appeared in public. On the contrary, Toffler writes, many excellent amateur
performers do exist. Also, the amateur movement is an ex-
emplary training ground for musical talent. In addition, amateurs strengthen professionalism because they are more knowledgeable about and interested in music than is the general
audience, do regularly attend concerts, and show the highest
appreciation of real musicianship.[55]

The evidence does bear Toffler out. Yet, some professional musicians, possibly fearful of the competition and
touched by an elitist attitude, instead of encouraging amateurism as a bulkwark against and a corrective to the star
mania, have described it as harmful. To give one instance,
Margaret Hillis, founder of the American Concert Choir in
New York and, later, the Chicago Symphony Chorus, has
described her own and other professional choruses as doing
"absolutely wonderful work." To her, all amateur choruses
were "a disgrace," especially when they performed with professional symphony orchestras.[56]

Similar attacks by professional musicians were launched against amateur orchestras and chamber ensembles. For example, Thomas Scherman, director of New York City's Little Orchestra Society, wrote, in 1965, that the amateurs who manned the orchestras of small cities and towns served to corrupt the artistic experience: "I contend that the more the audiences in those smaller communities are subjected to mediocre musical fare (I am talking now of quality of performance), the less they will demand the best in live music.... I would prefer to see fewer orchestras in the country, but those orchestras capable of higher musical ideals [because they contain only professional players and ban amateurs entirely]."[57] All such musicians did was to encourage the conclusion of many members of the public that amateurism meant second-rate. Moreover, increased attendance at these professional musicians's concerts did not necessarily ensue. That segment of the public embracing this conclusion usually found its safest alternative to the amateur was the certified star. Only incidental benefits came to other musicians when they served as accompanists to the one or two performers the audience had really turned out to hear and see.

Of considerable significance in the creation of a problematical public are unilateral aesthetic standpoints that subject the entire musical experience to narrow tests of artistry. For example, in the postwar period, certain coteries of like-minded composers or musicians have been prone to articulating aesthetic presuppositions intended to prove their creations or musical activities have excellence. By stressing a limited range of principles that best define their pursuits, they of course, give themselves value while denigrating the values of those who oppose them. Experimental musicians, in particular, have found it necessary to establish their meritoriousness in this manner, for they must convince others of their right to receive performances, jobs, subsidies, and whatnot.[58] Thus, when the public does not take readily to their propositions, compositions, or music-making, the weapons are at hand for scapegoating it. A reciprocal animosity results. In short, the music world may help to nourish its own monster.

Exacerbating the condition that he only means to report on, Harold Schonberg, who had a wide readership, defended art music, in 1978, from the attacks of Senator Claiborne Pell. The senator had declared federal money was being wasted on the arts, with no ensuing benefits to the majority.

Witness, for example, what Joseph Machlis writes in
The Enjoyment of Music, certainly one of the most employed
college texts in introductory music courses: "When we fully
understand a great musical work we grasp the 'moment of
truth' that gave it birth. For a moment we become, if not the
equal of the master who created it, at least worthy to sit in
his company. We receive his message, we fathom his intention. In effect we listen perceptively--and that is the one
sure road to the enjoyment of music."[63]

Since only rare (if any) individuals fully understand
in the manner just prescribed--grasping that moment of truth,
receiving the composer's message whole and fathoming his intention with certainty--many listeners may decide that if they
cannot understand this transcendent truth, they can at least
give the appearance of understanding it. Therefore, the most
outrageous avant-garde offerings are politely applauded. The
most hilarious passages in compositions by Haydn, Beethoven,
Bartok, and others evoke, at most, suppressed titters.

Schuyler Chapin describes a nationwide tour of the
NBC Television Opera, in 1955, where all the operas sung
were rendered in excellent English translations and with care
for diction. Newspaper reviewers were enthusiastic; people
turned out to fill the halls. Yet, few audiences were responsive to Figaro. They listened in rigid silence. Why? "Because they did not think it proper to laugh in an opera house
and they were not clued to the idea that Mozart might be
funny." Chapin himself then took to explaining before performances that Figaro was a comedy satirizing the Establishment, the My Fair Lady of its day. At last people began to
applaud "warmly, and one could sense that they were beginning to relax, which is exactly what they did. The laughter
and audience participation were such that at the great de-
nouement, when Figaro is confronted with his mother and
father and sister, Adler [the artistic director] had to fold
his arms and wait patiently for the laughter and applause to
die down."[64]

Other commentators have spoken of encountering audiences so fearful of being considered stupid or narrow-minded,
that they played it safe by reacting uniformly to works of diverse meaning and by politely approving with their applause
sounds they really found unpleasant.[65] Without doubt, this
has resulted in the most momentous problem in American

musical life. When such audience behavior prevails, it stifles emotions and denies pleasure to the listener. No interchange between composer, performer, and listener results; each remains isolated, constructing harmful fictions about their place in the music world. The composers go their own way. The performers schedule music heeding their own imperatives, watchful of ticket sales, and guessing about audience preferences. The listener makes a fetish of one or two stars and a narrow selection of compositions, or may discover less and less delight in the listening experience.

There is a further dimension to the audience's reactions. Applause can indeed be polite. However, if the emotionally arid and pleasureless experiences mount up, the public ceases to attend concerts at all, thus making its true opinions known to composer and performer. Yet, if conditions like the ones described increase and become dominant over two or three decades, then the problematical music public may well dwindle to no public at all.

The chances that such a total shrinkage will take place are slender. Not taken into account are the listeners who will continue to have a strong positive love for compositions from one or more stylistic periods. Then again, there are those listeners, however small their number, who will always welcome adventurous or new experiences. Finally, although the general music public may at times tend to bestow its affections on certain highly publicized individuals, it has normally counterbalanced this tendency with a common sense appreciation of fine musicianship wherever it occurs--whether in a young singer called on at the last minute to substitute for a star-- as has happened at the Metropolitan Opera, or in an unknown conductor suddenly appearing to replace an ailing director of prominent stature--a not at all uncommon event.

Notes

1. Two of my previous books discuss why and how this divergence took place: Sweet Songs for Gentle Americans (Bowling Green, Ohio: Bowling Green University Popular Press, 1980); A Music for the Millions (New York: Pendragon, 1984).

2. For a detailed examination of American musical life from the beginning of the 20th century through World War II,

see Nicholas Tawa, Serenading the Reluctant Eagle (New York: Schirmer, 1984).

3. Glenn Rice, of Stockton, California, letter printed in Musical America (January 1978), p. 4.

4. Douglas T. Miller, and Marion Novak, The Fifties (Garden City, N.Y.: Doubleday, 1977), pp. 135-136.

5. Samuel Lipman, Music After Modernism (New York: Basic Books, 1979), p. 222.

6. Dennis Alan Mann, The Arts in a Democratic Society (Bowling Green, Ohio: Bowling Green Popular Press, 1977), p. 6; Edward Shils, in Culture for the Millions?, ed. Norman Jacobs (Boston: Beacon, 1964), p. 10; Richard Higgins, "British philosopher says self-interest corrupts Western liberty," Boston Globe, 28 October 1984, p. 14.

7. Daniel Yankelovich, New Rules: Searching for Self-Fulfillment in a World Turned Upside Down (New York: Bantam, 1982), p. 1.

8. Mann, The Arts in a Democratic Society, pp. 4-5.

9. Christopher Small, Music, Society, Education (London: Calder, 1977), p. 164.

10. Donal Henahan, "Dip in Concert Audiences Trouble Impressarios," New York Times, 21 December 1968, p. 48.

11. The Performing Arts: Problems and Prospects, Rockefeller Panel Report on the future of theater, dance, and music in America (New York: McGraw-Hill, 1965), pp. 3-4, 184-185.

12. Fred E. H. Schroeder, Outlaw Aesthetics (Bowling Green, Ohio: Bowling Green University Popular Press, 1977), pp. 39-40; Jon Roush, in The Arts in a Democratic Society, pp. 33-34.

13. Alvin Toffler, The Culture Consumers (New York: Random House, 1973), pp. 48-53.

14. Harlan Hoffa, "On Education," Musical America (September 1974), p. 27.

15. John Booth Davies, The Psychology of Music (Stanford, California: Stanford University Press, 1978), p. 214.

16. Leo Steinberg, Other Criteria: Confrontations with Twentieth-Century Art (New York: Oxford University Press, 1972), p. 56.

17. Mel Scott, The States and The Arts (Berkeley: University of California Press, 1971), pp. 93-94. See also, Dale Harris, "100 Years at the Metropolitan Opera," Ovation (September 1983), p. 15.

18. Max Kaplan, "Sociology of the Musical Audience," Music Journal (January 1961), p. 60.

19. Toffler, The Culture Consumers, pp. 128-29, 37, 41, 44.

20. Ibid., pp. 248-249.

21. Ibid., p. 23.

22. Howard Klein, "Record Is Set by Audience in the Park," New York Times, 27 July 1966, p. 41.

23. Marya Mannes, in Pop Culture in America, ed. David Manning White (Chicago: Quadrangle, 1970), pp. 50-51.

24. Sigmund Spaeth, in the Music Journal (April 1963), p. 98; William J. Baumol and William G. Bowen, Performing Arts--The Economic Dilemma (New York: Twentieth Century Fund, 1966), p. 36; Alix Williamson, "The Problematic Art of the Musical Publicist," Music Journal (January 1965), p. 78.

25. Robert Cumming, in the Music Journal (September 1965), p. 4; Toffler, The Culture Consumers, p. 277; Beverly Sills, in Horizon (January/February 1982), p. 28.

26. Philip Hart, Orpheus in the New World (New York: Norton, 1973), p. 40.

27. John Rockwell, "At 25, Lincoln Center Makes Plans for a Lively Future," New York Times, 21 October 1984, section 2, pp. 1, 19; Schuyler Chapin, Musical Chairs (New York: Putnam, 1977), pp. 170-204.

28. Milton Goldin, The Music Merchants (Toronto: Macmillan, 1969), pp. 205-206.

29. Winthrop Sargeant, "Musical Events: Requiem of a Lightweight," New Yorker, 5 January 1963, p. 78.

30. Herbert Hecsh, "The Year of the Edifice Complex," Music Journal (September 1965), p. 48; see also, Baumol and Bowen, Performing Arts, p. 40; Richard Barri, "1969: The Year of the Edifice Complex," Music Journal Annual (1969), p. 45.

31. Goldin, The Music Merchants, pp. 207-208.

32. Unsigned news item. New York Times, 28 October 1984, p. 44.

33. "Issue of Arts Center: Pop or Symphony," New Jersey Supplement, New York Times, 28 May 1972, p. 69.

34. Goldin, The Music Merchants, pp. 208-209.

35. Harold C. Schonberg, "Have Cultural Centers Benefited the Arts?," New York Times, 11 July 1983, section 2, pp. 1, 26.

36. George Seltzer, The Professional Symphony Orchestra in the United States (Metuchen, N.J.: Scarecrow, 1975), p. 268-269.

37. John Rockwell, in the New York Times, 13 July 1976, p. 40.

38. Robert Cumming, in the Music Journal (March 1966), p. 4.

39. Goldin, Music Merchants, p. 208.

40. Baumol and Bowen, Performing Arts, pp. 95-96.

41. Edward Shils, in Mass Culture Revisited, ed. Bernard Rosenberg and David Manning White (New York: Van Nostrand, Reinhold, 1971), p. 68.

42. David Cwi, "The Symphony Subscriber and Single Ticket Buyers: How Do They Differ?" Symphony Magazine (December 1983), pp. 48-49.

43. Harris Green, "The Subscription Crowd Must Go!" New York Times, 7 June 1970, section 2, p. 13.

44. Norman Singer, letter to the New York Times, 21 June 1970, section 2, p. 15.

45. Richard Barri, "Opera for the People," Music Journal (October 1972), pp. 114-17.

46. William Barry Furlong, Season with Solti (New York: Macmillan, 1974), pp. 47-48.

47. Harry Ellis Dickson, "Gentlemen, More Dolce, Please!" (Boston: Beacon, 1969), pp. 156-158.

48. For more on this subject, see Richard Sennett, Authority (New York: Vintage, 1981), pp. 15-22.

49. Richard Schickel, Intimate Strangers (Garden City, N.Y.: Doubleday, 1985), p. 253; Lipman, Music After Modernism, pp. 241-242; Hilde Somer, "The Market for Modern Music," Music Journal (January 1961), p. 32.

50. Hans Kreitler and Shulamith Kreitler, Psychology of the Arts (Durham, N.C.: Duke University Press, 1972), p. 261; Schickel, Intimate Strangers, p. 28.

51. Christopher Lesch, The Culture of Narcissism (New York; Warner, 1979), pp. 55-56.

52. See Ovation (March 1983), p. 6.

53. John Rockwell, All American Music (New York: Knopf, 1983), p. 65. See also, Ralph Shapey's complaint about the star system working against the performance of American music, in Cole Gagne and Tracy Caras, Soundpieces (Metuchen, N.J.: Scarecrow, 1982), p. 378.

54. Small, Music, Society, Education, p. 163.

55. Toffler, The Culture Consumers, pp. 224-225.

56. Heidi Waleson, "Paying the Piper: Orchestras on the Road," Symphony Magazine (June/July 1984), p. 32.

57. Thomas Scherman, "Little Orchestra in the Community," Music Journal Annual (1965), p. 109.

58. For a lengthy discussion of this subject, see Howard S. Becker, Art Worlds (Berkeley: University of California Press, 1982), pp. 131-133.

59.   Harold C. Schonberg, Facing the Music (New York: Summit, 1981), pp. 444-445. The observation was actually made on 5 February 1978.

60.   Gene Lees, "The Dotage of American Raido," High Fidelity (January 1978), p. 16.

61.   Tibor Kozma, "Music vs the Majority," Music Journal (March 1963), p. 101.

62.   The Performing Arts: Problems and Prospects, pp. 1-2.

63.   Joseph Machlis, The Enjoyment of Music, 5th edition (New York: Norton, 1984), p. 7.

64.   Chapin, Musical Chairs, pp. 118-120.

65.   See Victoria Bond, "New Music's Scholarly Friend: A Talk with Joan Peyser," Symphony Magazine (February/March 1983), p. 29; Walter Kerr, The Decline of Pleasure (New York: Simon & Schuster, 1962), pp. 284-285; Barbara Hall, "Rockefeller Speaks Out for Arts Education," Boston Globe, 15 January 1984, p. 52.

Chapter 2

THE PUBLIC'S CANONS OF MUSICAL TASTE

When speaking about the general music public, critics tend to fall into the habit of seeing it as a bulky and uniform aggregate of people with the same myriad problems and the same suspect preferences. In truth, no two people have identical likings or identical failings. As shown by the many men and women I have interviewed, every music lover, however dedicated to serious listening, blends shortcomings with virtues in relation to music. They cannot help but admire certain performers for their personable traits as well as their musical abilities. They will favor particular performance practices, musical styles and composers, tending to find in other practices, styles, and composers a failure in integrity, technical competence, or expressive communication. Whatever the modes of listening, they may be an outcome of nature (the quality of the mind, senses, physiology, and nervous system they are born with), or of nurture (the upbringing, education, and social, economic, and other conditions that influence and modify their nature).

Writers on music who voice individual judgments, or those of a special coterie, on musical matters do have ready vehicles for exposing their views. On the other hand, the general music public voices a collective judgment (in reality, a generalized summation of innumerable not-completely-identical individual judgments) and can make its views known mostly through attendance or non-attendance at concerts, purchase or non-purchase of recordings, and listening or non-listening to broadcasts over radio and television. Let me again stress that what we see as the public's aggregate discernment is the gist of myriad opinions, shaped under diverse circumstances, the whole not always explaining or defining its parts. Of necessity, the public's decision must find expression in terms of the marketplace, a form of agreement that unitizes it but in no way shows the relationship of each music lover to the art loved. Regrettably few other means are provided for expressing the collective judgment, save for this distortive one.

Few truly impartial investigators have probed deeply into the conditions influencing the public's judgments. Contemporary composers, performers of new music, and friends of both complain about the test of the marketplace for artistic works, not caring to admit that artistic works have always experienced such testing throughout history. Misleading conjecture and preconceptions passing as truths frequently dilute the trustworthiness of explanations about why the public behaves as it does.

In the American democracy, the nature of most normal individuals is assumed to be more or less similar; the ability to discern and enjoy whatever constitutes excellence is a shared aptitude. When education and cultural exposure causes a segment of the American society to turn to art music for its pleasure, then a degree of respect must be given to its power of discernment and critical judgment. This was certainly part of Abraham Lincoln's meaning, in his Gettysburg Address, when he said that the American nation was "dedicated to the proposition that all men are created equal." Surely included in that proposition was the idea that every individual seriously concerned over any issue is entitled to an equal chance to advance his or her views and to an equal treatment for these views.

Even when most infuriating to one or more of the art-music sets, remarks from members of the music public require continuous and solicitous consideration. Certainly some of the more prominent contemporary American composers and musicians have also made statements meant to provoke, which they expect to have taken seriously. Since the Menckenian twenties, hitting out at the American public has been a favorite sport amongst intellectuals and artists.

In March 1975, a member of the music public sent a letter to the New York Times in response to an American composer's bland assertion that television and modern life had killed all sensitivity to artistry and new music in the American audience. The respondent's retort was that the contemporary music favored by the composer had "been dead for the last

50 years." Moreover, the majority of today's "serious composers" are "complete poseurs," whose mediocrity is concealed
by useless techniques. At the same time, their cause is supported by "weak critics" who find significance in their works.
On the other hand, he writes, popular music and jazz "live."
Their audiences care about them, as former audiences cared
when a Mozart, Wagner, or Sibelius wrote a new work. "But
when Cage or Crumb offers his latest 'ionisations,' or whatever, who gives a damn?--apart from a sad little band who
desperately want the universities, with their musical chairs,
to believe that the trash they have produced is significant."[1]

The letter writer is by no means entirely right. Nevertheless, his letter touches upon several themes expressing the
judgment of a host of listeners: most twentieth-century compositions are seen as uninspired stylistic exercises and sponsored by sycophants; instead of excited anticipation and ful-
fillment, indifference greets every new work and emptiness
is the residue after listening to it; no significance can accrue
to any composition unacceptable to the general music public;
especially unacceptable have been the dissonant, percussive,
and rhythmic experiments of Edgard Varèse (Ionisation), the
chaotic noises of John Cage, and the bizarre sound effects of
George Crumb.

Whether such criticism is justifiable misses the point.
For devotees of the three composers to call the letter writer
and his like asses is counterproductive. They have denied
any respect for his sincerity, discernment, and critical judgment. No dialogue ensues, just back-and-forth vituperation.

The letter writer states a view repeatedly voiced by
much of the public, when given a chance to speak. He and
others like him have heard all sorts of "ionisations" over the
years and found no real value in them, whatever the artificial value attributed to these works by the few. Concertgoers get no fair return in pleasure for their money and for
the time and attention expended in listening. Therefore, to
them the worth of such works is low, the degree of excellence
nil. The music is shunned rather than sought after. The
democratic mandate authorizing the composers to act on behalf of those expressing disapproval has been withdrawn.
Moreover, disapproval is widespread. Keeping this in mind,
we must surmise that henceforth support for the "ionisations"
will probably continue to take on the aspects of something

forced, restricted, and fabricated--none of it reflecting normal human inclinations.

Some attempts at explaining the conditions under which the criticism of music is justifiable only add to the confusion. To give an instance, Leonard Meyer has written: "The merits of a composition is tested ... not by the theoretical constructs upon which it is supposed to be based, but by the only real, 'empirical' verification available: the ability of experienced, sensitive listeners to understand and respond intelligently to the implicative sound relationships presented."[2] Yet, who is to define sensitivity and what is an intelligent response? To attempt an answer is to open up Pandora's box.

We must assume that the letter writer and his fellows are concerned music lovers. They are reacting to certain identifiable modes of artistic expression. They indicate some regard for sound, the way it is regulated to make one person a composer and another a noise maker. They have been introduced to new musical compositions that do not merely validate their own way of hearing things. They can be presumed to have listened to music, including at least some of the new music, over several decades. And they have found certain compositions to be wanting. They grant none the right to say they have not listened deeply, or repeatedly, or with open minds--therefore making their opinions irrelevant. Such an observation may be applicable to some people but never to all!

It is hazardous for anybody to express certainty about the right and wrong of the twentieth-century cultural experience. Ours is a society where the freedom allowed composers to explore whatever styles they wish has come to be associated in the public's mind with widespread and unrelieved aesthetic and stylistic confusion. Who is to say what recent music compositions possess excellence and result from urgent creative drives? Surely, not Milton Babbitt on Cage's works, nor John Cage on Milton Babbitt's works, nor Charles Wuorinen on Philip Glass's work. Although, on the one hand, a yardstick about what constitutes music and musical worth seems essential; on the other, the creative person wishes to work untrammeled by authoritative rules to which he or she does not subscribe. Regrettably, where once there were hundreds, now there are thousands of composers issuing tens of thousands of compositions in multitudinous, usually irreconcilable styles.

The most informed convictions about this music making conflict with each other.

Only one thing appears certain--musical compositions
come into existence in order to have somebody listen to them.
If composers or performers labor to please their ear alone
and form their own solitary audience, no problem exists. It
is when they expect an audience other than themselves to
give attention to their music that conflict arises and accusation and counteraccusation form the dialogue between the musicians who demand acceptance and the public who refuses to
grant it.

In a provocative article, published in 1984, Adrian Corleonis quotes the question once posed by Ferruccio Busoni:
"Are concerts there for people, or are the public there for
musicians?" Beginning with Schoenberg, writes Corleonis,
audiences were confronted with new music in strange and non-
comprehensive styles, whose "expressive power" was "inaccessible without an auditory apprenticeship augmented by reading and a grasp" of a composer's development. "When nearly
every considerable composer of the last half-century demands
this sort of apprenticeship the number of aspirants drops off
dramatically. With the stylistic fragmentation of modern music, the audience for new music thinned and diversified."[3]

Like the letter writer mentioned earlier, other members
of the music public tire of the hectoring they receive and the
dogmatic advice offered them about music they should or should
not like. They, too, on occasion become letter writers. In
1981, the critic William Youngren, in Fanfare, wrote that Aaron
Copland was "at best, a minimally gifted composer," that composers like William Schuman, Roy Harris, and Leonard Bernstein were tedious, and that a great deal of American music
was not worth hearing. On the other hand, he found one
composer (for whose music the general music public had no
enthusiasm) to merit extraordinary praise: "Elliott Carter is
the only American composer whose career I follow with continuing interest and excitement."

The replies came quickly. Most of the writers seemed
to be "experienced, sensitive" music lovers able to comment
"intelligently" about music. One person wrote: "In holding
up Elliott Carter as a paragon of virtue, Mr. Youngren seems
to be confusing obscurantism and inarticulateness with integrity, the muddled and distorted implication of this being,

apparently, that if it's simple and direct, if it can be grasped
by the layman, it can't be any good. I thought this elitist
non sequitur had been laid to rest with the passing from
vogue of Boulez and Stockhausen." He advises: "Please,
let's not whip any dead horses--contemporary 'serious' music
is in enough difficulty as it is." Another person, revealing
democratic sympathies, wrote advocating tolerance for all view-
points, rather than an indulging "in prideful disdain of some
kinds of music or" resorting to writings on music which allow
the authors to display "their knowledge of minutiae in an apparent attempt to silence critical response." Scarcely a person wrote in defense of Youngren or in praise of Carter's
music. [4]

What I have just stated is not to be taken to mean the
public is always right, simply that its reactions and the reasons behind its reactions to music must be taken seriously if
it is the intended audience and ultimate payer for the music
it hears. Its input is required for the effective operation of
the American democracy's checks-and-balances system as applied to the arts. Persuasion through education and constructive argument, and a reconciliation of differences are the expected approaches of those who differ with the general music
public, not dismissal or confrontation.

Ultimately, this public will be the arbiter of what music
lives, dies, or is worthy of resurrection. As Abram Chasins
writes: "Despite the abuses hurled at the musical layman in
those mythologies of music which for too long have passed as
histories, his record is one of astute judgment. He has no
trouble in selecting the best composers and their best works,
if not immediately, then promptly. His choices, his favorites,
remain the standard items of our concert and opera repertoires, from Bach through Stravinsky. This same plain music
lover has also been responsible for the fate of contemporary
music. If he found a work interesting enough to hear again,
it lived. If he came to love it, it became a popular classic
in its own time, according to an age-old incontestable process
still going on right now."

I once asked Elie Siegmeister, a composer worried over
the growing gap between contemporary artist and audience,
if the audience was always wrong in its assessment of new
music. He replied: "No, certainly the general audience is
not wrong when it continues to dislike certain works or styles.

Mostly I agree that the audience may sometimes be slow to
grasp something new (such as Le sacre du printemps or Varèse
in the 1920's and '30's, or Ives for longer than that). But
give them [sic] time and the real things will reach their minds
and hearts, and the artificial things will still be rejected."
The audience that now accepts Ives, Bartok, and Stravinsky's
music, "still can't stand such things as Erwartung ... [and]
Cage's Apartment House-Renga (whatever its name is), and I
can't either. In the long run, the audience is right," despite
the realization that this same audience "also unfortunately
goes in for gobs of schmaltzy treacly stuff that conductors
dish out in carload lots."[5]

   Those of us with considerable training in and experience
with art music may not always agree with the general public.
We often find ourselves in disagreement over its reception of
the contemporary American and other music we happen to enjoy. We should also try to remember that its cultural attitudes
may result from ignorance and thought-management--due to
lack of experience, unfamiliarity with particular works and
styles, and manipulation by cultural entrepreneurs through
enticing advertisements, planted articles, and arranged radio
and television interviews, all of which play on human weaknesses. In addition, we must keep in mind that the resolution of the situation does not come from condemnation or from
concluding an elite alone can ever comprehend artistic expression. It comes by working to insure that the public constantly
hears a wide variety of music, by letting war-horses rest and
seeing to the public's repeated exposure to selected but unfamiliar compositions, and by persuasive, non-technical, and
unpretentious explanation.

   If enough of the public still remains unpersuaded, if
too many people select themselves out of the audience for a
given musical style, then compromise is necessary, sufficient
to win minimal support to sustain a composer's output or a
performer's proclivities in programming and interpretation.
To insist the public is wrong, after all attempts to interest
a significant portion of it in a particular style or work have
failed, produces a situation which the criticizer cannot possibly win.

WHAT IS MUSIC?

The most audacious explorations of novel sound ever

carried out in the history of music have occurred in the second half of the twentieth century. Again and again, composers working in diverse nonconformist styles have tried with
the greatest conviction to clarify for listeners the intent of
their creative experimentation. Yet, because most listeners
find difficulty in experiencing these composers' inner imperatives, they cannot but remain mystified. If music for a composer is anything he or she says it is, then music for listeners also is anything they say it is. It follows that music for
the one is not necessarily music for the other. To the extent
their understanding of what constitutes music diverges, a
failure has resulted in the one absolutely essential function
for music's existence, in communication.

    We come upon music as a set of symbols on a page--it
is not music. We speak about music as a concept, a universal or abstract idea--it is still not music. Music can have
life only as sound and only when somebody listens to it. If
musicians fail to perform a composition and if no listener hears
it, the work is, in effect, dead. Obviously, music is something you <u>hear</u>, and only incidentally, if at all, something you
see, smell, or touch. When sense-stimuli other than aural
ones take on equal or greater importance, then it is better
to designate the experience as some form of performance art,
not music. Silence assumes sound at either end of the silence,
or it really is not musical silence but a strategem intended to
make you aware of unpredictable and transient noises within
the time-limits of the silence arbitrarily defined as music, as
in John Cage's <u>4'33"</u>. Here, the term <u>music</u> illustrates a concept alone, not an orderly pattern of tones. Such conceptual-
izing joins other serious philosophical speculations about musical aesthetics, many of them offshoots of European intellectual theories, about which the American public has been historically distrustful or indifferent.[6]

    In 1977, Harold Schonberg wrote an article in the <u>New
York Times</u> that attempted to sum up the definitions of music.
The composer Henry Cowell was quoted as giving a subjective
definition: "Any succession of sounds, tones, or rhythms, or
combinations of them, which is intelligible either emotionally
or intellectually to a given listener, is music." (A major draw-
back to this definition is that it opens the way to saying anything that any person says is music to him or her is indeed
music, thus making nonsense of the entire concept and closing off all discussion.)

Objective definitions stressed organized or ordered sound, as in the explanation from the pianist Harold Bauer: "Music is a succession of sounds by varying pitch, intensity, and duration, selected, combined, and arranged in a predetermined form with the object of reflecting the composer's emotional reactions to his environment." Walter Koons, author of The Mystery of Music, stated: "Music is a particular kind of abstract thought that thinks in patterns of tone and time, expressed in sequences of single or multiple sounds." On the other hand, no definition is possible, owing to the extraordinary divergences in the contents of contemporary works, stated others like Louis Gruenberg and Carl Engel. Pondering these various definitions, Schonberg then wondered what could be agreed about and wrote: first, that music is sound; second, that it has some kind of expressive aim; third, that it has some sort of rhythm. He ended up with the definition: "Music consists of abstract sounds rhythmically organized for expressive purposes."[7]

If we ask how the general music public defines music, we encounter first the idea that it is a skillful and orderly embodiment of someone's creative imagination. Note the commonly held insistence on demonstrable competency and regulated direction. Next, music comprises identifiable tones that listeners find expressive, comprehensible, and gratifying. Last, these tones are given an explicit organization--melodic, rhythmic, harmonic--articulated over a period of time, an organization that the public can perceive as a musical composition.[8]

Human physiology and mental quality seem to affect what the ear readily recognizes as intelligible progressions and mixtures of tones. For two thousand years, writes Leonard Meyer, music theorists have tried to discover a "natural" explanation for music based on acoustical data. In the twentieth century, however, adovcates for the new music that overthrew traditional triadic and tonal theories abandoned this justification, maintaining that musical styles are learned. But learning is not arbitrary, insists Meyer, for the central nervous system is not neutral: "It selects and orders stimuli in terms of its own capacities and structural organization." Considerable evidence, experimental and cultural, indicates that the central nervous system, in conjunction with motor systems, "predisposes us to perceive certain pitch relationships, temporal proportions, and melodic structures as well

shaped and stable." For example, the octave, fifth, and
fourth are basic intervals in all cultures.[9]

The more a piece deviates from what is accepted as
"natural," the more seemingly unrelated the tonal combinations, the greater the number of aural phenomena the mind
is asked to process at one time, the more complex a work appears to the listener. Continuous reexperiencing of the piece
over a period of time may cause the listener to accept the new
aural experiences, assimilate the strange tonal data, and lessen the complexity. On the other hand, if the work remains
unassimilable, unpredictable, without discernable structure,
it will continue to be heard as noise, not music.

The psychologist John Booth Davies writes of a curious
reaction to noise on the part of some listeners. Noise to them
can be interesting or not depending on whether it is intended
to be taken as "music." Concerts have been given where
"musicians" stand on step-ladders and throw objects at glass.
"It is a tribute to the gullibility of some sections of the public that they turn up and listen to it," he concludes. Yet, a
similar "concert" of a gang of demolition men working in the
street is "unlikely to attract an audience of people wishing to
listen to their music." Although it is true that musical theory
represents a set of invented rules, Davies writes, these rules
"define the area within which the artistic endeavor takes
place." Rules make possible aesthetic deviation, confirmation,
expectancy, and deliberate rules' violation for aesthetic purposes. They are all "critical events as far as musical recognition is concerned." Without rules, utter liberty exists,
where "pure chance reigns, and a chain of purely chance
events is without meaning. In summary, there can be no
art without some kind of constraint."[10]

Most members of the public that we are writing about
would not have heard anything they would define as music in
the concerts described above. After reading their letters to
various periodicals, after listening to their comments at the
conclusion of concerts, and after interviewing many of them
over a period of over two decades, I must infer that musical
pleasure for the scores of people with whom I spoke ensues
from sound relationships harmonious with their, not the composer's, sense of order. A musical composition proposes an
order that must strike their ear as right, as effective and
rational expression. On the simplest level they derive pleasure

from the orderliness of an unassuming melody or dance-rhythm pattern or euphonious harmonic progression. This is one level of understanding they can all share, a level of perception of the beautiful we should not belittle. It is as true for the late-twentieth-century audience, as it has been for audiences in previous centuries.

Having in mind unhinged sound-experiments like John Cage's Musicircus, Walter Kerr wrote, in 1962: "Man's mind has a bias, a leaning, a predilection: it thirsts, without thinking twice about it, for order.... When arrangements go wrong ... a spirit dominated by so powerful a compulsion cannot help but kick and scream and swear and despair in just as powerful a sense of frustration."[11]

Melody can become more and more complicated, whether by itself, or combined with rhythm, or heard as part of a series of harmonic progressions. Insofar as one continues to sense some order that seems right, the music can give pleasure and strike the ear as beautiful. If the sense of order lessens, if the complexity or the seeming disorder prevents the music from reaching out to touch listeners, ugliness may replace beauty and produce displeasure.

Commenting on the American audience for art music in the eighties, Robert Ehle observed the acceptability of some noise (drums, cymbals, etc.) in music. However, he also observed that "the most intrinsically musical music would be that which is based to the greatest degree upon the property of sound called pitch and its simplest and most audible extensions: the harmonic series, consonance, small whole number ratios, tonality, and so on. At the other extreme, the least intrinsically musical music would be that which ignores or defies to the greatest extent possible all of these dimensions. Such music would, in the extreme, use no instruments capable of producing pitch, and would partake of none of the basic pitch phenomena listed above. It might be totally percussive or totally rhythmic. In a somewhat less extreme case, it might be built out of pitches, but might ignore or contradict all of the pitch-related phenomena listed above."[12]

Normally, listeners depend on the direct perception of attractive sound to appreciate a composition. Less significant are the words of an apologist who tells them through what theory a work is to be understood. They care little about "truth through ugliness," about perceiving the outrageousness of the modern world in something called music, about Zen's selflessness, and about irrational chaos as aesthetic experiences. They turn instead to the works of Beethoven, Brahms, Verdi, and Tchaikovsky, which offer a perceptible sense of order, a sympathetic projection of their humanity, a content that they feel more truly tells them who they are and that, at the same time, is a source for enjoyment. When they say a musical composition is a serious work of art, they mean, at least in part, that the work's expressive and rational content has some depth, and appeal transcending the moment, and even a degree of complication--but it is comprehensible complication. If the music's attractiveness is transient, with fluffy content, or dependent on sensationalism, in the long run they decline to designate it as artistic.

The public's designation of certain works as representative of high art is based neither on analyses of scores nor on critical theories about art but on intuitive understanding. Jacques Barzun, concerned with rescuing culture from the clutches of theorists and scholars, has written in praise of this intuitive understanding, which "does not analyze, does not break things down into parts, but seizes upon the character of the whole altogether." The understanding "derived from the experience is direct ["valuable for" its "direct effect on the head and the heart"]; and because it lacks definitions, principles, or numbers, such an understanding is not readily conveyed to somebody else."[13]

Here is a further reason why the public must speak through the marketplace. In accord with what was said earlier about its judgment, the public's intuition is but the sum of countless individual intuitions. Because these are direct insights derived from the music itself, they render impossible any complete explanation in words. Perforce, the conveyance of music's cumulative effects needs must resort to the everyday world of supply and demand.

THE ROLE OF MUSIC

Polls and surveys have consistently shown the majority of the American people predisposed to the arts, despite the fact that a much lesser number constitutes the arts-public. For example, a New York State survey, in 1972, and a

delight in following the regulated rearrangements of musical
materials, and the achievement of spiritual rapport.

   She and others like her, predictably, will find less
pleasure in music that keeps the emotions constantly on edge,
that sounds so complex or chaotic nothing links up musically
with anything else, and that fails to transport the listener
in mind and spirit. However often compositions unacceptable
to this audience win prestigious prizes, however prominent
the teaching positions their composers occupy, this public
may find the music ugly, low in value, and without function.[19]

   This judgment does not preclude others from finding
positive values in such works. Yet, at the same time, art
music in America operates in a buyer's market offering a vast
selection of music commodities. The woman just described,
and the many with similar inclinations, will choose to buy
elsewhere. The limited public for difficult-to-assimilate works
can create only a small market for the music it favors. Demand remains weak, distribution limited, and appreciation of
worth restricted. Only reversal of present valuation by a
future generation, such as happened to the music of Johann
Sebastian Bach, can alter this condition. Such a reversal
will be long in coming, if at all, for the twentieth-century
works that depart considerably from traditional practices.

   None of what was just said should cause the reader to
conclude that the larger music public, because it disfavors
most post-tertian art music, always wishes to limit its listening experiences to a handful of long familiar compositions.
On the contrary, indications point to curiosity about lesser
known works and gratitude for variety in programming. For
example, a survey by the National Symphony of its subscribers revealed a desire for less airings of works like Beethoven's
Fifth Symphony and Tchaikovsky's Fourth Symphony, and more
airings of little performed works from all historical periods.
The glaring exception was music in an aggressively twentieth-
century idiom.[20]

   To give a second example, around 1982-1983, it seemed
that every violinist was playing Beethoven's Violin Concerto.
At the end of a Boston Symphony presentation of this concerto, featuring an internationally acclaimed soloist, subscribers seated around me wondered why so much music by Beethoven and Mozart (they had had a surfeit of Mozart's piano

concertos, as well, in Boston's concert halls) was being heard, when, as one put it, "all kinds of terrific music was lying around waiting to be picked up." They brought up the names of works mostly from the nineteenth and early twentieth centuries. Again, although they did mention early Stravinsky compositions, Bartók's Concerto for Orchestra, and a couple of works by Copland and Barber, they cited no twentieth-century works composed in advanced idioms.

Abram Chasins maintains that because Americans, especially the younger ones, have grown up with a variety of different musical styles sounding in their ears--art music, jazz, rock--they have next to no stylistic prejudices: "They have no hesitation or inhibition about playing a Jelly Roll Morton record immediately before, or a Blood, Sweat and Tears album immediately after, a Vivaldi concerto."[21] I have frequently found confirmation of Chasins's observation. Typically, a woman of around 32 years of age, married, and with two children commented to me about her love for "symphony, opera, jazz, and some pop," particularly when heard in live performance. Music from whatever of these sources was a "form of joy which is felt as a feeling of excitement; or it can lead me to tears." As for art music: "I think the music of Beethoven (especially) and Bach (not always) is very beautiful. Symphony music can often be thrilling and when I hear it, it seems to become a part of my whole being."

An "authority" on music may have led listeners like this woman to "great" works. However, they learn to admire these works "out of a spontaneous uprush of awe and affection, a swelling of heart and mind," writes Walter Kerr. To question their perceptions, when honestly stated, is nonsense. He writes: "Taste is either personal (yours, mine, Henry's) or it does not exist.... Taste is never a law. It is always an entirely private love." Two conditions influence taste: "One of them is affinity, the other exposure." As for affinity: "Each of us is born with a neurological and psychological radar on which some signals are readily received and others remain faint. We are complexes, here and there sensitive, here and there not; and there is little we can do to alter our natural wave lengths." Add exposure in depth over a time period, a sampling of the richness in the arts, and an exploration of those enriching experiences giving the most pleasure and we see taste develop.[22]

Negative reaction to avant-garde compositions is not always attributable to close minds. A forty-year-old music lover who frequented concert halls and whose appreciation of music went beyond "a sound bath," said of the obstinate silences in Cage's 4' 33": "It's fun for a minute and amusing, but I would never want to repeat the experience. You hear it once, then its most important element is always too predictable." The apparent non-relatedness to each other of the many incidents in the unpredetermined Fontana Mix annoyed her. She did sincerely wonder whether her annoyance arose "because beautiful to her means music ... written during the Classic or Romantic eras," and whether clarity of structure "makes a piece appeal to me." Furthermore, she said, she had often asked herself if her "excitement over a particular composer, conductor, or orchestra" was because she was "stuck in a rut," or because her musical education was limited, or "simply because someone of some repute" told her what she should appreciate. "I see it as being none of these things and yet at the same time perhaps being all of them" was her conclusion. She also recognized within her an unashamed giving way to "bare-faced, unabashed, personal enjoyment," especially to sensuous string passages, soaring melody, and rich orchestral sounds--a reaction for which she could not account but which she would not alter.

With the three women just quoted, the desire for art music is clearly established, as is an entirely personal love for it. Regrettably, as will be shown, elitist and educational bias, big-business economics, and mass-media's selling of personalities and excitement have often denied them exposure in depth to a variety of enriching experiences. Insofar as this denial has taken place, democracy has also been denied.

Fortunately for these women, a modicum of exposure to art music has occurred, and this exposure has added beauty to their routine existence. As Dennis Alan Mann explains: "One of the more important goals of American democratic society is to enrich the citizen's everyday life. Art which is integral to society can add to the quality of our everyday experiences. It can beautify, it can illuminate, it can delight, and it can bring [in Leslie Fiedler's words] ... 'moments of release from the ordinary burdens of everydayness and even a rationality, and a better understanding of (our) own lives.'"[23]

I asked all three women whether they agreed with a passage in the Rockefeller Panel Report on the performing arts, which went as follows: "While the arts do not make society or its individual members more energetic or efficient, they do tend to make both wiser and happier--inwardly healthier, outwardly more alive. The arts are a source of simple enjoyment and delight, hence, of refreshment and renewal. They are also educating and civilizing, can provide a sense of the grace, power, enchantment, and beauty of which the creative impulse is capable. And, at their greatest, the arts are exalting, with some of religion's moral and mystical power. These are the terms in which the arts are best justified."[24]

They endorsed most of the statement, but questioned whether music really made them feel wiser and more educated. As one of them said: "People don't listen with the theories of composition in their minds, even if they know them. They listen for the physical impact and the emotion they hope is there. There's also the excitement of a performance. Let's face it, you get a lot of pleasure from watching performers on the stage. Knowing how something is put together and always following the form while you listen is interesting but not that important. When you're through listening, if you feel you've been hit in the gut, then it's a real powerful sensation and the music's great."

My notes show that most of the listeners I have interviewed confirm her conclusions. To summarize my findings, visceral and emotional response, whether to popular or art music is given the highest priority--instinctive and unreasoning abandonment to sheer sound and transportation in feeling into an intensely pleasurable state are prime requirements for a significant listening experience. This experience is produced mostly by works that balance repetition of old with introduction of new material, that balance traditional patterns of sound with fresh departures from these patterns, that contain recognizable tones, melody, and harmony organized within a tonality, and that eschew namby-pamby rhythms, or no rhythm at all.

Some articulate interviewees granted art music a much profounder role in their lives, saying it allowed them to rise above mundane existence and achieve a state of ecstatic delight. I was reminded of something Ernest Becker wrote, in Escape from Evil (1975), that culture lets a human transcend

himself in "complex and symbolic ways ... by finding a meaning for his life, some kind of larger scheme into which he
fits," thus raising him "above nature."

PUBLIC TASTE: CONSERVATIVE, MODERATE, OR RADICAL?

The destabilizing events lived through by late-twentieth-
century American society have left it with much less confidence in itself. Along with cold and hot wars, social and
economic crises, and ethical and moral upheavals, society has
also had to cope with an attempt to overthrow all high-cultural
systems. The rejective tendency on the part of artists has
especially characterized the fifties, sixties, and most of the
seventies.

With easier breath, Calvin Tomkins observed a change
toward stability in the arts at the beginning of the eighties,
saying: "This is a great relief. Subversion has not always
been thought to be art's main function, after all, and our society could use some reassurance."[25] He undoubtedly had
the art-consumer particularly in mind when he made this assertion.

As background to what Tomkins has written, we find
that a firmly implanted suspicion of any attempt at extreme
alteration of our attitudes and institutions has surfaced many
times during the three-hundred years of the United States's
history. As often as not it has produced deplorable results.
For example, when Douglas Miller and Marion Nowak wrote
about the McCarthyism of the fifties and the support it received from a majority of Americans, they explained it as a
manifestation of the "deep-rooted anti-radicalism in this nation's history.... From the 1790s when the United States
first established a workable constitutional government to today, radicalism has been in disrepute."[26] What Miller and
Nowak needed to add was that this same anti-radicalism eventually was also a potent force in bringing down McCarthyism
when it hit a peak of extremism in the political right.

With the impermanence of the postwar decades, when
every societal precept became unfixed, the reversion to conservatism grew, even as social reformer and cultural avant-
gardist insisted upon the bankruptcy of the past and the

need for revolutionary modifications of the status quo. Amidst
the ensuing confusion, one found many men and women yearning to retreat into the past, whether in music, painting, or
literature--to the artistic products of a time when people
seemed to know what they were doing and where they were
going, or so the fiction went.

Note Lionel Trilling's mention of the large number of
students in the seventies who took an interest in Jane Austen:
"We can readily suppose that the young men and women who
so much wanted to study Jane Austen believed that by doing
so they could in some way transcend our sad contemporary
existence, that, from the world of our present weariness and
desiccation, they might reach back to a world which, as it
appears to the mind's eye, is so much more abundantly provided with trees than with people, a world in whose green
shade life for a moment might be a green thought."[27]

Surely a similar supposition can apply to the strong
back-to-the-"authentic" Baroque, back-to-the-"authentic"
Medieval, and other back-to activities manifest in today's music world. It applies as well to the devotion of individuals
to single composers like Guillaume de Machaut, Heinrich Isaac,
Alessandro Scarlatti, and Luigi Cherubini, and to the preference of others for the euphonious music of Classicism or Romanticism over cacophonous Modernism.

An urge, such as that described above, toward the music of the past is a conservatism that in its best manifestation
is sustained by men and women capable of reacting positively
to the requirements of older expressive modes and who need
these modes to clarify some present sense of dislocation. For
these men and women, modern art provides only further psychic disturbance. A living tradition, which is conservatism
at its most vital, comprehends the opposition of the two inter-
acting influences just mentioned, juxtaposing yesterday's
creative realizations and today's nonfulfillment of being, and
fostering a tensile balance between these antipodes. Without
this opposition, conservatism appears hackneyed or a contriv-
ance for evading the claims of the self.

In short, mere escape from spiritual conflict and domination by unthinking habit vitiate conservatism and ossify
tradition. As Jon Roush once wrote tradition "requires constant re-creation as well as study," and "a dialectical tension

between past and present." If divorced from the "recurrent expressions of" the people "who participate in it," tradition can have no substance.[28]

In 1968, a composer dismissed the past, in print, as having no relevance to contemporary living. Quickly a response came from a music lover who said the past was indeed relevant. Compositions by composers like Mozart and Beethoven can "have relevance to any contemporary civilization. Why? Because they grab you where it counts; they reach into your heart and do something to it."[29]

We cannot state with certainty how many of today's audiences listen out of habit and a desire for escape, or because they, like this music lover, find older music most relevant to their present human condition and modern music not relevant at all. Assuredly, most individuals exhibit some degree of both. To be guarded against is the blaming of the dominant conservatism of the general public on the former with no consideration of the latter.

The arch-examples of American musical conservatism appear in the presidents of the United States. None of them have liked post-triadic music. One or two have had no ear for any music at all. Most, like President Johnson, preferred popular music and folksongs, varied with light symphonic fare--Strauss's waltzes, Brahms's Hungarian Dances, and so forth. Any deeper liking for art music centered mostly on nineteenth-century compositions. For example, John F. Kennedy's favorite music comprised works of the nineteenth and early-twentieth centuries that had historical, literary, or pictorial associations, among them Debussy's Afternoon of a Faun, Ravel's La Valse, Berlioz's Overture to Benvenuto Cellini, Gounod's ballet music from Faust, and Mussorgsky's Boris Godunov.[30] These are all artistic works created to reach the general art-music public of their time. They retain characteristics appealing to large audiences today.

Carl Dahlhaus writes that older works like these and any modern music of real significance are "characteristically 'multivalent.'" They "can be heard on different levels of understanding without losing" their "sense and effect on the lower levels. Works like The Magic Flute or The Creation are directed at the naive as well as at the reflective hearer."[31]

One must give some heed to the assertion that the conservative majority of the general music public decides the
future existence of all proposed artistic advances, constantly
measuring the new against the old, granting life to what measures up and casting away the rest. Although Martin Gottfried
had the modern theater in mind when he wrote about the role
of conservatism, his comments do apply to the music scene.
He states: "No true development is possible unless there is
a constant building upon foundations that were tried and
proved. So artistic adventures are dared, tested against
current values, and when developed, accepted. Those that
fail are discarded (sometimes mistakenly, to be retested long
afterward against later values). Some are mistakenly accepted and prove ephemeral. In all cases, the right wing
provides the challenge for the left wing's proposition and a
defeat at its hands usually will prove fatal.... In any case,
the proving process is the function of the right wing, and
the general audience ... of any period is a basic part of that
wing. In its role of mere attendance, simple enthusiasm or
rejection, the public is essential to the development of the
theater [and art music]." There is no such thing as a traditional left wing, Gottfried points out.[32]

The traditionally-minded make important contributions to
the current music scene. First, theirs is the task of winnow-
ing what is legitimate and lastingly important. Customarily
with more than a little forbearance, they listen to what is offered as new but harbor a skepticism ever ready to condemn.
Few works, and those that are the most finished and refined,
and the most satisfying to a generality of listeners, earn
their accolade. In contrast, artistic radicals, who are a minority of the listening public, tend to accept whatever works
strike them as most original, with less concern for crudities
and what that originality preempts. They are sometimes [and
possibly unfairly] characterized as always "onto something new,
bored with what is already passé," showing "no concern for
the lasting strength of maturation, ... looking for new pastures, once the seed has been planted in the old."[33]

Whatever innovations that the conservative majority
shows itself ready to assimilate soon reappear in a number
of other works, travel from city to city and country to country, and find themselves transformed, tested, and polished in
thousands of variations. Secondary composers receive encouragement to cultivate and mature the innovations, although

they cannot help but "dilute" the "original excitement."
Lastly, "with each reapplication of the new idea--as revolution moves into trend and finally into tradition--the step"
that music has taken "broadens from a foothold to a horizon-
wide extension." When the advance is finally digested, it has
become a part of the mainstream, accepted by musicians and
the general public. [34]

Is today's general public invariably conservative? Its
older elements more than its younger elements is an accurate
first response. The older the listener, the more he or she
may be confused by and apprehensive about the lengthening
trail of intricate and weird twists that his or her life has tra-
versed. Resiliency is probably down, along with spryness.
Method, order, and stability loom as desiderata. Where is
one certain to find them more than in the past? Hence, conservatism, the seeking of reassurance and peace in the sounds
of Bach and Chopin.

When still young, say under thirty-five years of age,
the listener is more apt to be sound in body, vigorous in
mind, flexible in attitude, and confident in the ability to face
up to disturbance. He or she may have a greater willingness
and capacity to deal with the measure of insecurity and seeming disorder that inevitably accompanies the new in art. [35]
Hence, the likely absence of intimidation when confronted with
the sounds of the musical avant-garde. Finding more young
than old people at concerts of new music is not unusual; nor
is finding more old than young people making up the audiences
of symphony and opera associations dedicated to the tried-and-
true.

All this said, a significant portion of the general music
public, old and young, does not reject modern music out of
hand. Often, it is not so much the antagonism of the public
that keeps contemporary works from being programmed, as it
is the timidity of music directors and managements of performing companies, who are oversensitive to a few adverse criticisms. On this matter, Philip Hart writes that, although the
"silent acquiescence of the many" may be involved, more likely
it is the complaints of the trustees themselves or of major
donors, not the general audience, which keeps a work off
the list. For example, when Lukas Foss was music director
of the Buffalo orchestra, his innovative policy, says Hart,
was blamed out of all proportion for the orchestra's ills.

Other factors were ignored: "A stern lecture from a donor
to a trustee at a country-club cocktail party, or a stream of
letters to the newspapers--even if from only a score of patrons
out of thousands--can carry more weight with management appraisal of artistic policy than can the passive acceptance, or
even cordial welcome, of the vast majority of the audience.
In symphony affairs, as elsewhere in matters involving public
response, the adage of the squeaky wheel prevails."[36]

    A 1950 poll of Indianapolis's concert subscribers showed
that 50 percent of them wanted about 9 percent of the programming to consist of American music; 30 percent of them
wanted 9 percent of the programming to consist of "extremely
modern" music. A poll of Seattle's opera audiences as to the
choices for programming for the next year, taken in 1965, involved more than 1,600 persons. Among the top 25 choices
were twentieth-century works: Wozzeck, Peter Grimes, The
Ballad of Baby Doe, and Vanessa.[37] Save for Wozzeck, none
of these oepras could be considered to have an overly aggressive modern sound.

    Further testimony comes from the composer Otto Luen-
ing, who saw a need for cultivating the curiosity of listeners,
not giving them the same old thing over and over again so
as to glorify conductors and soloists. He asserts that he
used to present new American music in Tucson and always
filled the hall. "So nobody can tell me there isn't any interest in new music, because I've done it." Along the same
vein, Richard Barri, director of New York's Opera Theater,
speaks of an untapped real public for opera, which wants to
be entertained and to understand the action and language.
It wants communication, involvement, and identification with
what is performed, and, given these, will countenance the
new and different.[38]

    Lukas Foss's Time Cycle (1960) represented an extreme
stylistic change for the composer, towards a complex, dissonant, and highly chromatic music. The conductor Leonard
Bernstein made an extra effort to prepare the work for presentation with the New York Philharmonic. He went out of
his way to discuss Time Cycle with the audience immediately
before he conducted it, and offered to repeat the work at the
end of the concert for all those who cared to stay. "A near
miracle occurred after the Friday afternoon concert, which is
peopled chiefly by apathetic ladies for whom concert-going

generally appears to be more a social obligation than a cultural adventure," writes Allen Hughes. "Some 400 members
of that very audience stayed to hear the repeat of 'Time
Cycle.'"39

If even some of the "apathetic ladies" stayed to listen,
then surely the case for getting the public to accept unfamiliar music is not hopeless. Not all the music public, nor
all the new music, to be sure, but enough so that the assumed adamancy of the general listener against hearing any
contemporary work, let alone ever enjoying it, can be seen
as the fiction it is.

AN ACCEPTABLE NEW MUSIC

By the year 1985, the aggressive modernism that characterized so much of the art music written in the twentieth-
century had begun to seem outmoded. The sort of melody and
harmony with which the general audience has always identified
seemed to be returning to its former favorable position.
Twentieth-century American composers whose works conserved
some of music's traditional values were less apt to be dismissed
as irrelevant to contemporary concerns. John Alden Carpen-
ter, Douglas Moore, Randall Thompson, and Samuel Barber,
among others, were discussed and their works performed with
greater understanding and sympathy than had been the case
in the first three decades of the post-World War II years.

A younger generation of composers (John Corigliano,
David Del Tredici, and Steve Reich--to name three), at least
in several major compositions, tried in fresh manner to build
on the styles of the past, although with a careful admixture
of selected post-triadic procedures. Yet, perplexity and contention befogged the movement. The thinking and modes for
discussing contemporary works employed by writers on music
had been conditioned by the attitudes of the atonal or experimental composers and turned out to be unsatisfactory when
contemplating this neo-traditional trend. What appreciation
of it was evident in the writing of critics centered on manifestations of originality, seriousness, and integrity--three buzz-
words of modernists.

The seventies and eighties have found composers like
George Rochberg utilizing musical quotations from the past

as discrete parts of a larger composition--as if the strengths
of Josquin, Monteverdi, and Mozart can act like threads of
life spun into a contemporary fabric. Other composers, like
Philip Glass, have stripped away every fleshy superfluity in
order to present the skeletal rudiments of harmony and rhythm
in repetitious patterns. Still other composers have completely
repudiated the present and take their entire inspiration from
a specific historic style--whether Medieval, Renaissance, or
Baroque.

Yet, the task remains for some one of this younger
generation of composers to push composition to a position of
achievement where allusions to earlier practices cease as coun-
terfeits and exist as invigorating resources that help achieve
a vital and unified artistic goal. The result would be fresh
compositions wholly of the present day, though also descendants of older works. Moreover, this music must also have
proved consequential to substantial numbers of listeners.

A few writers on music insist that such compositions
already exist, written by various composers active during the
century. Cited are works by Ives, Griffes, Copland, Barber,
Piston, Moore, Schuman, Creston, Mennin, Ward, Persichetti,
Corigliano, Dello Joio, Glass, Reich, and others. Regrettably,
the picture is by no means clear. The writers disagree with
each other. Argumentation continues at white heat. Even
those works that have proved pleasing to audiences get desultory performances. The grip of avant-garde ideology, the
dictate of financial profit and loss expectations, and the prejudices of conductors and other musicians in power preclude
an honest testing of much of this music through repeated and
widely diffused presentations.

As for the American music lovers themselves, note the
remark of Dora Romadinova, a Russian music critic specializing
in contemporary music, who spent several months in America.
She observed that American audiences genuinely regretted
their inability to understand the more radical of the modern
works; they wanted to do so but just could not.[40]

Notes

1. Ralph E. West, Jr., letter in the New York Times,
9 March 1975, section 6, p. 92.

2. Leonard B. Meyer, Music, The Arts, and Ideas
(Chicago: University of Chicago Press, 1967), p. 266.
3. Adrian Corleonis, "Ferruccio Busoni," Fanfare
(January/February 1984), p. 107.
4. See Fanfare (March/April 1981), pp. 3, 6; (July/
August 1981), pp. 2, 6-8.
5. Abraham Chasins, Music at the Crossroads (New
York: Macmillan, 1972), p. 5; Elie Siegmeister, letter to the
author, dated 21 July 1983.
6. J. Meredith Neil, Toward a National Taste (Honolulu: University Press of Hawaii, 1975), p. 6; Davies, The
Psychology of Music, p. 56.
7. Harold C. Schonberg, "Define Music," New York
Times, 23 January 1977, section 2, p. 15.
8. The first definition of "music" given in Webster's
Third International Dictionary corresponds closely to that of
the public: "The art of incorporating pleasing, expressive,
or intelligible combinations of vocal or instrumental tones into
a composition having definite structure and continuity."
9. Meyer, Music, The Arts, and Ideas, pp. 288-289.
10. Davies, The Psychology of Music, pp. 19, 95.
11. Kerr, The Decline of Pleasure, p. 171.
12. Robert C. Ehle, "The Evolution of Musical Style,"
The American Music Teacher (January 1983), p. 20.
13. Jacques Barzun, "Scholarship Versus Culture,"
Atlantic (November 1984), p. 99.
14. Philip Hart, "Art Surveys: To See Ourselves,"
Musical America (August 1974), p. 15.
15. See the report of Charles B. Fowler, in Musical
America (November 1977), p. 16.
16. Edmund Fawcett and Tony Thomas, The American
Condition, New York: Harper & Row, 1982), p. 320.
17. Lucy R. Lippard, Overlay (New York: Pantheon,
1983), p. 5.
18. This and other reports from which I quote were
selected from over a thousand in my possession, collected
over the last 18 years at the University of Massachusetts/
Boston. They were written by men and women ranging in
age from 18 to 65 years of age, most of them members of my
daytime and evening music classes, scarcely any of them having specialized musical training. Although a majority of the
reporters were born and brought up in the New England
states, some 200 of them came from other, widely scattered
areas of the United States. An examination of the data showed

no regional differences in attitudes. Permission to quote
them was granted so long as I did not identify them by
name.

19.   For further discussion of the significance of prizes,
see Barbara Jepson, "After the Pulitzer, Then What?" New
York Times, 28 October 1984, section 2, pp. 23-24.

20.   Unsigned editorial: "Audiences Request Wider
Repertoire," Musical America (June 1954), p. 12.

21.   Chasins, Music at the Crossroads, pp. 24-25.

22.   Kerr, The Decline of Pleasure, pp. 288-289,
293.

23.   Dennis Alan Mann, in The Arts in a Democratic
Society, ed. Mann, p. 5.

24.   The Performing Arts: Problems and Prospects,
pp. 6-7.

25.   Calvin Tomkins, "Skowhegan," New Yorker, 20
September 1982, p. 94.

26.   Miller and Nowak, The Fifties, p. 23.

27.   Lionel Trilling, The Last Decade, ed. Diana Trilling
(New York: Harcourt Brace Jovanovich, 1979), p. 209.

28.   Jon Roush, "The Humanities Museum," in The Arts
on Campus, ed. Margaret Mahoney (Greenwich, Conn.:   New
York Graphic Society, 1970), p. 35.

29.   Henry T. Blasso, Bronx, N.Y., letter to Music
Journal (September 1968), p. 18.

30.   See the New York Times, 20 July 1960, p. 59; and
8 August 1960, p. 9.

31.   Carl Dahlhaus, Analysis and Value Judgment,
trans. Siegmund Levarie (New York: Pendragon, 1983), p.
26.

32.   Martin Gottfried, A Theater Divided (Boston: Little, Brown, 1969), pp. 21-22.

33.   Ibid., p. 23.

34.   Ibid., p. 23.

35.   For further discussion of this matter, see John A.
Kouwenhoven, Half a Truth Is Better Than None (Chicago:
University of Chicago Press, 1982), p. 220.

36.   Hart, Orpheus in the New World, p. 402.

37.   "Concert Subscribers Polled in Indianapolis,"
Musical America (October 1950), p. 24; Rolf Stromberg, in
Musical America (January 1966), p. 143.

38.   John Rockwell, "An Influential Musician at 80,"
New York Times, 15 June 1980, section 2, p. 30; Barri,
Opera for the People, p. 17.

    39. Allen Hughes, "Leonard Bernstein," *Musical America* (January 1961), p. 110.

    40. Donal Henahan, "Russian Music Critic Criticizes Critics," *New York Times*, 21 April 1968, section 2, p. 17.

Chapter 3

EDUCATING THE PUBLIC TO ART MUSIC

The post-World-War-II years, as was said in the first
two chapters, were problematical ones for art music and its
practitioners. As we have seen, the actual American democracy did not always put its beliefs into practice, nor consistently build upon the premises intended to justify its existence. Most Americans, for whatever the reasons, had negligible interest in knowing any of the fine arts. Moreover,
what public for art music did exist demonstrated several im-
pediments that diluted the quality of its listening experience.
Was formal education a way to remedy the situation, wondered
Americans dedicated both to the principles of democracy and
to the strengthening of the arts in the popular mind and affection.

The usual American view of what cultural education
should be all about was rarely free from ambiguity and uncertainty. Usually in contention were the democratic imperatives
to insure equal access to what many thoughtful people regarded as the finest cultural productions of humanity and
the offsetting pressure to heed what was perceived as the
will of the majority, however culturally debilitating the realization of that will was. Here, a political principle intruded
into areas it should have entered only with circumspection.

In regard to this conflict, several misapplications of the
meaning of democracy loomed. In theory, educators might believe in presenting what they understood as culturally excellent to all men and women, and in educating them in its value.
By so doing, they might wish to heed what seemed a consensus of opinion by the most respected representatives of Western civilization, past and present. In practice, however,
they tended to allow their schools to deemphasize those cultural products which they thought the majority of Americans
did not prize. A corollary to this was an assumption, which
concealed itself in the recesses of their minds, that since

73

majority rule must always prevail, then they might safely assume the eventual demise of art music as it has existed in
the United States.

Such thinking weakened the mandate to afford all humans a means for cultivating whatever incorporeal faculties
each of them possessed to their maximum extent. Educators
were tempted to settle for less than this in education, in order
to stress what had immediate, tangible, and practical value.
They thereby increased the possibility of domination of cultural aspects of American society by persons indifferent to
refinements that could possibly make whole the human spirit.
They also may have encouraged suspicion of the few who exhibited sensitivity toward some of the highest manifestations
of artistic expression.[1]

More than a suspicion that events were moving swiftly
in this direction grew in the late sixties, when a questioning
of all traditional values spread like wildfire thorugh the country. The musical compositions of Bach, Beethoven, Bartók,
and Barber, maintained the spokespeople for revolting youth
and the academics with antennae attuned to the current intellectual climate, were not demonstrably superior to those of
popular-music composers and arrangers, nor pertinent to contemporary society. Every sort of music had legitimacy, with
perhaps the music that was least tainted with elitism having
the greatest legitimacy. Besides, excellence was in the eye
of the beholder. The long-standing tendency in most American
secondary schools to favor popular music over art music was
thus strengthened. (One was not inevitably superior to the
other. However, both were needed to present Western civilization in its entirety.)

About the same time, not all but considerable numbers
of Americans decided that the essence of their individual existence was better defined through a materialistic lifestyle,
not necessarily based on those human values that included the
arts. Instead of aiming to rise higher than one's physical
self, one aimed at a lifestyle "based on eating sushi, playing
pinball, and wearing penny loafers," writes Emily Hiestend.
Her harsh and rather overstated criticism continues: "The
flaw with this otherwise appealing scheme is that it overlooks
the main events of life--wrestling with chaos--and suggests
that to form beliefs from utter confusion is as easy as picking
the right shade of paint for the foyer." Originally a marketing

word for consuming, signifying an array of goods one might
examine and select from, lifestyle replaced "the rugged enterprise of a soul engaged with the universe," substituting the
acquisition of goods as the fashionable means for achieving
"the good life."[2]

Critics like Hiestend maintained that, for many men and
women, living a full life did not require the contemplation of
a canvas by El Greco or listening attentively to a string quartet by Mozart. To them, these were choices equal to a thousand and one other choices, like learning to scuba-dive or
gambling at a casino in Atlantic City, choices that anyone
could make or not make as one wished.

At the beginning of the 1970s, Leblanc, a manufacturer
of music instruments, surveyed its advisory board of "music
educators of distinction," on the role of future music education. The board agreed that from kindergarten through the
twelfth grade, music had to be made to conform to students'
needs and lifestyles. Every kind of music should be taught,
centered on understanding musical language (not necessarily
literature). Furthermore, the board found altogether too
many music teachers "out of touch with reality" and not keeping abreast of changing lifestyles.[3]

In secondary-school education, administrators at times
made choices, as did parents and their children, which indicated that, as far as they were concerned, the arts were a
part of a less important lifestyle, and a snobbish one, at that.
In contrast, they and a majority of Americans had chosen
athletics as a vital feature of the "American way-of-life."
Thus many secondary schools and colleges, either overtly
or covertly, sought out, nurtured, and placed a higher value
on athletics, providing athletes with as excellent coaches as
could be hired. They spent quantities of money on athletic
equipment, practice fields, gymnasiums, and stadiums, and
saw to a great deal of media coverage. School administrations,
alumni organizations, the mass media, and students often idolized an outstanding athlete, while paying scarcely any attention to a student who demonstrated extraordinary attainments
in literature, painting, or music. The educational focus was
on physical activity and skills at the expense of cultural
knowledge and perception of the presumably subtler nuances
of human experience.

Jesse Jackson, upset because young black Americans were being educated to favor athletics over learning, said over WNEC-TV, on 9 December, 1984: "It came to me that whatever one does 24 hours a week, or without interruption, and with discipline and determination and drive, one becomes good at it. So if we pursue art and science and literature with the same passion we do football, basketball, and baseball, we can slam-dunk a thought. You know we have the same capacity.... Democracy does not guarantee success. It does guarantee opportunity. You have to keep opportunity alive. But effort must always exceed opportunity."

Unfortunately, many of our secondary schools allowed students a poor chance for advancement in the arts, either denying them arts courses altogether or directing creative energy into narrow channels--football marching bands, for instance. By so doing, they checked democracy by lessening opportunity for a student's full development. In addition, the possibly creatively gifted student might have been deterred from the arts, even when instruction was offered, since economic reward, peer-approval, and societal recognition would not necessarily result.

A number of twentieth-century educators did not always heed what a Stanford University professor, Elliot Eisner, said about the arts. In an article on deciding what to teach in our schools, Charles Fowler wrote, in Musical America, of Eisner's claim that the arts offered the young student a variety of ways to record what the senses perceived about the world and the different ways of perceiving it. He then quoted Eisner as stating: "The realization that the arts represent one of the ways through which humans construct and convey meaning and that the creation of art forms requires the use of judgment, perceptivity, ingenuity, and purpose--in a word, intelligence--seems to have escaped most those who have commented upon the state of education...."[4]

One should add to this that those who enjoyed art music said its importance lay in the exploration of areas of human experience and feeling untouched by the other arts and by popular or folk song. It tried to represent the inner world in less simplistic terms than music intended for entertainment alone, by more fully utilizing the resources of sound. To critics who said: "Prove its value!", the reply came that

nothing could ever easily be proved, not even 1 + 1 = 2.
Nor was it required in the ordinary conduct of human activity that convictions underlying civilized society be proved
as indisputable beyond the possibility of doubt. Such proof
was impossible. What alone could be advanced was a degree
of corroboration and a show of sufficient reason in support
of these convictions. Justification of this sort of art music
was accessible and to be found in the cumulative perception
of men and women who have concentrated their attention upon
the social, artistic, and intellectual features of Western civilization. Their consensus was that such music marked a stage
of thought and feeling representative of that civilization at
its best. For this reason, at the minimum, it should be presented as an important component of school education.

MUSIC EDUCATION IN SECONDARY SCHOOLS

At the beginning of the 1980s, the federal government
issued an assessment of elementary and secondary school students, finding that three-quarters of the students (at three
levels--9, 13, and 17 years of age) valued music as an "important realm of human experience," and had a high degree
of awareness of, and sensitivity to, it. Seventy-two percent
of the 17-year-olds had taken at least one class in music, and
thirty-three percent had participated in a vocal or instrumental
group for at least one year. Participants in musical activities
also did better than other students in all studies, and those
who had participated most in the arts had achieved the most.
A definite interrelation with socio-economic background was
noted. Students with parents having some education beyond
high school and those attending schools in economically advantaged urban areas (and thus in districts able to afford to
offer more, varied, and sequenced courses) were above national levels. In contrast, students living in the Southeast,
those attending schools in disadvantaged urban areas, and
those with parents having less than a high school education
were below the national levels. Girls outshone boys in music
at every age level. Disquieting to the compilers of the report, however, was the uniformly poor showing of older students in identifying and classifying all musics both historically
and culturally.[5] In short, it was necessary to raise the question of the direction and quality of this teaching, whether in
art, folk, or popular music, and what sort of sound was sig-
nified by the term "music."

In 1984 came a new federal study of course-offerings
and enrollments in the arts and humanities in the secondary
schools. Ninety percent of the high schools, it was found,
offered music instruction, usually in the form of performance
(band, orchestra, instrumental ensemble, and chorus), and to
a much lesser extent in courses in theory, composition, ar-
ranging, and conducting. Half the schools offered instruction
in cultural appreciation of some sort. Almost seventy percent
of the seniors had taken at least one course in the arts while
in high school. Not surprisingly, rural schools had much
fewer offerings in the arts. Again a correlation was found
between students interested in the arts and those with an
advantaged socio-economic background. [6]

The findings in these two reports were regrettably deceptive. A converse side was evident to Ernest Boyer and
John Goodlad, who made public their own reports in 1983 and
1984, respectively. For instance, they noted that in most
schools the arts were the last to enter and the first to depart from curriculums. Almost one-third of all students had
never taken any arts courses. What is more, ten percent of
the schools offered no musical instruction whatsoever. When
carefully examined, even the surprisingly large number of
courses in some schools could be reduced to similar, if not
identical, offerings, as was the case in the several courses
given in vocal or instrumental ensemble.

Questioned was what the two-thirds of the student body
who took arts courses had actually heard and learned. If a
student joined a chorus or band, what did he or she really
understand about the arts, or music for that matter? Moreover, grading in arts courses was so inflated, content was
so diffuse and standards were so low that academic esteem was
absent. Interest centered on performance for entertainment
purposes. Students came away with negligible knowledge of
artistic compositions. [7]

In American high schools, values inclined toward the
commonplace. Educators whose views coincided with those of
the majority were put in power and had little conception of
what the arts might mean to education--so said critics of secondary education. [I have been astonished at the number of
school principals, assistant principals, and guidance counsel-
lors that I have met who were originally physical-education
teachers or athletic coaches.] These critics censured high

schools for stressing performance at the expense of listening
to and learning about any music, not just art music in particular, despite the fact that most graduates would end up not
as performers but as listeners.[8]

Music should be seen again as of permanent value,
writes Samuel Lipman, a writer worried about what he saw as
the erosion of standards through which one might assess cultural expression and experience. The purpose of teaching
music, he states, is "not as a form of self-expression or as
leisure-time activity, but as part of the great tradition of
learning and culture. The goal is training audiences, not
just--and perhaps not even primarily--musicians; training
and honoring music lovers and teachers of music, not just--
and definitely not primarily--performers."[9] This complaint
was increasingly voiced from the late seventies on, and not
only by cultural conservatives.

The American educational system from past to present,
writes Erich Fromm, in To Have or To Be? (1981), has trained
the young in knowledge proportionate to the wealth or position they may achieve in their future. Each may receive a
"luxury-knowledge package to enhance their feeling of worth,
the size ... in accord with the person's probable social prestige." But this does not mean students are put "in touch
with the highest achievements of the human mind," or with
the deeper meanings of Western tradition. Rather, students
receive "a vast smorgasbord of knowledge ... and in the
name of spontaneity and freedom are not urged to concentrate
on one subject."

The earliest American schools, in the history of the
United States, had been considerably influenced by religious
attitudes, with morality and right-thinking as prominent curricular desiderata. The arts had found no place in the teaching. Later, a business manner of looking at education prevailed. Schooling was meant to ready students for the real-
life siuations they would have to face.[10] Although the arts
were regarded as useful accomplishments for a young gentle-
woman seeking to attract a future husband, they were classi-
fied as adornments to gentility and their study not overly
emphasized. At the same time, they were considered to be
of no use to a young man whose main concern had to be getting on in agriculture, commerce, or industry.

Beginning with Lowell Mason's first attempt to introduce music instruction into Boston's public schools, in 1838, a gradual but grudging acquiescence to vocal music instruction in the classroom spread through the country. Some school administrators may have been stung into leniency by Ralph Waldo Emerson's criticism of nineteenth-century education: "We teach boys to be such men as we are. We do not teach them to aspire to be all they can. We do not give them a training as if we believed in their noble nature." Early on, singing was advocated as promoting health, psychological well-being, and morality (through the singing of uplifting texts). Then choruses (often designated as glee clubs) and bands entered the picture. By the mid-twentieth century also in place were orchestras, general-music courses in the intermediate grades, and elective music-appreciation courses in high school--more often, to be sure, in urban, less often in rural, school systems. In the second half of the twentieth century many music instructors made attempts at interspersing art works, mostly in the form of simplified arrangements, amongst the popular repertoire towards which high school choruses, bands, and orchestras usually gravitated.

Since its commencement, in 1936, the Music Educators National Conference, an association with members from every state, had worked toward raising standards in performance and in what was performed. Directors of bands, orchestras, and choruses in every state were encouraged to exhibit their students in ensemble performances at annual conferences on the district, state, regional, and national levels. The more praiseworthy directors tried to present balanced programs that included past and contemporary compositions representative of the best in folk, popular, and art-centered expression. During these conferences, the directors also attended workshops in order to further their knowledge of available literature and rehearsal techniques. Of course they also exchanged practical information during informal get-togethers. Over the years, I have attended many of these conferences, both as an observer and participant.

A common topic of conversation was their constant battle with school principals over scheduling music, any music, in the regular teaching hours and the less-than-adequate sum of money allocated the music program, save for the football marching band. Widespread was the complaint that school officials backed by teachers of science, mathematics, history, and English (who felt that college-bound students, especially, would waste the school day on dispensable even frivolous matters) advocated making over all music instruction into extra-curricular, after-school activities, for which no academic credit would be given.

Arts programs sat in the back of the academic bus-- assigned a second-class educational citizenry. This was emphasized by William Schuman, when he reported on research findings as to the acceptability of the performing arts in the curriculum. These findings had been published by the educational division of a major corporation. He quoted the conclusions as stating: "Serious questions were raised regarding the ability of the school system to fit an [arts] program into their present curriculum, due to time scheduling problems and also their ability to pay for such a program. Most teachers and curriculum advisors we contacted felt such a program might be highly desirable, but not critical to the development of the learner, and were most concerned lest time be subtracted from the basic education courses...." In similar vein, Charles Fowler concluded that the arts "have always been forced to fight for their usually meager slice of the annual budget," and "to defend their place in the curriculum. They have struggled against schedules that often prevented them from reaching the students who needed them most. They have expended endless energies trying to impress the power structure that their subject matters are worthy of being counted equal to the more acceptable 'legitimate' fare. Arts educators have probalby written more articles justifying their existence than all the other educators combined."[11]

In addition to the problems just named, music educators had also to deal with principals and school counselors who sabotaged general music and appreciation classes by dumping students with disciplinary problems into them (for want of another place to put them), then accusing the music teachers of inability to teach and maintain order. When hiring new music teachers, the marked interest of school administrators was in their ability to control unruly students or their willingness to act as entertainers and submit to public-relations needs. Musical attainments came second. Thus was unleashed a series of events where the response to one troublesome problem created another that made the situation worse.

As might be expected, these educators were also aware

of the predominant attitudes and prejudices of a vocal portion
of their constituency (whose volume level increased deafeningly
in bad economic times) which described the teaching of the
arts in derogatory fashion and saw in their elimination a preferred means to cost-cutting and to tax savings.[12]

Among themselves, concerned high-school music directors often expressed anger over administrators whose judgments of musical worth rested on successful public-relations
presentations. The band director was prized for the ability
to stage attention-grabbing half-time shows at football games,
the band's success in amusing businessmen during chamber-
of-commerce luncheons, and the "volunteering" of the director's and students' services to march in community-sponsored
parades, not the least of which were the annual "Santa Claus
parades" aimed at increasing Christmas retail sales. The
choral director was prized for his or her ability to stage colorful Christmas pageants, entertaining vaudeville productions,
and simplified versions of currently popular Broadway mus-
icals.[13]

Witness the remarks of Harlan Hoffa, chairman of the
art-education department at Pennsylvania State University,
about how the arts, still considered "special subjects" by
educational planners, were "the first to be called up for the
PTA extravaganza and the first to be shot down by the
school board's Finance Committee." He finds, however, that
the arts teachers themselves have contributed to this lament-
able situation, by acting "as if they were special. They have
tended to the special interests of special students but have
blatantly ignored those who are not specifically arts-oriented."
Furthermore, they have no involvement with other subjects
like history or social studies. Over-specialization, he claims,
makes them feel important but the isolation also hurts them.[14]

The educational administrator took note of this isolation
and felt uneasy. At the same time, the bureaucratic mind
was made more comfortable with other branches of learning,
where studies were technological or intellectual. He or she
prized learning if it was also objectively testable, essential
for survival, or necessary to the business community. Music had limited applications, no survival virtues, and slight
usefulness to the business community. Other than the learning to sing or play an instrument, it was a subjective pursuit and unamenable to objective testing. As the composer

William Schuman pointed out, in a speech given before the
National Conference of the Association for Supervision and
Curriculum Development, in 1968, public educators found
music less than significant because it failed to prepare the
young for future vocational or practical employment. It
could not have a high priority in an educational system whose
primary aim was "to develop skills necessary for economic security."[15]

When conservative fiscal policy and the back-to-basics
movement became equally prominent, as they did after the
mid-seventies and into the eighties, then the opportunity to
study music lessened. In April, 1985, the director of the
music program in the Boston public school system told me that
in the early seventies, he had 140 vocal, instrumental, and
classroom music teachers available to service 18 high schools,
24 middle schools, and 79 elementary schools. Owing to a
growing fiscal crisis, the school committee had to cut back on
the number of teachers in the system. Because music was
judged the least vital of the city's educational programs, the
pruning of music teachers was severe and out of all proportion when compared with that of teachers in other areas. By
1982, seventy percent of the music teachers had been dismissed; only 42 remained. To give a second example, Baltimore, Maryland, in 1982, had 39 fewer elementary music teachers than in previous years, and only 26 vocal-music teachers
left to cover 127 elementary schools. Meanwhile, the school
board of Prince George's County, Maryland, had eliminated
17 of the elementary instrumental music teachers. The board
previously had tried to wipe out the entire instrumental-music
program, but community pressure had forced it to reconsider
the action. As it was, only 20 instrumental teachers were
left in the county. A final example, New York City's school
system employed 2,200 music teachers in 1974. Forced to put
its finances in order, the city found cutting out music teachers a relatively painless way to retrench. Ten years later,
only 793 remained in the system. Typically, when cutbacks
of this nature occurred, accented was the widely accepted
tendency to admit only students with talent or strong musical backgrounds into whatever musical programs were allowed
to continue, while ignoring the rest of the student body.[16]

Two obvious consequences of music's lack of esteem were
the weakening of a sense of purpose and self-respect amongst
music educators and the attraction of less-than-talented

candidates to the profession of music teaching. Although the
training of school-music teachers had never really stressed
the acquiring of knowledge and love for music literature, a
large proportion of the young school-music teachers who entered the profession in the sixties and seventies had even less
sympathy for art music than had older teachers. When assigned to teach courses in music appreciation, they were more
comfortable transmitting snippets of a composer's biography,
legends surrounding a famous composition, the "program" of
an instrumental piece, the plot of an opera or ballet, and
the macro-structure of a movement. This was also subject-
matter that lent itself to convenient-to-correct and "objective"
testing (like true-or-false questions). These teachers reflected the prevalent attitude of most Americans, that any
music--art, folk, or popular music--could be found to have
expression, emotional power, and persuasiveness. The first
goal of education was to teach the aesthetic perception common to all musics.[17] No instructional balance had to be struck
between different musics.

The effect of such thinking was the downplaying of
art music (especially when the teacher had little understanding of it), or the mechanical going-through-the-motions of
teaching it (when the teacher was assigned its instruction).

Samuel Lipman was one of several educational critics
alarmed by the trend toward dismissing the pursuit of music
as a significant activity. It seemed to him that music increasingly took the guise of "ego therapy" for the "socially disadvantaged" or appeared as a pabulumized version of artistic
expression, all in the name of democracy. Lipman took especial umbrage at the publication Coming To Our Senses (1977),
the report of a panel chaired by David Rockefeller, Junior,
and sponsored by the American Council for the Arts in Education. Out of 334 pages, Lipman writes, only three clauses,
not sentences, touch on the music of the "great composers."
The report's approval is given almost entirely to "innovative"
programs like those involving jazz, rock, and soul music, and
after-school piano and guitar sessions. Every area of music
study was made equal, with some [presumably the nonelite]
subjects more equal than others. Emphasis was given to
forms of self-expression and "unsophisticated mock-artistic
creation." Criteria for determining the quality of musical activity, he said, were impossible to establish.[18]

Lipman is too limited in his views. Innovative programming involving jazz, rock, and soul music should not
ipso facto be discouraged. Instead, it is the question, already mentioned, of balance that must be raised: is art music receiving its fair share of funding, of adequate space
and equipment for teaching, and of properly trained teachers
with love for artistic compositions and skill in communicating
their love to students?

The weakening of the arts on the secondary-school
level received encouragement from colleges and universities,
whose admissions policies operated to exclude music. College-
entrance examinations had no arts components. The student's
grade in music frequently was deliberately left out of grade-
point averages reported to admissions committees. Both
college-bound students and high-school teachers, whatever
their private feelings, quickly got the message that a student's
involvement in the arts did not pay off when it came to selection by the college of one's choice.[19]

Awareness of this discrimination against the arts grew
in the eighties. The Education Equality Project of the College
Entrance Examination Board issued a report, in 1983, entitled
Academic Preparation for College: What Students Need to
Know and Be Able to Do. The report urged that the arts
be granted equal footing with academic subjects since they
are needed to "challenge and extend human experience," and
represent "a unique record of diverse cultures" and "provide
distinctive ways of understanding human beings and nature."
The compilers of the report wanted the arts valued as "creative modes by which all people can enrich their lives both by
self-expression and response to the expressions of others."
Artistic compositions are "complex systems of expression" requiring "careful reasoning and sustained study that lead to
informed insight." They enhance the quality of life, stimulate
the imagination, encourage flexibility in thinking, foster disciplined effort, and build confidence in one's self. Therefore,
to be cultivated in all students hoping to enter college is,
among other things, the ability to understand and appreciate
different artistic styles and works from representative historical periods and cultures.

The report failed to alter attitudes. Secondary-school
administrators, teachers, and students still thought that reports of this sort were little more than window dressing.

College-entrance criteria and attitudes that downgraded the arts continued as before. Worried about the military threat from Communist countries and the industrial and technological competition from other advanced nations, however friendly, American political and economic leaders, in the 1980s, want less "foolishness in education," and greater stress on "basics," like writing, science, mathematics, and computer training.

What of the future? Even those school administrators making a sincere effort to give at least equal representation to art, alongside folk and popular, music must realize that a decreasing number of their teachers will have an adequate knowledge of or a great affection for their subject. In a majority of schools, instead of stressing outstanding compositions representative of every type of musical expression, past and present, non-American and American, the temptation may continue to be to stress whatever music will serve as an adjunct to sports and public-relations activities, performed by student music groups that exist outside the serious educational orbit. What classroom teaching is attempted is likely to be superficial, begrudgingly done, placed in ridiculously brief time slots, and without follow-through over a period of time. In addition, the instruction, whatever it may be, will reach students who, for the most part, have little or no background in or experience with high culture. No reinforcement will ensue outside of the classroom of whatever they might have studied, even when that study has taken place under the best teachers.

"Classical music" continues to bore students. Yet, when questioned, students have murky ideas of what it is, confusing it with jazz, big-band, ballroom, and folk music. Almost all of them prefer the most recent popular, to any other kind of music, although this preference is less marked in girls.[20]

By high-school age, it is much less easy to broaden cultural behavior. The influences from the surrounding American society prove more difficult to overcome. Instruction should begin in the early primary grades, when minds are impressionable and still open to myriad experiences, without the psychological blocks that are operative later. Repeated listenings to a limited selection of compositions, preferably ones with striking rhythmic characteristics and agreeable melody and harmony, should extend over the entire school year. Insistent promotion on radio, television, and other entertainment

media has served commercial music well. A similar promotion
of art music in the classroom, alongside other types of music
is needed. In particular, students should acquire knowledge
of all aspects of music in America, and the myriad shapes it
has come in. Furthermore, in responding to this music, students, especially the younger ones, should not find their
manner of appreciation circumscribed, particularly when they
form an audience for live performances. If music spontaneously moves them to dance, sing along, conduct, jump up
and down, and shout their approval--fine! These are all
modes of understanding, as legitimate as, if not more legitimate
than, comprehending structure and style. The educator must
keep in mind that the ends of education are altered behavior
and a profounder grasp of the world without and within the
individual, not the exacting of the pound of flesh, known as
testing, which destroys the aesthetic experience.

MUSIC IN HIGHER EDUCATION

In the last third of the nineteenth century, a number
of American colleges and universities began to offer courses
in music history, theory, and composition. Some of these
institutions and the several conservatories of music, most of
whose doors opened for the first time shortly after the end
of the American Civil War, also sponsored applied-music studies.

By the latter part of the twentieth century, music
courses were ubiquitous in the liberal-arts curriculum. The
more modest schools with any pretensions to teaching the
liberal arts had monetary capital barely sufficient for their
needs. They, nevertheless, did at least offer courses in music history and appreciation, though usually with barely adequate equipment and, not infrequently, with lackluster instructors. Their student bodies usually consisted of young men
and women from the least affluent and least educationally
oriented social groups. Many entrants into college were
young people often psychologically and academically ill prepared to cope with studies on the university level.

A few fortunate universities had won splendid reputations for the excellence and the variety of their educational
efforts in music. They had ample funds to channel into the
arts. As a matter of course, they hired scholars, composers,

and musicians with national or international reputations to teach their students. They also provided superior music facilities, and therefore succeeded in attracting the most capable of the high-school (and private-school) graduates.

Between the handful at the top and the larger heap at the bottom came the preponderance of educational institutions, whose music offerings varied from the outstanding to the erratic or mediocre, with evidence of all three sometimes discoverable in the same school. Their student bodies boasted some unusual students, but more often the run-of-the-mill products of the secondary schools.

All of these colleges and universities, in the second half of the twentieth century, had to respond to a trifurcated mandate. First was the idea of the university as a transmitter of civilization's cumulative knowledge and culture, in particular those central to a society's values and continuing identity. Second was the imperative, in a democracy, to reach out to all young people, from whatever class or ethnic group, and whether sufficiently prepared or not by their secondary schools for higher education. Somehow institutions of higher education had to help them overcome whatever their social, economic, and educational limitations and place them in the ranks of well-educated Americans. Third was the peculiarly American inheritance manifested in the predominantly practical mind-set of the society, which assessed all education, whether theoretical or applied, mostly in terms of its possible utilization in advancing the economy, fortifying the nation against aggressors, or augmenting the professional social services by producing medical doctors, lawyers, and the like.

My intention in this chapter is to examine the relation of music instruction in colleges and universities to the general student, not to the student majoring in music, and the way that relation has been affected by the American democracy.[21]

As a starting point, it is useful to look at the observations on higher education made by William J. Bennett, who headed the National Endowment for the Humanities until the end of 1984, when he became Secretary of Education. Mr. Bennett, an educational conservative, is anathema to a crowd of college and university provosts, chancellors, and presidents, in part for obtuse remarks like the one he made about the privileged financial status of students, in part for the sharp

censures he levied against contemporary American curriculums.
Higher-education curriculums, he maintained, were a catchall
for every description of nonsense, with the humanities downgraded and the basic traditions of Western civilization deem-
phasized. Intellectual junk-food was substituted for what
should have been the central purpose of all institutions--the
transmission of culture. Sharing a similar viewpoint, Leonard
Kriegel, English professor at City University in New York,
has spoken of the "intellectual flotsam" evident in contemporary curriculums: "Courses in the humanities become manifestations of race, of ethnicity, of regionalism, or of class.
And by allowing all values, all opinions, all feelings, all ideas
--no matter how ridiculous or ill-conceived--to be considered
equally, we made humanistic education a minor branch of
what might be called 'arts of living.'"[22]

These remarks bear a close resemblance to those voiced
by Hiestand and Lipman, quoted earlier. They make reference to the first of the three educational legacies, which they
insist is being supplanted by the other two. Yet, are Bennett and Kriegel right? And how does what they state relate
to art music?

Immediately after World War II the college population
burgeoned, owing to an expanded birth rate, a general increase in prosperity, and a widely shared conviction that as
many young people as possible should enroll in college. The
G. I. Bill of Rights made possible the attendance of former
members of the armed forces who might otherwise never have
attended a college. In addition, enormous amounts of money
supplied by federal and state governments, foundations, and
industry helped educational institutions to expand facilities,
hire additional faculty members, and offer scholarships and
loans on liberal terms to entering students, thus fueling the
rise in college enrollment. College attendance in 1900 amounted
to around 237,000 young men and women. Forty years later,
the figure had grown to one and a half million; by 1950, to
over two million; by 1970, to almost eight million; and by
1983, to around twelve million.[23]

Most of the extra millions of students came from families
whose members at worst demonstrated various stages of illiteracy, or at best boasted high-school degrees. Slender means
and unfamiliarity with most forms of literature and high culture characterized them. Theirs was a mass culture revolving

around the entertainments of radio, television, movies, and
youth-catering night spots and concert halls. Music to them
comprised the popular ditties of the day.

To these millions, college was a way to learn a market-
able skill and a means for climbing the ladder of success to
well-paying occupations. Rounded and cultural educations
were incidental to their main purpose. Not surprisingly, over
one-half the entering students expressed indifference to the
arts. As Margaret Mahoney observed, even though two-thirds
of the freshmen might state that they entered college "to seek
a philosophy of life," most of them really thought the arts irrelevant to the search and proportionally few of them enrolled
in arts courses unless distribution requirements forced them
to do so.[24]

When this indifference was coupled to the youth-oriented
revolt against authority and all traditional values, in the sixties and early seventies, it resulted in hostility to all received
wisdom. Whether Johann Sebastian Bach or Milton Byron Babbitt, art composers no longer were thought to represent the
best in music. "There is no best," was a common rejoinder.
Taste was subjective. Her best and his best had equal validity, comments Henry Blasso, writing in 1970. He further
states that students were making a shambles of culture as
their elders had known it, substituting emotional, immature
judgments of the moment for the considered, mature judgments
of serious thinkers over the years. Cultural nihilism was the
result.[25]

Students increasingly insisted that they be amused with
the music they knew and favored. Some schools began to
conduct in-house polls in order to learn what popular performing groups were most approved. These were hired. Of
course ticket sales for these groups met with tremendous success.

Describing Michigan State University at East Lansing,
in the late sixties, Jim Roos states: "The programs which
account for such [great] financial success follow the not-too-
unusual formula of fame and fad." Michigan State popular-
music concerts drew an average of 6200 students, and sometimes as many as 7500 students, the great majority of them
freshmen and sophomores. The concert series featuring orchestras and ballet companies was much less successful.

Chamber music "bombed with the students." As few as 150
people might attend, with ninety percent of the audience consisting of faculty members and outsiders.[26] It was a picture
that continued to portray a number of colleges and universities
twenty years later.

Michigan State's situation, in other words, was not
unique. The "student power" movement that gathered force
in the sixties, persuaded those educational officials most beset by anxiety to comply with students' demands, especially
in those areas which seemed to them peripheral to education's
main mission. Music in the opinion of many of them was certainly peripheral.

It was a case of those in need of education and cultural
enrichment determining the content of their education, however narrow and uninformed the viewpoint influencing the determination, and nullifying the idea of art music as proper
enrichment. As we shall see, such accommodation of students'
demands would occur not only in extracurricular but in curricular matters affecting the fundamental character of American higher education.

In short, if the operation of democracy meant that students would determine what musical culture was to be espoused, then colleges and universities might cease to transmit any form of art music. Majority rule would operate with
a vengeance. As a consequence, one aspect of American society's core identity, that is to say the sum total of its musical character, could entirely comprise its most commonplace
elements. Because this music represented the ever fluctuat-
ing present, with no past and future, then it would be an
identity without a history and without a goal.

I do not mean to imply that all students, or even more
than half of them, advocated such an outcome; simply that
the implications of this cultural direction, especially within
the context of increasing sophistication in the profit-hungry
and amoral entertainment industry, pointed to an eventuality
where the works of art composers were ruled out in advance.
From its beginnings, the American nation had put emphasis
on checks-and-balances in order to deflect the force of majority rule. Needed now were educational checks-and-balances
to restrain the movement toward complete musical homogeneity.
Could administrators and professors supply this restraint?

As the number of students in higher education grew
into the millions, a greatly augmented teaching staff was necessary to deal with this growth. Thousands of additional
faculty members were recruited. Regrettably for art music,
most of these thousands had had the same economic, social,
and cultural backgrounds as the students they were hired
to teach. Moreover, in the seventies and eighties they represented a new generation of instructors whose cultural education, in the universities they had attended, had been con-
stricted by their backgrounds, by the denigration of the
worth of art music, and by the rise of elective courses allowing them as students to avoid music altogether or to choose
to enroll in music studies towards which they were already
favorably inclined. Of the trifurcated mandate, I spoke of
earlier, the first was depreciated, the second distorted, and
the third made a subliminal advisory for academic decisions.

Quite a few of the new additions to the general faculty,
some of whom became administrators or heads of important
committees, learned to talk fluently about art music but were
absent from the majority of concerts offered at the university
and in the community. Some of them also heeded "the cries
of relevance" and surrendered whatever commitments they
had to the arts and literature "under the rubric of curricular
reform." They occasionally sponsored, instead, courses "in
magic, astrology, rock music, Yoga, Zen, and meditation."
One result was that untenured instructors might find themselves vying with each other for the largest enrollments by
offering commonly liked courses that were easily passed.[27]

In general (and I speak also from personal experience
with eight colleges and universities), of all the departments,
the music department usually had the poorest equipment, the
most limited library collection, the smallest offices, and the
least backing. For every institution taking pride in and sup-
plying liberal funds to its music department, ten could be
signaled out as acting in a dilatory or deliberately unforth-
coming manner when it came to the discipline's needs. For
example, requests for tape recorders, pianos, practice rooms,
and concert space would go unheeded, while science labora-
tories and sports complexes got the nod.

It has already been mentioned that a small percentage
of the academic community attended orchestral and operatic
performances. The scarcity of young people and faculty was

even more noticeable at chamber music concerts. One does not need to look further than some of our better known institutions to find examples of this noninterest in music. Brandeis University, to cite one instance, had a fine record for support of its music program. Yet, the composer Seymour Shifrin could still testify to how troubled he was because the Brandeis "community of scholars" did not "find it within their purview to be curious and even seeking to know what is happening in the arts." Few felt an obligation to music, what obligation there was going to the plastic arts. Among the faculty, he saw "pompous asses" who were "suspicious of the enterprise of the arts in the curriculum of the university." Again, Pennsylvania State University is by no means the most backwards when it comes to music. However, the painter Harold Altman was able to say: "One thing that bugged me in the past was the lack of appreciation for the creative arts in the university. In this university in particular, the sciences were the important thing." Then he adds: "You know art is a frill; music is a frill. But making the better computer and finding a better insecticide is important."[28]

To give a final example, Princeton University is noted for its contributions to contemporary American music. Despite these contributions, the composer Milton Babbitt states that the lack of curiosity about music, especially contemporary art music, at Princeton went back to the fifties: "We thought we could talk to the scientific and academic community in general by attracting them to a sense of our worth. We attempted to talk about music in a way we believed would make sense to them. We discovered that if there was anything they resented more than taking music seriously, it was taking talk about music seriously. I know of no scientist here in Princeton who has even so much as attended a concert of our music."[29]

It was invariably the case for administrators to react to cost squeezes or drops in arts enrollments with a lopping off of music programs and a dismissal of music faculty, while at the same time those courses seen as relevant to job getting, national defense, and business remained protected, however much their enrollments also dropped.[30]

Like their counterparts in the secondary schools, professors of music found it necessary to defend their subject as an academic discipline, that is to say as a study that imparted verifiable knowledge by influencing the qualitative

character of a student's mental faculties. How did this defense affect the general student who might be influenced to
join the future audience for art music? The young people
enrolling in music courses immediately found themselves buf-
feted by a number of contradictory educational crosscurrents.
In the name of rational objectivity, they were introduced to
the history of various musics and musical styles. However,
they also found themselves entangled in aesthetic theories deal-
ing with the nature of music and artistry. Instruction was
given in the way a composition was formed and how it was
to be conceptualized in order to understand it. If all else
failed, mystiques of the creative process, of the composer as
a supramundane being, and of the musical work as significant
beyond the limits of all possible knowledge helped to obfus-
cate and, by implication, add a veneer of profundity with
which to intimidate the recalcitrant student and the skeptical
non-music faculty.

Although art music was normally at the center of this
instruction, a smorgasbord of other musics, each with its own
history, style, aesthetic theory, and mystique offered an in-
digestible mélange of information in the usual introductory
survey courses for non-majors.[31] This hodgepodge of musical instruction became especially prevalent after the fifties,
when art music began to be seen as a form of elitism, and
colleges and universities moved to shore up their democratic
credentials.

A pitifully small number of graduates from these music
courses discovered a love for art music. They had not always had teachers with a passion for and a quick discernment
of their subject; teachers who not only thought out an orderly
scheme for presenting their instructional materials but also
analyzed their students' limitations and capabilities; teachers
who encouraged direct, excited, and intuitive involvement with
sound; and teachers capable of fitting the necessarily limited
scope of one course into the universal human impulse for musical expression. The likelihood was strong that students
would take their final examinations and take away no subjective understanding of any of the unfamiliar musics in which
they had received instruction.[32]

To be sure, effective teachers existed, capable of imparting their knowledge to, and firing the enthusiasm of, students. Prominent in the academic scene, however, were three

types of music educators whose presence had been much less prevalent during the first half of the century: the musicologist, the art composer, and (for want of a better term) the go-getter.

Most serious music departments, after World War II, gradually were dominated by musicologists dedicated to the "rational and systematic investigation" and analysis of all music, writes Charles Hamm.   They conceived of music "as a rational thing that can yield its secrets to intellectual analysis."   This narrowly defined approach "was first and most easily accepted for older music, but in time ... was accepted by many as a valid and even necessary attitude toward newly composed music."[33]

Trained by European musicologists and, later, by Europhilic American music scholars to transatlantic ways of thinking, American musicologists tended to pledge their allegiance to West European music and its objective explication, states Richard Crawford, not to music in America, nor to the relation of music to audience, nor to the internal and emotional effects of sound.   Distrusted was the personal and subjective and anything having a suggestion of the sociological.[34]   Fostering the strong feelings attendant on a student's successful personal encounter with music was not a function that musicologists felt they should assume.   Indeed, it might mean the cheapening of art music.   Quite a few of these members of the music faculty played a significant role in denying students the essence of what constituted the musical experience.

After World War II, teaching alongside the academic musicologist was the academic composer.   Tensions between the two inevitably developed.   At times, these tensions came to such a peak that the composer had to be fired by an institution where musicologists were dominant in the music department, and the musicologist had to be fired where composers were dominant.

The academic composers commenced with a subjective, if not a self-centered vision of music.   They, more often than not, taught in order to receive a salary that would enable them to continue composing.   They usually resented the committee-work imposed upon them by the university, the required contact with music students uninterested in becoming composers, and the necessity for teaching the general student.

They might also feel that they had been hired so that the
school could profit by their reputation as composers, thus
making them a commodity and vulnerable for displacement by
another composer seen as having a greater reputation.[35]

They were often irritated, if not angry persons when
facing the classes populated by members of the general student body. Their instruction might be unthought out, un-
structured, or biased toward their own compositional view-
points.[36] To be sure, this was not true of all composers,
but certainly of enough of them to make it a frequent source
for complaint amongst students. The non-composers on the
music faculty were irked at what they interpreted as free-
wheeling instruction and made the problem of the composer-
teacher a persistent topic of conversation at higher-education
conferences. The end result, as far as the student was concerned, was a lessening of curiosity about music even as he
or she learned to avoid further study with certain composers.

Because in most institutions high emphasis was given to
excellence in scholarship or creativity in granting tenure, the
musicologist or composer with a respectable record of achievement in publication or production of new compositions but with
a poor record of teaching might easily be frozen into position
and thus continue to perpetuate his or her failings vis-à-vis
the general student. Democratic dialogue that encouraged a
sense of community and fellowship, and joint participation in
a journey of discovery would take place in few classrooms.

Beginning with the sixties, a third type of music-faculty
member, the music go-getter, was increasingly in evidence,
not perhaps in the most prestigious institutions but certainly
in lesser private colleges intent on attracting applicants for
their freshman classes, and in public colleges sensitive to the
criticisms of prosaic politicians to whom crowded classrooms
and lecture halls were the surpeme test for successful teaching. Theirs was a personality influenced by the revisionist
and populist ideologies. Art music, they might consider to
be merely a decorative appendage to the lifestyle chosen by
certain of the educated and affluent classes. The sincere
musicologist and composer resented their necessary involvement with music as a commodity; the go-getter accepted the
situation and tried to profit by it.

The picture I now draw is a composite that features the

diverse elements making up this type. Scarcely ever is the
complete go-getter sort found in reality, at least not blatantly.
Nevertheless, many academics will recognize some delineations
of themselves in the portrait.

The two and a half decades beginning with 1960 were
ripe for such an individual to appear. These were years that
produced an overabundance of university graduates holding a
master-of-music or -arts, or a doctor-of-music or -philosophy
degree. As competition increased for academic positions, so
also did the strenuous efforts to gain some fame, from whatever source, in order to distinguish one's self from the crowd.
The imperative to look out for one's own welfare affected even
the most sincere and honest of the music graduates. Besides
teaching, they knew of the existence of few professional alternatives through which to make a living.

We should also keep in mind that, although in 1964 three
out of four college students with high honors pursued academic careers in arts and sciences, by 1985 only one in four
did so. Harvard College, to give one instance, saw a 77 percent drop in seniors going on to scholarly post-graduate study.
The top students abandoned the arts for the better-paying
and more numerous positions in industry and commerce. This
lack of top-notch students was especially true in music, where,
in the best of times, positions were few and insecure, and job
alternatives, nil.

Even as graduate schools experienced a drop in the
number of highly capable students in the arts, their total enrollment continued to hold up. A report on the arts and humanities, issued by the National Research Council, that came
out in the mid-eighties stated: "Although the number of top
students who become scholars has been declining, the number
of doctoral degrees being awarded has dropped only slightly."
Michael Spence, dean of Harvard's arts and sciences faculty,
worried about the caliber of students in the humanities. William G. Bowen, president of Princeton University, put it suc-
cinctly: "Too many Ph.D. candidates and not enough quality."[37]

In music, doctors of philosophy were graduated who
could hardly read a note of music and who possessed minimal
knowledge of, and no great affection for, the literature of
art music. Nevertheless, as one new member of a Michigan

university's music faculty declared to me between sessions,
at a national music conference held in 1985: "No matter how
poorly trained some of my buddies were, most of them managed to graduate. And, boy, did they know how to hustle
the product and promote themselves."

Some go-getters ostensibly were music historians or
composers, but neither publishable tomes nor imposing compositions came from their pens. The go-getters tended to
pursue the main chance, that is to say whatever seemed to
offer the most advantage and make him or her the most acceptable to administrators and students. They willingly taught
non-majors, sometimes to avoid the challenge of courses with
complex subject matter.

They took over non-technical appreciation classes.
Also, they constantly sampled the academic waters and advocated programs most likely to meet with widespread approval
(not, regrettably, programs that addressed the educational
deficiencies and needs of students). Because they were en-
terprising sorts of persons, they went after and in too many
instances got what they wanted. Even though syllabi, required listening, and assigned-reading lists might look impres-
sive, the content of every course they conducted was altered
in the actual teaching so as to make it more relevant to the
interests of students. They introduced new student-favored
courses mirroring various aspects of contemporary America's
mass culture. Recreation by reviving and giving fresh life
to the spirit gave way to the aim to please on the most acceptable level.

Although the discerning student detected shallowness
and was offended by soft grading, the majority of young people considered them good people and were inclined to give
them excellent evaluations at semester's end. Neither a sensitive awareness of musical worth, nor an honest acquaintance
with and an understanding after study of any music, whether
art, folk, or popular, was in the cards. A real broadening
of cultural horizons by venturing into lesser known musical
waters never truly occurred.

About the last point, a rueful Erich Fromm comments,
in To Have or To Be?, that a number of people have come to
desire contact with tradition and "teachers who can show them
the way. But in large part the doctrines and teachers are

either fraudulent, or initiated by the spirit of public relations ballyhoo, or mixed up with the financial and prestige interests of the respective gurus. Some people may genuinely benefit from such methods in spite of the sham; others will apply them without serious intention of inner change."

Even as the go-getters restricted the direction of the educational process, they subverted the meaning of democracy by debasing it through lowered standards and miscellaneous offerings. Admittedly, their counterparts existed in other departments. However, their potential for harm was of the greatest consequence to art music, especially when they presented it in a noncommitted manner. If students had a good time in their classes, they nevertheless graduated with little respect for some of the most serious utterances in music.

From a larger perspective, the transmission of culture, in particular the transmission of involvement with art music, lost through default. Owing to the fragility of democracy, the loss was an important one. The go-getter provided no restraint to majority rule. The level of taste and discernment remained unaltered, not only in music but in all of the arts.

The survival of an American democracy having a claim to civilized distinction demanded leaders dedicated to the ideals from which the nation drew its strength. These leaders were an integral part of the checks-and-balances meant to counter the domination of the usual, the ordinary, and the trivial in democratic culture, a domination that Alexis de Tocqueville had warned about 150 years ago, in <u>Democracy in America</u>. If the colleges and universities failed to produce these leaders, from where would they come?

A PARADOXICAL ENLIGHTENMENT

After detailing the failures of administrators, general faculty, and music departments in relation to art music, I must also concede to several seemingly contradictory functions that higher-education institutions accepted as stemming from their mandates. From the mid-fifties until the late seventies, a prosperous America contributed large sums of money to institutions of higher education. As they pondered how to employ some of their newfound disposable income, enlightened administrators and trustees were quite aware of their responsibility to transmit the culture of their society. They felt their institution was expected to reach out to the entire academic community and, in many instances, to the surrounding civic community with public offerings of the finest products of their civilization.

When and where funding was abundant, school officials gave practical expression to their democratic commission by, among other things, building cultural centers for the arts. They sponsored fine-arts exhibits, dramatic productions with and without music, and instrumental and vocal concerts of every description. The number of cultural projects were scaled up or down depending on the available money. The administrators and trustees of many of the less wealthy institutions dispensed with the building of new centers, but did try to institute some sort of concert and dance series, if only to prove that their institutions, too, could demonstrate refinement in thought and taste.[38]

This effort on the part of colleges and universities was admirable. For one, performances were sponsored of compositions that were otherwise ignored, dismissed as insignificant, or avoided. American music from the distant past to the current avant-garde benefited highly from this sponsorship. Less prevalent than in commercial-music circles was the desire to play it safe and to program mostly a handful of tried-and-true works from the past. Another benefit was the conscientious attempt made at authenticity, performances that reproduced a work in accordance with the composer's directions and in an idiomatic playing style, true to the time and place of the work's first realization. The spur to this quest for authenticity was the research findings of musicologists busily engaged in scholarly reconstructions of the past. No musicologist, unfortunately, could tell with complete accuracy how any work had once sounded. Yet, the attempt to recapture the original ambience and reinstitute original performance practices was laudable, especially when it enhanced expression and respected the need to communicate with a twentieth-century audience. A third benefit was the mitigation of the star-system common elsewhere. Lesser known performers from within and outside the school had a chance to appear before audiences. Indeed, by the seventies, a majority of musical performances were given under college and university auspices. A final benefit was the bringing of art music to widely scattered

areas of the United States, where music lovers might otherwise have been denied live concerts by professional musicians.
No longer did every one have to travel to a large, sometimes
distant, urban center in order to attend a concert of excellent quality. Moreover, admission to the school-sponsored
performances was usually either free or pegged at a low ticket
price. Thus, the building of new audiences for art music
was advanced.

Nevertheless, an immense number of colleges and junior
colleges made scarcely an effort to encourage art-music performances. Moreover, in a majority of colleges and universities, however much was spent on centers and art-music performances, the academic situation, as already described, between students, administrators, non-music faculty, and music
faculty, tempered the benefits. At one extreme was Indiana
University, with ample facilities, a well-nourished music program, and performing groups which included a professional
calibre symphony, extensive opera productions, and resident
professional chamber ensembles and soloists. More than 600
concerts and recitals and eight or more new opera productions
took place every year.[39] At the far more densely populated
other extreme was the University of Massachusetts at Boston,
with no facilities to speak of, an impoverished academic music
program, and a minuscule concert series (for which no administrators and hardly any faculty or students turned out) made
possible mostly through performers volunteering their services.

After the mid-seventies, the money-wells dried up for
many higher-education institutions, as they had for public
school systems. College and university administrators who
had resisted active students' demands for currently popular
amusements and who had sponsored art-music concerts even
when poorly attended, found themselves without a monetary
surplus. Much less was left over after meeting the bills for
what were considered the essential academic programs. The
number of art-music contributions to extracurricular academic
life had to be reduced. As a result, the "activities fee" paid
by students increasingly became an alternate source for the
funding of concerts.

Schools with strong leadership and an aware student
body managed to maintain the quality of their musical offerings. Not surprisingly, in other schools, the temptation, and

sometimes the necessity, to cater to young peoples' tastes
grew. Students insisted on taking a hand in the bookings,
and, as Robert Jones states, soon "rock artists" were "in,
classical artists out," whether they came from without or
within the school. Jones continues by saying that Joseph
Lippman, vice president of Herbert Barrett Management, once
asked a university committee in charge of booking: "Tell me
something. Do you have a music department in this university?"

"Oh yes!" the committee members replied. "We have
the best in the state!"

Lippman then said: "Well, what the hell do you have
it for? You people are turning out pianists and violinists
and singers and harpsichordists and cellists and you don't
want to hear them. So why are you turning them out? There
are enough people already performing who can't get engagements. Your position is amoral. Why don't you shut down
the school and save yourself four or five million dollars a
year?"[40]

The now up, now down status of art music in higher
education will undoubtedly continue in the foreseeable future.
Educators must never forget that the American democracy
premises the existence of a will to learn about the unknown
on the part of its citizenry. To teach them everything and
anything brings on chaos. Educators should consider what
knowledge is of importance to transmit from old to young and
should classify the underlying topics which form the basis for
liberal study. Consideration should be given to subjects that
provide springboards to further learning and that try to give
life a meaning beyond the obvious.

Art music does meet these requirements, because it sig-
nifies more than the giving of instant pleasure and the allure-
ment of the immediately apprehended. It does ask for some
industry in the study of its expressive modes in order to
yield up the many-layered pleasures it can offer. The outstanding art composers in our Western civilization have met
with and responded to the world around them with insightful
works of the imagination. Their compositions should be taught
as far-ranging explorations of man's emotive and psychic nature. Our finest musical compositions, like our greatest poems,
plays, novels, paintings, and sculptures, are not superfluities

having only decorative significance; they are basic to our
education, because they put us on the road to becoming hu-
mane individuals and, therefore, responsible citizens.

"Why study classical music?" asked Charles Fowler. He
answered: "Because the apotheoses of human achievement in
musical art are found in works such as Bach's Art of the Fu-
gue, in Beethoven's Ninth Symphony, in Britten's War Requiem,
or any number of other great works. We must offer every
person in this society the right to climb those mountains,"
through education available to all Americans. We defeat democracy when only affluent communities sponsor worthwhile
programs in their schools. Thus, does art become reserved
for the elite. Fowler continues by saying that other students,
not reached by the arts, get the message that they are too
stupid, untalented, or poor to study it; or "by its absence
... that [it] isn't important enough to bother with." As it
is, fewer and fewer Americans get to know art music, and
more and more detractors try to retire it from education curriculums.[41]

We must avoid the pessimism of Thomas Berger, the
novelist, who claims the masses today show the same mentality
as that of peasants from the Middle Ages, and who finds that
popular education insures the triumph of illiteracy and the
pollution of intellect. As Richard Schickel said, after refer-
ring to Berger's statement, we hate to back ourselves into an
elitist corner, however despairing our view.[42]

Even if an elite will always exist, the least we can do
is to give everybody the chance to join it, though few may
elect to do so. This we try to do by attempting to enhance
each individuals interior space--that is to say, the psychological area which comprises not only what he or she requires,
esteems, and struggles to achieve, but also the blocks and
constraints of circumstance that diminish them. At the end,
I suppose, I must concur with Schickel's declaration that in
any society with a pretense to greatness an elite of some kind
"is vital to its healthy functioning as the knowing repository
of its highest intellectual and artistic attainments, as the caring (if sometimes misled) sensors of what, in contemporary
culture may be worthy of that great tradition."[43]

Notes

1. For further discussion of this aspect of democracy
as related to the arts, see Etienne Gilson, Painting and Reality (Cleveland: World, 1959), pp. 223-225.
2. Emily Hiestand, "May I Have a Word With You?"
Boston Globe Magazine, 23 February 1985, pp. 15-22.
3. See the Music Journal Annual (1972), p. 218.
4. Charles B. Fowler, "Deciding What to Teach,"
Musical America (October 1983), p. 413.
5. Charles B. Fowler, "Musical Achievement: Good
News and Bad," Musical America (May 1982), pp. 212, 24.
6. Charles B. Fowler, "The Arts in Our High Schools:
New Data," Musical America (January 1985), pp. 22, 35.
7. Ibid., pp. 336-37.
8. W. C. Greckel, "Music Misses the Majority," Music
Journal (December 1972), p. 521.
9. Samuel Lipman, The House of Music (Boston:
Godine, 1984), p. 273.
10. Barbara Hall, "Rockefeller Speaks Out for Arts
Education," Boston Globe, 15 January 1984, p. 53.
11. Amyas Ames, "The Political Power of the Arts,"
Music Journal (September 1970), p. 36; Schuman, "The Malady Lingers On," p. 31; Charles B. Fowler, "On Education,"
Musical America (February 1975), p. 7. See also, Nancy
Stevens, "Young Audiences Is Twenty-Five," Musical America
(February 1977), p. 13.
12. See Robin M. Williams, Jr. American Society, 3rd
ed. (New York: Knopf, 1970), pp. 319, 334.
13. During the fifties and sixties I was a music super-
visor in three Massachusetts public-schools systems and regularly participated in music-educators' conferences, from district to national. The comments made on these pages stem
from personal experience and the experiences of directors
from other states, who were friends or acquaintances made
during conferences.
14. Hoffa, "On Education," pp. 14-15.
15. William Schuman, "The Malady Lingers On," Music
Journal Annual (1968), p. 31.
16. See the report on cuts in public education, in Musical America (February 1983), p. 10; also, the New York
Times, 21 December 1984, section C, p. 1.
17. Hart, Orpheus in the New World, p. 441.
18. Lipman, The House of Music, pp. 271-272.

19. Charles B. Fowler, "Deciding What to Teach," _Musical America_ (October 1983), pp. 12-13.

20. See, for example, the surveys discussed in Ruth Zinar, "Musical Taste of Adolescents," _Music Journal_ (January 1973), pp. 10-11; also, Charles B. Fowler, "Classical Music Is Singing the Blues," _Musical America_ (June 1985), p. 12.

21. The relation of the young composer-in-training to institutions of higher education is discussed at length in my book _A Most Wondrous Babble: American Art Composers, Their Music, and the American Scene, 1950-1985_ (Westport, Conn.: Greenwood, 1987).

22. Chester E. Finn, Jr., "Colleges must heal themselves," _Boston Globe_, 19 February 1985, p. 15.

23. Godfrey Hodgson, _America in Our Time_ (New York: Random House, 1976), pp. 53, 96; Fred M. Hechinger, "State Schools Becoming Less Free and Easy," _New York Times_, 27 March 1983, section 4, p. 20.

24. Robin M. Williams, _American Society_, 3rd ed. (New York: Knopf, 1970), p. 341; Margaret Mahoney, ed., _The Arts on the Campus_, p. 22.

25. See the report of Henry Blasso, in the _Music Journal_ (January 1970), pp. 24-25.

26. Jim Roos, "Music at Michigan State--Are the Students With It?" _Musical America_ (August 1968), pp. 6-7.

27. Robert Brustein, _The Culture Watch: Essays on Theatre and Society, 1969-1974_ (New York: Knopf, 1975), p. 22.

28. Morris Risenhoover and Robert T. Blackburn, _Artists As Professors_ (Urbana: University of Illinois Press, 1976), pp. 19, 156-157.

29. Jeffrey G. Hirschfeld, "Milton Babbitt: A Not-So-Sanguine Interview," _Musical America_ (June 1982), pp. 16-17.

30. Fawcett and Thomas, _The American Condition_, p. 318.

31. Risenhoover and Blackburn, _Artists As Professors_, pp. 39-40; Eric Larrabee, "Artist and University," in _The Arts on Campus_, ed. Margaret Mahoney, p. 41; Charles M. Fisher, "The Performing Arts in Akademia," _Music Journal_ (April 1968), p. 37.

32. Howard Hanson, "Cultural Challenge," _Music Journal_ (January 1961), p. 5; Walter Simmons, in the _Sonneck Society Newsletter_ (Spring 1978), p. 12; Norman Lloyd, "Music and Education," in _The Arts on Campus_, ed. Margaret Mahoney, p. 86; Jon Roush, "The Humanities Museum," in _The Arts on Campus_, pp. 29, 36.

33. Charles Hamm, in Dictionary of Contemporary Music, ed. John Vinton (New York: Dutton, 1974), s.v. "Musicology and Composition."

34. Richard Crawford, American Studies and American Musicology, I.S.A.M. Monographs #4 (Brooklyn: Institute for Studies in American Music, 1975), pp. 2, 13-14.

35. Larrabee, "Artist and University," p. 42; Philip Friedheim, letter to the New York Times, 29 August 1971, section 2, p. 18; Elliott Carter, The Writings of Elliott Carter, ed. Else and Kurt Stone (Bloomington: Indiana University Press, 1977), pp. 280-282.

36. Vittorio Giannini, in the Music Journal Annual (1962), pp. 33, 72; Eugene Cook, "Penderecki: The Polish Question--and Others," Music Journal (February 1977), p. 42.

37. Richard Higgins, "A Warning to Academia," Boston Globe, 30 April 1985, pp. 1, 6.

38. Chapin, Musical Chairs, p. 107; Kozma, "Music vs the Majority," p. 86; Risenhoover and Blackburn, Artists as Professors, p. 3.

39. Jack M. Watson, "The College's Role in New Music," Music Journal Annual (1965), p. 58; Risenhoover and Blackburn, Artists as Professors, p. 43.

40. Robert Jones, in Musical America (July 1975), p. 15. 15.

41. Fowler, "Classical Music Is Singing the Blues," p. 16.

42. Schickel, Intimate Strangers, p. 294.

43. Ibid., p. 295.

Chapter 4

ON BEING A MUSICIAN IN AMERICA

Frustration and financial instability are endemic among American musicians, save for the few who occupy the catbird seats. Every year, however great their love for music and promising their talent, thousands of young vocalists and instrumentalists must abandon the music profession for the more certain rewards and securities afforded by jobs in business and industry.

Around a half a dozen years of hard study may produce a competent woodwind or brass player; at least a dozen years, a competent string player. Many who demonstrate strong musical potential, especially for a string instrument (violin, viola, cello), fail to develop their gifts. They know that after giving all they have to mastering their voice or instrument, their recompense will almost certainly be an inadequate wage for occasional or seasonal employment. "The incentive is not there," once said John Corigliano, former concertmaster of the New York Philharmonic. A further detriment to involvement with serious musical study is the dominant attitude amongst many Americans that puts self-fulfillment and immediate gratification first as recompense for any undertaking.[1] It is fortunate for the art-music world that some young people do decide to risk the life of a professional musician.

From where does the professional instrumentalist or vocalist come? A prime requirement for the nourishing of most budding musicians is a home where music is valued, a child is allowed to commence study at an early age, and constant practice is insisted upon (an autocratic, not democratic, parent is often the grey eminence behind every successful musician). Interestingly, as far as art music is concerned, that home has usually contained immigrants to America whose origin was an East-European, Iberian, or Mediterranean country, or their

immediate descendants.[2] For example, Elmar Oliveira, a concert violinist who won public attention in 1984, explains that
his Portuguese-immigrant father adored music and was a frustrated violinist, but his work was carpentry. He was determined that his two sons would study the violin, no matter
what. Both did, and Elmar Oliveira's brother was now a member of the Houston Symphony.[3] Carol Rosenberger, a pianist,
says her earliest memories were of persistent piano practice
and little else: "I remember standing at the keyboard up
above my head. I started formal lessons right after my fourth
birthday. The sound always drew me. I reached up and
touched the keys. A friend of my parents who was a piano
teacher watched this for a while and said, 'You might as well
start her lessons.'" Her study continued for twenty or so
years, despite costly lessons.[4]

To reach the top, a performer needed equal quantities
of ambition, aggressiveness, and stubbornness. In a demo-
cratic-capitalistic society, a tough competitive spirit and a
readiness to exploit every opportune situation are essential
to getting ahead. One well-known concert manager thought
that talent alone "may only count 20 percent," toward success. Another manager once stated: "Artists have to feel
that playing music on stage is absolutely the only possible
way they can spend their lives. Someone with a beautiful
voice who comes to me and says, 'I thought I'd try singing,'
I forget immediately. I discourage everybody. Those who
won't be discouraged perhaps have a chance." A majority of
the extremely talented quickly "recede into obscurity," owing
to the lack of ambition, writes Bernard Holland. "They see
the extramusical rigors that success requires and either lack
the drive or--depending on your viewpoint--are too intelligent
to proceed."[5]

Contemplating the fine graduates of the Juilliard School
of Music, Marianne Costantinou said that, after years of loneliness and absence of free time, a handful would succeed as
soloists, some would join orchestras, several would teach
privately or in some school, and the rest would play at wed-
dings, bar mitzvahs, and birthdays or enter another profession.[6] Many ended as freelance musicians, picking up playing
assignments where they could find them and frequently living
hand-to-mouth in barely adequate housing. Tim Page writes
of the New York scene: "Freelance musicians play Broadway,
Carnegie Hall, recording sessions, churches, smaller opera

companies, nightclubs and bars, and even on friendly streets.
Marya Columbia of Manhattan, a young violinist, holds a degree from the Mannes College of Music. She has played with
the Bel Canto Opera, at Atlantic City, and in many area restaurants. But, for some years now, one of her main sources
of income is the money she makes playing on the corner of
West Broadway and Spring Street, in the heart of SoHo."
Eine Kleine Nachtmusik was a corner favorite. [7]

All the musicians just described were certainly not equal
in talent. What, however, the American democracy had sometimes failed to grant them was equal opportunity to prove
themselves before an audience and allowing the most talented
to gain the recognition they deserved.

GETTING STARTED IN A MUSIC CAREER

On the whole, one aim of young American musicians has
been to gain fame as a soloist. Although realistically the
great majority of these musicians have to find employment as
ensemble performers and music teachers, the training and the
mind-set given them predisposed them to seek positions only
a fraction of them could hope to occupy.

The quest for fame caused them to depart from the towns
and smaller cities and congregate in large urban centers, where
they hoped their big break would come. In an article, published
in Ovation (April 1986), a less than sanguine pianist, Emanuel
Ax, estimated that the break depended five percent on talent,
five percent on very hard work, and ninety percent on luck.
He also complained that the pressure to have commercial success
as a virtuoso bothered him because the emphasis was so wrong.

Arrival on the music scene was heralded by a debut
concert, which could be given anywhere. However, a first
concert appearance in New York City was normally a sine qua
non for the aspiring but unknown musician. This musical
rite of passage theoretically should have allowed the young
man or woman an opportunity to present his or her performing
credentials before a sophisticated audience and, if they proved
bona fide, to be accepted into the rank of artist worthy of
continuing attention. Unfortunately, most instrumentalists
and vocalists could afford neither the trip to New York, nor

the hiring of a hall, nor the necessary advertising for a debut. Even if they borrowed the large sum of money necessary
to display their talents, they had no assurance that anybody
would come and listen to them. In short, the gifted musician
might find the right to a full realization of his or her potentialities denied.

A debut could turn into two hours of tortured isolation,
since at times no one at all showed up. The New York critic
Harold Schonberg once recalled a pianist's debut without benefit of manager or publicity, in Carnegie Recital Hall, where
only three people made up the audience. In the middle of
the presentation, the unfortunate pianist underwent sudden
mental collapse and sobbed his defeat and grief into the empty
hall. Another New York critic, Edward Rothstein, remembered
another pianist's debut where the audience consisted mostly
of mentally retarded people bussed in to fill some of the seats.
Regrettably, as the pianist performed, they walked around,
chatted, called out to each other, or tried humming along
with the music. Yet, even if a performer had been lucky
enough to have had more than one or two listeners, and these
had proved musically knowledgeable, the chances were good
that after the concert he would return to the darkness from
which he had sought to emerge.[8] As is obvious, the coeffi-
cient of risk affecting debuts was usually at an oppressive
level.

Most first appearances took place without sponsorship
and with pitiful results. Some were handled by managers,
like Norman Seaman or New York Recital Associates, who specialized in debut presentations, provided the aspiring musicians alone took the risks. Edward Rothstein found these
managers similar to "vanity" publishers, where the artist
"publishes" his or her own work after footing all the bills.
They also did not guarantee success. Nobody would promise
a knowledgeable audience or the presence of a newspaper
critic (by the 1980s, in New York, only the Times was reviewing debuts). Managers like these offered the novitiate
a service only.

Almost all successful debuts were those of players who
had been selected out of many candidates, after being audi-
tioned by some reputable sponsoring organization. The organization then reserved the hall for the debut and later presented the artist in other recitals. One such organization,

Young Concert Artists, had helped launch the careers of
Pinchas Zukerman, Paula Robison, and Murray Perahia. Another, Pro Musicus, supported recitals on condition that the
musician later played gratis at community concerts with free
admission. Concert Artists Guild rewarded the winners of
their auditions with around eight New York debuts each year.[9]

To give some details about one legitimate organization,
Young Concert Artists was founded in 1961 by Susan Wadsworth, in order to ease the player's transition from school to
concert career in a circumscribed market where competition
was fierce and competitors many. Wadsworth says that Young
Concert Artists arranged for New York debuts and scouted
colleges, orchestras, women's clubs, and museums to discover
performance slots for its protégés. "It was slow going," she
said, "because they hadn't heard of us or our soloists. They
reasoned that if you're going to engage an unknown at a low
price you might as well take a local high school student who's
a promising pianist. Why bring someone from New York?
But the caliber of the musician we were presenting was always terrific." Fifteen years later, the reputation of Young
Concert Artists was established. Public and private grants
helped it pay for a New York concert series and for some 300
other concerts. Other organizations had also begun to sponsor its young musicians in the concerts that they gave.[10]

However, the sponsoring concert organizations were few
and could assist only a very limited number of musicians.
Most players remained ensnared in a system that denied them
access to audiences.[11] As the pianist Boris Bloch explained,
in 1981, all unknown soloists found the going tough. Unfortunately, art music was less and less a focus on American musical life. "People in this country who present concert series
have a concert budget of, say, $20,000 a year, for five or
six attractions. Basically, all of them do not want to hear
about anybody they have never heard of."[12]

The concert public, denied the means for further en-
lightenment, knew mostly the standings of outstanding artists,
who were frequently written or talked about in the media.
Soloists were either promoted into the star category or remained unmentioned.[13] If not yet a star, the impression had
to be given that you were about to become one. If the player
was part of the roster of an artist's management firm, bro-
chures were carefully put together and advertisements placed

in trade publications, like Symphony Magazine, and in Musical
America, advertising the artist's name and credentials, showing what he or she looked like, quoting from the strongest
positive reviews of previous performances, and listing the
artist's recordings, if any.

Prior to her achieving star status, the singer Marilyn
Horne says that hardly anyone was willing to give her a helping hand. She cites as an example her difficulty in getting
together enough money to further her career in Europe. Her
father asked people in her home town, Bradford, Pennsylvania,
for help, but the prominent citizens connected with the arts
claimed that she had insufficient talent. "That hurt and
hurts still," said Marilyn Horne many years later. After she
became an internationally acclaimed star, her home town finally
granted her recognition: "In 1979, Bradford, Pennsylvania,
declared a Marilyn Horne Day, and I stood on a platform listening as some of the very citizens who'd refused me twenty
years before praised me to the skies. I felt little joy. The
people who might have been most touched by the tribute--Dad,
Mom and Dick--were gone and, frankly, I'd have traded all
those accolades for just a little support when I'd most needed
it."[14]

The young Marilyn Horne's desire to go to Europe is
understandable. For the most part, America tended to waste,
not foster, its artistic talent. Even after the building of new
cultural centers, the expected increased demand for performers failed to accommodate the number of soloists seeking engagements. The opportunities for performance, whether in
concert or opera, on radio or television were much greater
in Europe than in the United States, as also was the ability
to assimilate the new talent that came along every year.[15]

Witness also what Beverly Sills had to say about launching her career. She says that when she was trying to get
started, in the late forties, she dreamed of becoming "an
opera star," but found herself singing mainly in Broadway
productions. The possibilities for a young operatic singer
in the United States were limited owing to the scarcity of
opera companies and to the lack of interest in unfledged
American singers in those companies that did exist. J. J.
Shubert, the theatrical producer, advised her to give up a
serious career and become a music teacher or go to Europe
to gain experience and win attention. The Metropolitan, he

said, treated American singers "like poor relations compared
to European singers," and the country "was European-oriented
as far as culture was concerned."[16] She, like so many other
American musicians, had to leave for Europe.

By the middle sixties, West Germany alone had 600 American musicians as regular members of its opera companies, of
which 250 were singers--"an eloquent indictment of our [Amer-
ican] musical culture," said Tibor Kozma.[17] Around 1960,
Westminster Records decided to record Douglas Moore's opera
The Devil and Daniel Webster in Vienna. The music director,
Kurt List, easily secured the services of American singers
working professionally in the area to make up the entire cast,
principal singers and chorus. All of them were highly qualified for the roles they took on.[18]

Whether instrumentalists, singers, or conductors, American musicians also felt it necessary to make the hegira to
Europe in order to prove themselves and to encourage their
own country to take them seriously. In addition, there they
could practice their profession to the full and, what is more,
get paid for it. When Marilyn Horne decided to leave America,
she had these considerations in mind, plus the conviction that
Europe provided the best training and the most varied experiences for young singers: "I don't believe Americans should
start their careers singing in America, particularly since most
of our operatic repertory still comes from Europe. Young
singers must go to Europe and learn the languages and styles
right there." The best the Metropolitan Opera would offer
her, after she had made successful important appearance in
the United States, was a small part with the company. What
is more, she would have been doomed to remaining a small-
part singer. She refused, won a tremendous European reputation, and in ten years returned as a principal singer at the
Metropolitan.[19]

In the postwar period among the first leading expatriate
American singers in Europe were Edith Lang of the Hamburg
Opera, Evelyn Lear and Thomas Stewart of West Berlin Opera,
Teresa Stich-Randall, Jean Madeira, and Eugene Conley of
Vienna Opera, Gloria Lane of Paris Opera, and Chloe Owen
of Milan Opera.

For black-American artists, a European career was even
more necessary. Paul Moor wrote, in 1960: "Larry Winters

has developed such a following that the fortnightly Berliner
Kulturspiegel gives his guest appearances almost unprecedented
star billing: 'Lawrence Winters in ...' Winters, a Negro, jokes
about not making up for the roles he is given but making
down--and, incidentally, says he has never once encountered
racial prejudice in a German opera house." Furthermore, Moor
said, "Two other Negroes whose superlative attainments have
won them secure positions are the soprano Lenora Lafayette
... and the contralto Lucretia West; surely these are two of
the most sumptuous, opulent voices in the world today."[20]

Music competitions seemed to promise a leg up to winners.
Theoretically they offered a democratic solution to the problem
of how to provide equal opportunity to the unknown and unsponsored artist.   They were acceptable and their weeding
out process fair so long as those who were indeed best tech-
nically, musically, and interpretatively did come out on top,
and those with lesser but also praiseworthy abilities were
singled out and rewarded according to their levels of excellence.

Several major cities boasted international competitions--
the Tchaikovsky contest in Moscow, the Wieniawski contest in
Warsaw, the Queen Elisabeth contest in Brussels, the Enesco
contest in Rumania, the Villa-Lobos contest in Brazil, the
Leventritt contest in New York, and the Van Cliburn contest
in Texas, to name seven significant ones.   Such contests,
warned Henri Temianka, encouraged the development of a class
of professional contestants, who turned up in any of the thirty
or forty international contest centers, searching for recognition.[21]

Recognition, however, did not come easily, even if a
competition were won.   After the pianist Van Cliburn won the
Leventritt Competition in 1954, he still could get nowhere in
concert circles.   Though suffering considerable depression,
he then entered and won the Tchaikovsky contest in 1958.
Possibly winning an important contest in the leading communist country had something to do with it, but immediately the
American agencies of mass communication lionized him and he
became a familiar name to all Americans.   His return to New
York City was greeted with a ticker-tape parade and meetings
with officials from the city, state, and federal governments,
from business, and from the arts.   "Every orchestra and concert association in the country fell all over themselves trying

to engage him. Record companies lined up at the door, Hollywood besieged the office, the television networks never got
off the phone. Everyone, it seemed, needed Cliburn that
minute," comments Schuyler Chapin.[22]

Another Tchaikovsky contest winner was Elmar Oliveira.
Although he had already won the Dealey Young Artists Competition and the Naumburg competition, the biggest boost to
his career came in 1978, with the Tchaikovsky win. An invi-
tation to the White House followed. He was immediately booked
to tour the world and play over 100 concerts.[23] Less dramatic were the wins of the violist Paul Neubauer. First, he
conquered at the Tertis International Viola Competition, in
1980; then, in 1983, at the Whitaker International Competition.
The eventual outcome was a principal's chair, at the age of
21, with the New York Philharmonic.[24]

The description just given of contests is nevertheless
onesided. Considered from the viewpoint of the countless
numbers denied the first prize, contests can raise havoc with
careers. For one thing, except for judgments on technique,
all other judgments can be subjective in nature and a reflection of a judge's personal tastes. Politics and prejudice also
exercise their influence.

Contests have been winner-takes-all affairs, despite the
fact that a hairline might separate the one victor from several
rival contestants. These others would bear the onus of failed
would-be artists. Their chances for places in the sun might
be denied; the injunction to deal justly with all and reward
each according to his or her deserts, disregarded.

The year that Van Cliburn won the highest honors in
the Tchaikovsky competition and was greeted with a ticker-
tape parade in New York City, another American, Joyce Flissler, took seventh place in Moscow, among violinists who had
come from all over the world. Some people, like Paul Moor,
thought her lesser placement was perhaps owing to national
and political considerations. Significantly, the noted Russian
violinist David Oistrakh considered her an instrumentalist of
the highest caliber, and Flissler immediately was asked to tour
several Russian cities, where her playing was greeted with
frenzied enthusiams. However, when she returned home, no
reporter interviewed her, no television crew recorded her arrival, and no official greeted her publicly. What was even

more disheartening, not a single inquiry was received by her manager and not a single engagement resulted. Then, in 1960, the Russians had her tour their country again, and she achieved such a dazzling success, that the Associated Press filed a story about her. Some American notice was taken of her, but no concert management pressed her advancement, and she was denied a Carnegie Hall recital unless she herself financed it. She decided nobody in America cared to hear her as a soloist and began to make a living by playing in an orchestra and freelancing.[25]

The concert pianist Ruth Laredo was more fortunate, although her beginnings were quite inauspicious. "I tried out for everything and lost in every major competition including Brussels, the Naumberg, Leventritt, and National Federation of Music Clubs. I've had to work hard all my life, and I'm glad everything seems to be falling in place.... It's a lot harder to develop your career without a flashy contest victory or two," she said in 1974. Her good fortune was to have the highly respected Rudolf Serkin, her teacher, advance her career. A debut with Stokowski and the American Symphony and an engagement with the Philadelphia orchestra resulted, followed by engagements with other orchestras, a recital at Lincoln Center, and recordings of Ravel and Scriabin.[26] She, however, was the exception, not the rule.

Serious criticisms of competitions, other than the ones mentioned, have been raised. Stephen Drury, a pianist, says such contests encourage performers to play like machines, able to repeat a given interpretation under any condition, without that element of spontaneity essential for vivid communication. Others say that contests reward musicians whose playing style is quick, clean, conformist, and inoffensive, that they favor technical perfection over musical insight, and that truly great but individualistic musicians like Artur Schnabel, Rudolf Serkin, and Vladimir Horowitz could never have won a contest.[27]

THE MUSICIAN'S ORBIT

An opinion sometimes voiced by observers of the American art-music scene is that a major virtue of American musicians resides in their command of instrumental and vocal technique. When some American musicians have augmented this virtue with a firm intellectual grasp of the music and insight into its expressive content, they have managed to gain international acclaim. Coming to mind are singers like Sherrill Milnes, Robert Merrill, Frederica Von Stade, Jerome Hines, and Jessye Norman; and instrumentalists like Paul Jacobs, Peter Serkin, Paul Zukofsky, Richard Stolzman, and Lynn Harrell. One should add that American musicians of their caliber would have had a more difficult time winning recognition before World War II, when a European orientation prevailed amongst American cultural leaders. This is not to say that recognition came easily in the postwar period, merely that the anti-American bias had somewhat abated and the mechanisms for discovering talent, imperfect and few as they were, had increased.

How does one describe the ideal relationship between performer and music lover? That the music lover would hear no music without the performer is a truism. Since so much is owed the musician, since audiences are so directly dependent on him or her for the aesthetic experience they desire, in a sense the musician turns into a benefactor to whom they owe a measure of gratitude. Like a magician, he or she is expected to conjure a music score into life, a score that would otherwise remain only the composer's idea, unheard and unknown. The performer is always concretely there, before the audience, responsive to whatever warm and grateful applause is showered upon them--the physical incarnation of what the music lover values in music--there, even after the music ceases.

Mundane existence unfortunately intrudes upon this image. How to achieve and retain this kind of rapport has always been a major concern for musicians. Keeping your finger on the public's pulse and giving consideration to what it wants to hear, maintain several writers, is a key to achieving the rapprochement. When constructing programs, the audience's tastes are to be considered or no audience will be there to listen. Either perform before a paying audience or perish is the motto guiding the pragmatic musician.[28]

Such advice obviously requires a <u>caveat</u>. An ever present danger is that the performer may experience him or herself only as a commodity that must be sold in competition with others--a consequence that Erich Fromm warns about. Performers may shape themselves into a person concerned less with deep artistic probing, more "with becoming salable." They adapt completely to the personality market: "I am as

you desire me" is a guiding principle, writes Fromm.   There
can result a cessation of inner questioning, a loss of artistic
identity, and a "stunted emotional life."[29]

Excellent as American performers are, on occasion some
do exhibit the symptoms that Fromm describes.   As a result,
their playing may suffer from the uncommitted sound they
produce, which has slight connection with human personality
or emotions.   Quite a few of them play smoothly, sophisti-
catedly, even brilliantly, but in a noninvolved manner.   In
studying a work, some tend to intellectualize about it after
separating the whole into its component parts.   As Joe Goldberg commented in 1981: "The current style [of performance]
is cooler, more analytical."[30] For every Charles Rosen who
succeeded with this approach during the postwar years, there
were countless other musicians who thereby failed to catch
the audience's fancy, since the usual music lover puts feeling
first.

Even while American vocalists won positions abroad and
some attained to the highest operatic positions, certain similar
reservations were expressed about the same singers who
crossed the Atlantic.   Philip Hart mentions that they were
found to be excessively "glossy" and facile.   Lacking was the
development of "individual personality among our young opera
artists." Well trained vocally, capable of singing in any language, they nevertheless sounded impersonal to Europeans.
In like manner, Andrew Pincus writes of the pianist Malcolm
Frager: "Critics remark on the cleanness and honesty of Mr.
Frager's playing.   But, especially as he has matured, few
call him charismatic or exciting." And in reviewing a performance of the Bloch quartets by the Portland String Quartet, Harlow Robinson complained that the players' attitudes
were serious to the point of being overly deferential.   They
had thought a lot about the music: "Indeed, it sometimes
sounded as if they had thought too much and felt too little."
Bloch's music is deeply expressive, sad, and tragic, but not
cerebral.   Changing moods have to be realized or monotony
results.   Yet, Robinson complained, these players failed to
capture this emotional level: "The real problem was that the
playing was rather dry and thin; one wanted a richer, juicier
tone, particularly from the first violin and the viola."[31]

The capacity to adapt to the changing expressive requirements of the music and to grasp a work's overall emotional

structure might elude the performer, even if he or she decided to stress feeling in an interpretation. Commencing particularly in the late seventies, and a reflection of the newfound romanticism that modernists had started to appreciate,
a number of performers tried injecting greater amounts of
emotion into their interpretations, not always convincingly.
To give an instance, the pianist André Watts was judged by
Bernard Holland to have "a sort of hotline between the inner
passions and the keyboard," but to lack a "sense of scale,
an ability to be patient, the prudence that might allow his
ideas to grow naturally." Watts was comfortable in tightly
knit works like the Scarlatti sonatas, but in music that allowed him more freedom of expression, like Chopin's B-flat
minor Sonata, "Mr. Watts tended to summon up huge hand-
fuls of emotion and simply fling them in our faces" without
any "feeling of cumulative power." When playing some Liszt
studies, he "created thundering disjointed bombast." John
Rockwell speaks of a similar reaction to the playing of the
Concord String Quartet. Young American-trained musicians,
he said, were evidencing a "driven, pressed, and intense"
performing style. The Concord Quartet epitomized "this style
to the point of parody, particularly in the terrier-like and
unfortunately not always all that accurate playing of Mr.
Sokol." The execution of the fast movements was rigid, at
times affecting "ruddy passion." What the interpretation
lacked was grace, sensuousness, and real inner drama.[32]

Whatever validity such adverse criticisms had, they
normally were most applicable to those musicians not in the
first echelon. Moreover, because American and European
socio-cultural conditions were becoming increasingly similar,
critics could also have applied similar evaluations to European
musicians.

After World War II, the United States could also point
to its large share of performers who not only possessed tremendous musicality but also tried to preserve their artistic
integrity in the face of a burgeoning mass culture. A number
of them wished to think of themselves as artists alone, cus-
todians of the finest in musical thinking, and educators of
the endangered American art audiences. It was an attitude
which, in part, Americans had acquired from German aesthetic
thinking, beginning in the second half of the nineteenth century.[33] For these American artists, programming only the
most serious art compositions and avoiding anything smacking

of the frivolous were rules of conduct. Joining them, however, were certain musicians who hid their interpretive deficiencies under the weight of the musical substance they presented and the seriousness of their approach.

Complaints were quickly forthcoming about the incessant
playing of multi-movemented abstract works, the lack of contrast and variety, and the absence of lighter works of greater
entertainment value in the musical presentations. Nor were
the genuinely outstanding instrumentalists and vocalists ex-
empted from this criticism. Many a listener was suffering in-
digestion from the heavy diet. Although certain universities
and urban centers might produce concertgoers appreciative
of unalloyed sobriety, such music lovers comprised a tiny
portion of the usual American audience.

Fortunately for audience retention the idea of entertaining the art audience became more acceptable in the seventies
and, especially, in the eighties. As a sign of the change,
the pianist Earl Wild, in 1981, gave a program of "high salon
Romanticism," which "would have been hooted off the stage
during those severe days before the Romantic Revival; when
the approved kind of program had nothing but the last three
Schubert sonatas, or the 'Hammerklavier' and 'Diabelli,' or
the 'Goldberg' variations at slow tempos with all repeats."[34]
In short, performers, among them those dedicated to their
art, eventually did pay some attention to the desires of the
audiences they were addressing. Nor was this necessarily a
bad thing. The time had come for the stiff images of the
Temple of Music, the Revealed Musical Word, and the Conse-
crated Artist to begin fading into the past, and for musicians
to realize that music was created for people, not people for
music.

As has already been pointed out, listeners desiring the
highest and most serious art do exist, and where enough of
them can gather to make up an evening's audience, then an
uncompromising program can meet with approval. They may
even be growing in number. Witness the proliferation of
string quartets in the decades after the war and, what is
more significant, of music lovers willing to come to listen to
them. On the other hand, the chamber music audience is not
large enough to sustain all of the new chamber ensembles active in the postwar period. Their continuance would have
been less assured if it were not for the in-residence curricula

of several universities and schools of music, where quartet members are paid to give concerts and teach music students, while at the same time they are allowed a great deal of freedom to concertize elsewhere.

Twentieth-century economics (the expense of artists' fees, travel, concert-hall rental, stagehands, publicity, and program printing) requires that the presenters of nonsubsidized concerts attract as large a general audience as possible, lest they operate at a loss. Much of this expanded audience prefers assorted and contrasting programs. To chew on a lengthy sonata is fine, so long as there is also a garnish of shorter, colorful pieces of immediate appeal, like those that the Romantic musicians were expert at turning out.

What about an American repertoire? Older works by Gottschalk, Chadwick, MacDowell, Griffes, and Gershwin, to name five composers, would also provide the necessary variety. They certainly are not played with any frequency. A continuing European inspired bias, which declares them insubstantial, derivative, uninspired, or cheap, and therefore second rate, causes performers to shun them. As for the more contemporary American music, if one puts to one side the relentlessly avant-garde works, in which few listeners are interested, selected and accessible compositions by Copland, Barber, Creston, Dello Joio, Muczynski, Flagello, and Rzewski, for example, can prove quite effective in performance and do contain excellences not found in European music. Audiences have not rejected them, despite what some concert managers claim. Music lovers simply have not had the opportunity to hear them.[35] The passive or active connivance of prominent European performers, who occupy powerful positions in the American music world, of unimaginative patrons, who contribute large sums of money and influence the policy of their music associations, and of managers anxious to lessen financial risk by limiting repertoire to a select number of surefire hits has much to do with this state of affairs. In denying these American composers access to the general audience lies the conclusion that nothing of cultural excellence resides in the art music produced in the American democratic culture, a conclusion patently false and destructive to American self-esteem.

These same managers arrange the concerts to take place in scattered parts of the United States and decree a life of

nomadism for the musicians they represent, whose roaming
existence is frequently irksome. The cellist Yo-Yo Ma, for
example, says the life of a touring soloist is no luxury. For
him, it consists of wearying overnight stands, airplane flights,
waiting in terminals, scurrying to rent cars, gulping meals at
roadside restaurants, and other harassments. He wonders:
"Why do musicians go through all this, having to worry about
concerts and travel at the same time, playing pieces we [sic]
don't like, competitions, trying to rehearse when your ears
are still popping from the airplane ride? I used to think of
it as a challenge--seeing how many times I could play well
under the worst circumstances. Now I'm not quite sure."[26]

In addition to this, states Bernard Holland, soloists
had to please their local presenters, "a job which usually extends well after the concert." There were post-concert parties which had to be attended, where the soloist ate hors
d'oeuvres or cookies, however hungry for solid food he might
be, and chatted amiably with locally prominent citizens, however fatigued his senses. Indeed, "ineptitude at small talk,
the inability to charm local clubwomen and society leaders,
has been known to hurt beginning careers," writes Holland.[37]

Oral or written communication spread the word to other
local concert administrators and to orchestra conductors, describing what musicians were likely to please audiences. The
winning of a competition or an enthusiastic _Times_ review also
alerted them to viable candidates for their concert series.
Finally, regional and national conferences acquainted attendees
with available performers. As reported in the _Times_, in February 1984, when the Association of College, University, and
Community Arts Administrators met in new York's Sheraton
Centre, to attend workshops and lectures concerning management problems, also present were dozens of concert managers,
both well known and obscure. "They rented space and hawked
their wares--namely musicians--as if at a bazaar, but presenters looking for artists for their concerts do a lot of compara-
tive shopping and come to a lot of decisions."[38]

In the early eighties, the beginning soloist earned perhaps a couple of hundred dollars for a concert, that is to say
after his manager took over some twenty percent of the gross
and expenses another thirty percent. Fairly well established
soloists could earn $5,000.00 per concert (and chamber-music
trios or quartets about $9,000.00). On the other hand, once

"star" status was achieved, not uncommon was a concert fee of $20,000.00 or more. The extraordinary pianist Vladimir Horowitz, in 1942, used to earn around $2,750.00 per recital. Ten years later, the figure had risen to $8,500.00 for a recital at Carnegie Hall. Around 1976, Horowitz could demand 80 percent of the gross box office receipts--thus, in one concert earning $39,152.00. Although in February 1978 he supposedly donated his services for an "uncommercial" concert before President Carter, at the White House, Horowitz later made the President furious by seeing to the foreign distribution rights of the program, for which he extracted fees totaling $193,964.00.[39]

Money was one measure of artistic prestige. The more costly the engagement of a musician, the more he was perceived to command musical skill, imagination, and taste. Ticket prices inevitably rose to meet expenses and put the entire concert business in jeopardy. Because not all members of this public could afford the prices exacted for celebrity or, if they could afford them, garner one of the limited number of available seats for a performance, the tendency amongst this group was to stay home and ignore the less celebrated musicians. Besides, much of this public lived distant from the centers where the more famous personages chose to appear and had to make do with recordings and televised musical programs.

Concerned over this state of affairs and anxious to keep his fees low as a matter of principle, the pianist Anton Kuerti found that the comparatively modest charge for his services could be detrimental to his career. In 1976, he told Guy Freedman: "The outrageously high fees being charged today are ruining the recital business and also helping the symphony orchestra into bankruptcy. It has become irrational and purely a question of vanity and prestige. I have been told again and again that I am hurting my career by this attitude and that many leading concert sponsors will be reluctant to book anyone whose fee is less than $3,000.00 for an engagement. This makes it impossible to present recitals in moderate sized halls and one finds the superstars playing in vast spaces where intimate communication is out of the question."[40]

Making one's way as a general musician was normally a thankless undertaking. Most musicians would have agreed

with Jacques Barzun's comment: "When our children ask us,
twenty years from now, 'What did you accomplish in those
days?' we shall perhaps be glad to answer, like the French
revolutionist after the Terror, 'I survived.'"[41] Even at the
height of the American cultural explosion the U.S. Department
of Labor, in BLS Bulletin No. 1300, was advising parents to
dissuade their children from becoming musicians, since the
field was over-crowded and scarcely anybody in it could make
a decent living.[42]

About the same time (1962), Joseph Levine, then conductor of the Omaha Symphony Orchestra, observed that more
and more Americans were becoming interested in art music.
Nevertheless, he said, the millions of children who went into
music should not choose a musical career, because the professional musician rarely found adequate employment. About a
dozen orchestras offered full financial support to their musicians. Players in other orchestras had to find additional employment elsewhere. Nor was turning to musical composition
a solution. The American Music Center could find only sixteen composers who made more than $5,000 a year from their
works.[43]

Excellent instrumentalists and singers were engaged by
orchestras and opera companies for a season of a few weeks
then were made to look out for themselves during the rest of
the year. Herbert Hecsh, writing in the Music Journal, of
September 1965, saw this as "the dark side of building arts
centers--with its social, partying, ego-puffing activities,"
where communities proved "indifferent to minimal support of"
their musicians.

One instrumentalist complained: "Playing as much as I
can, I play about 26 weeks a year and counting odd jobs, too,
I make about $2,500.00 per annum in music. In eight years
of playing I've hardly recovered the cost of my education and
instrument." Another said: "Music and house painting--quite
a combination for a God given gift of music talent. But believe me, if it wasn't for painting I, my wife and child, could
not make it." Not surprisingly, Paul Hume, music critic of
the Washington Post, advised: "Do not go into music as a
career unless you are prepared to sacrifice any thought you
may have of making a decent living at it ... unless you are
ready and able to take on two, three, or four jobs in order
to earn a living sufficient to let you marry and raise a family."[44]

Twenty years later, studies found people in the arts still unable to earn very much from their profession, almost all of them forced to hold down one or two other jobs--as waiters, taxi drivers, teachers, store clerks, telephone operators, and so forth. In New York City, in 1982, when a job was available, union scale for a violinist was $60.00 per concert, plus $12.50 per rehearsal hour, hardly an example of munificent pay. In Boston, a newly hired member of the Boston Symphony earned the unusual salary of $36,400.00 a year, in 1983. However, almost all of the other musicians in Greater Boston, including more than a few superb instrumentalists and singers, were part of an immense pool of free lancers, performing with various choral groups, the Opera Company of Boston, the Boston Ballet, other opera associations, chamber orchestras, and ensembles hired to play in church and college concerts.[45]

THE CULTIVATION OF OLD MUSIC

One fresh industry that grew in the postwar years and offered welcome employment to instrumentalists, singers, and instrument makers centered on the "authentic" performance of musical compositions written before the year 1800. It normally involved the use of instruments, sound production, and ornamentation that partisans sincerely tried to make true to the period, place, and composer of a work. These partisans went one step further and claimed that faithfulness to the past produced an aesthetic experience more revealing of the real nature of the music than was possible through the then accepted incorrect manners of performing it, using modern instruments, oversized ensembles, and uninformed interpretations of the musical score. Behind the scenes (or the performers themselves) were musicologists specializing in the investigation of early music. They discovered fresh evidence and formed theories about what the different musics were like prior to the Romantic age--whether music of the Middle Ages, Renaissance, Baroque, or Rococo. (In the 1980s, the definition of early music would be extended to include pieces of Haydn, Mozart, and early Beethoven.)

The intense interest in the musical past coincided with the deepening instability in art music, owing to the general public's repudiation of twentieth-century works which abandoned tonality and consonance as commonly understood. The

more uncompromisingly modern that contemporary music became and the more heated the rivalry between competing
avant-garde camps, the more pronounced, it seemed, was the
attention given to the qualities, principles, and affinities
thought to belong to a different and more stable cultural
era.[46]

The interest also coincided with rising production costs
for music. The production costs for the performance of old
music might be made lower, because royalties did not have to
be paid and, at most a tiny group of musicians had to be
used. These musicians lacked reputations commanding large
fees. Performances could frequently take place under non-
commercial auspices (universities, churches, and museums),
thus keeping hall-rental expenses low and avoiding the necessity for paying high wages to often unneeded stagehands
and technicians, a condition prevalent when commercial auditoriums were used.

Other explanations for the strengthening of the early-
music movement, beginning in the 1950s, given by John Rockwell, were the arrival and proliferation of long-playing recordings, and the unfilled need for new sounds that could stimulate listeners. Baroque music, in particular, was reinterpreted
and authenticated by means of "brisk, rigid tempos and bright
chamber ensembles with a steady jangling, chordal harpsichord
continuo," as in Hermann Scherchen's recording of the Messiah.
It was a style that would sound dated in the 1980s, writes
Rockwell, due to the overly prominent harpsichord and stiff,
unyielding, machine-like tempos. A different authenticity
would prevail thirty years later, characterized by "a teasing,
expressive rubato, softer attacks, proper pitch and tuning,
greater vocal ornamentation, and more authentic instruments,"
as in the recordings of Nikolaus Harnoncourt and Gustav Leon-
hardt.[47]

Obviously, authenticity could not be a settled matter.
Its definition changed as tastes changed and as more accurate
information about the music in question was acquired.

The American democracy in its reception of this novel
approach to the past demonstrated some flexibility in its cultural processes. A minority had set off in a markedly different musical direction. Specialized ensembles had been organized to play for a specialized audience. Nevertheless, the

vastly altered rendition of early music also managed to win a
larger group of listeners from that general audience deemed
by many critics to be frozen in one repertoire, in one way
of presenting that repertoire, and in a state of mind that
valued music only when outstanding musical personalities performed it.   Numbers of young people who had grown up with
rock music found the strong metric pulsation and rhythmic
drive of Baroque music to be attractive to them.

The early-music movement was set into motion especially
in 1953, when Noah Greenberg founded the Pro Musica Antiqua,
in New York.   During the years that followed other ensembles
came into existence, with New York and Boston soon recognized as twin founts for the trend. [48]   To name just a few of
these groups, in New York were the Waverly Consort, Aston
Magna, the New York Cornet and Sacbut Ensemble, the Ensemble for Early Music, the New York Consort of Viols, and
the Concert Royal; in Boston, the Banchetto Musicale, the
Boston Camerata, the Boston Museum Trio, and the Friends
of Charles Burney.   By the year 1980, the performance of
early music from the Middle Ages to the Classical era was common throughout the United States.   In the course of one November week alone, for example, New Yorkers could listen to
several specialist groups: the Capella Nova with Burgundian-
Court music, Badinage playing Baroque music, Igor Kipnis in
a harpsichord recital, the Waverly Consort, the Viola da Gamba
Trio, the Musicians of Swanne Alley, a Domenico Scarlatti
program at the Third Street Settlement, and at Lincoln Center the Chamber Music Society in an all-Bach program and
Judith Blegen singing Baroque compositions. [49]

The renewed attention and better informed approach to
the musical past helped mitigate the ill effects produced by
bloated performances which distorted the meaning of the music from the past.   This had been particularly true for the
music of Bach and Handel.   Huge symphony orchestras and
choruses concertizing in large halls had prevented the listener's close association with sound originally intended to be
heard by small forces under chamber conditions.   By resorting to the more muted instruments typical of the period and
eschewing Romantic emotionality, vibrato, and other inappro-
priate practices, the early-music groups caused the compositions of Bach and Handel to sound newly made and offered
an alternate modernism to that of the contemporary avant-
garde, one more acceptable to the general music public.   A

commentary of Bernard Holland went: "Music seems bored
with its present [1983] and distrustful of its future, and for
solace and for confirmation, some part of it is turning to the
past. The avant-garde of this cultural retreat is the early-
music movement and its recreation of ancient instruments, ancient musical ways and, often, ancient dress and even life
style."[50]

Fidelity to the original score and usages surrounding
the score, it was hoped, would make the music more meaningful to a contemporary audience. Note Andrew Porter's assertion, in the New Yorker: "The music of any age speaks most
directly, most freshly to modern ears in the tones and idioms
of its composer--or at least in as close an approximation to
them as halls and instruments allow."[51] Furthermore, the
aesthetic experience of listeners, some early--music enthus-
iasts said, would be enhanced if they shared in the accumu-
lating knowledge about the music--how it was once performed
and how a contemporary ensemble aimed to reproduce the original effect. Instruction could come in the form of lectures
about the past era, demonstrations of the sound qualities of
the early instruments to be heard in a concert, learned program notes, and verbal explanations of individual pieces before
each was performed.

Warnings about the limitations of this last approach to
the appreciation of artistic works were already appearing in
the 1950s. Although he had paintings more particularly in
mind, Etienne Gilson, to give one instance, was worried about
the growing assertiveness of modern pedagogy in the arts and
about the insistence that aesthetic experience was teachable.
On the contrary, he maintained, whatever is teachable is only
indirectly related to the aesthetic experience and danger lay
in the belief that no distinction existed between enjoyment
and learning. If this were true, then the scholars who studied the arts of the past should have the greatest feeling for
beauty and the contemporary layperson could enjoy nothing
"without having first absorbed as much information as possible
concerning the objects of" enjoyment. Clearly, this is not the
case, he says. "There is a great deal of danger in letting
people imagine that they do not 'understand' art because they
'know' little or nothing about it." If the direct perception of
a work fails to produce joy, then reading and studying the
literature on the subject "in the hope of acquiring the aesthetic experience" will be in vain. Although reflection may

contribute to aesthetic intuition, "nature has set no scholarly
conditions to the enjoyment of beauty."52

In the performance of music, reservations were expressed
early on about how pedagogy untempered by creative and
imaginative impulse could kill the aesthetic experience. Lorin
Maazel remarked, in 1962, on the vogue of faithfully reproduc-
ing music as the composer wrote it and warned it often resulted
in a homogenized or machine-like art. Precision, accuracy,
and informed taste were not enough to bring music alive; they
might defeat "the very purpose for which people have always
congregated to hear music; that is to share in an experience
of Art." Predictable sameness, not participation in a musical
adventure, ensued when "the old music is executed as if it
were written by the Synthesizer."53

The emotional and intensely personal interpretation of
music was no longer acceptable, wrote Rose Heylbut five years
later, since taste now "forbids liberties and champions the
cool, cerebral approach" in the rendition of most music. Yet,
how did one perform accurately; who really knew how Bach
or Handel were performed? Possibly today's absence of interpretation and impersonal renditions reflected modern taste,
not the taste of the past, when all music was thought of as
emotional.54

Also brought into question was the faithful adherence
to specific "authentic" instruments during performance. Rosa-
lyn Tureck, the highly respected American pianist and harpsi-
chordist, pointed out that Bach and other composers were constantly changing the instrumental settings for some of their
works. Moreover, musicians of the time thought nothing of
switching parts--if a violin were not available, then a flute
would play the solo, etc. Why not have a clavier part executed on the piano, if so desired? It was absurd to attempt
filling Carnegie Hall with a harpsichord sound, and amplifying
the sound was an anachronism, not a solution. Recommended
was greater adaptability to different performing conditions.55

Warnings accumulated about how learning was hampering
musicality, about how a dryness of sound appealed more to a
cult than to the general audience.56 Harold Schonberg, for
example, cited Thomas Dunn's performance of Bach's B-minor
Mass in New York, in 1961, as an example of the sort of eru-
dition that killed music. A chorus of twenty was heard.

However, Bach himself had never asked for such a limit.
When Bach is quoted as asking for "at least" that number in
the chorus, he without question did not mean "at most."[57]
Ridiculous, writes Edward Strickland, was Joshua Rifkin's
reduction of the Bach chorus to only five people. The result
was anemic music worthy of the "Snore of the Year award."
Rifkin had cited as precedents the physical size and disposi-
tion of vocal parts in the chorus available to Bach, and the
possibility that illness might have cut the choristers down
even further. This, writes Strickland, was an absurdity;
or was it really "musical opportunism"? "The next step may
be to insist that Beethoven's Seventh be recorded exclusively
by orchestras led by deaf conductors."[58] Authenticity reduced to the utmost in absurdity would be the creation of a
new, more authentic audience that grows up isolated from the
modern world in order to maintain keen ears not contaminated
by traffic, subway, and airplane noises. It would listen to
musicians placed on the floor (not a stage) of unheated halls
devoid of electricity. It would wear the clothing of early
times, which absorbs and affects sound differently from today's clothing.[59]

One must keep in mind that when Bach, Mozart, and
other composers had written or spoken about the meaning of
their music, they had almost always dwelt on its emotional
content, with scarcely a word about form or structure. If
Bach's own playing of his music is described by contemporar-
ies as expressive, exciting, daring, free, strange, and colorful, why then did Anthony Newman, in August 1973, play
Bach's works, at a New York concert, without color or virility,
adhering strictly to the "thoroughly modern concept" of "sewing-
machine" objectivity?[60]

In the same way, when Mozart's music was given an
"authentic" rendition why should it strike the listener as
bloodless. Witness John Schneider's report on Jeffrey Kahane's playing of the C-major Piano Concerto, K467, in Atlanta, in October 1984: "Jeffrey Kahane delivered the Mozart
flawlessly, albeit in that unruffled, let's-not-get-excited style
of Mozart playing, with an inordinate amount of soft pedal,
that sets restraints on the projection of the music and conse-
quently on the listener's enjoyment potential."[61]

A close look at the question of authenticity was taken
by Laurence Dreyfus, in 1983. He found that the urge toward

authenticity of the postwar years encompassed performers,
musicologists, early-music instrument makers, publishers,
critics, managers and agents, sound engineers, and record
company executives. Treatise after treatise on performance
practice came out, each highly charged with a concept of authenticity intended to underly "every conscious act" of performance. Especially during the 1950s, it was first a regu-
lative ideal asserting "a supposed opposition to the self-
aggrandizing individualism prevalent in Mainstream musical
praxis. In the typical version of this widespread myth, the
individual Mainstream artist harnesses the musical text to his
or her own will, thereby glorifying self-expression at the expense of the composer's intentions. A musician humbled by
authenticity, on the other hand, acts willingly in the service
of the composer, thereby committing to 'truth.'" A study of
historical practices, which "are magically transformed into the
composer's intentions," replaces the empathetic and imaginative
reconstruction of music.

Unfortunately, states Dreyfus, things were described
more or less accurately but with no stock taken "of the biased
vantage point from which the (human) observer perceives the
phenomena." Emotional content was ignored in the name of
objectivity and letting music speak for itself. Wryly, Dreyfus comments on a new species of musical gratification--the
Freedom from feeling itself.[62]

All of this said, there always have been early-music
specialists who have thought deeply about embodying the authentic spirit of the original music in expressive performances
that do excite twentieth-century audiences. In truth, from
this standpoint, authenticity is welcome and provides an in-
valuable service. To such specialists we owe a large measure
of gratitude.

The most successful early-music groups--that is to say,
ones able continuously to gather in respectably sized audiences
--did pay attention to their listeners, while keeping their integrity as bona fide interpreters intact. And in the late
seventies and into the eighties, emotion was again in favor
with serious musicians, among them many who had previously
disdained it. Michael Jaffe, of the Waverly Consort, said in
1983 that while critics still came to his ensemble's concerts
"super-aware that God forbid we should use a wrong size
crumhorn ... the audience is much less concerned with such

matters." Despite complaints from diehards that the Consort
was too popular and was too interested in putting on a show,
Jaffe insisted his group did adhere to authentic guidelines,
although aware that nothing is absolutely certain. It also
believed in exploring a period in depth and putting stress
on variety and musical values, which had a winning effect
on its audience. [63]

Another highly successful group in the eighties has
been the Boston Camerata. Its leader, Joel Cohen, says:
"Early music was counter-cultural at first, and now [1983]
there are a whole host of 'official' ways to do early music.
But none of the very best performers of early music talks
about 'authenticity' at all; Andrea von Ramm, who staged
The Play of Daniel for us and sings the title role, goes ba-
nanas whenever she hears the word. It's only the third-rank
talents that want to codify everything. In the Camerata we
want to keep experimenting; I hope we never toe the line." [64]
Cohen and the Camerata present informal, relaxed concerts,
after which listeners are invited to talk to the performers.
They are completely aware that it is a contemporary audience
they are addressing. I remember a Camerata performance of
Purcell's Dido and Aeneas, with D'Anna Fortunato singing the
part of Dido, that was full of sensitive feeling, rhythmic
verve, color, and life--and true to the original. Half of
the large audience, myself included, rushed backstage to con-
gratulate the musicians, all of us carried away by the exhila-
rating performance.

In evenings such as the one described lies the vindication of the early-music movement. Performers honor both the
letter and intent of past musics and the psychological requirements of contemporary audiences. They uncover, preserve,
and introduce compositions of lasting value that are made to
come alive in a modern time. Their concertizing sounds ex-
citingly fresh, neither sterile nor hackneyed nor ersatz.
Their commitment to the past and present has produced more
than a cult following. As proof, the annual springtime Boston
Early Music Festival, in the first half of the eighties, has
managed to attract listeners numbering not in the hundreds
but in the thousands.

WOMEN AS MUSICIANS

During and after World War II, the number of women

in the American work force increased dramatically, to around
45 percent in the eighties. The realization also grew that although for obvious reasons single women had to work, more
and more married women had to join them, because owing to
monetary inflation husbands found it increasingly difficult to
support a family. Divorces, which burgeoned from the early
sixties onward, forced once-married but still child-encumbered
women into the job market. At the same time, a conviction
prevailed amongst more and more of the better educated and
professionally trained women that the be-all and end-all of
women's lives did not have to be centered in the home or in
the lowly positions traditionally allocated to them. By the
1980s, driven by this conviction, they numbered about 15
percent of all physicians, lawyers, and judges. A push was
on for women to become rabbis, priests, ministers, aviators,
nuclear scientists, elected officials, directors of corporations,
and so forth. Nevertheless, most women continued to hold
down the more boring jobs that led nowhere, to experience
wage discrimination, and to encounter varying aspects of male
chauvinism, whether outside or within the home; hence the
rise of militant feminism.[65]

Pertinent to our discussion of the American democracy
is an observation offered by Betty Friedan to Richard Reeves,
in 1979. She said it was no accident that the modern women's
movement began in the United States, since "the real ideology
that shaped the movement was the ideas of America--equality,
democracy, participation in the shaping of decisions that affect your own life." Ingrained in American thinking was "the
responsibility and the opportunity to mold your own destiny."
By joining together, women increased their influence on the
direction American society would take.[66]

The National Organization for Women was founded in
1966. it added its weight to the demands of Afro-Americans
that discrimination had to end. During 1971 to 1973, Congress
voted for the Equal Rights Amendment, and passed the Equal
Pay Act and the Equal Employment Opportunities Act. Land-
mark sex-discrimination court cases were settled against Corn-
ing Glass, the men's bar at New York's Biltmore Hotel, News-
week, the American Stock Exchange, American Telephone, and
Reader's Digest, to name six. However, for all the talk about
liberation and the right of the individual to choose to leave
home in order to fulfill one's self through work, most women
like it or not sought jobs because livings had to be earned.[67]

Traditionally, women made up more than half the audience for art music and most of the volunteers who promoted
and raised money for the various musical associations. They
populated subscription and educational offices, organized symphony and opera balls, sold goods to benefit their musical
causes, conducted auctions over radio and television, and performed myriad other tasks necessary for the continuing existence of symphony orchestras and opera companies. As mentioned in Chapter 1, these were functions that women were
less and less able or inclined to perform in the postwar years.
Illustrative of the new antagonism toward the "lady" image is
a voice with electronic-music composition by Doris Hayes,
called Exploitation, which was recorded by Folkways in 1983.
It denounced the mean and unjust use of women volunteers
and artists, who were required to donate time and effort without expectation of compensation.[68]

Women had grown up to feel guilty about seeking careers
in art music. If they became wives and mothers, whatever
talents they had were supposed to be made subservient to
the demands of husband and children. Often brought up as
an example was the gifted composer Ruth Crawford Seeger who,
after 1931, did little writing in order to devote herself to her
family. To this has to be added what the singer Frederica
von Stade said about problems of career and family: "Part
of the problem is fatigue levels, especially with small children
at home. I love having my children as part of my life. I
love trying to do it all. A lot of the time, that works. But
there are times when things collide, resulting in terrific fatigue." Also, as Joan Tower, the pianist-composer, pointed
out, in 1982, women have been diffident about pushing their
way into the art-music world because scarcely any models of
women's achievements in this area exist or are granted visi-
bility.[69]

One response of the more combative women was to form
musical organizations like the League of Women Composers,
which began life in 1974, and to hold women's festivals that
would showcase female musicians, like the International Women's
Arts Festival organized by Verna Gillis in 1975. Nancy Van
de Vate, an early chairwoman of the League, insisted advocacy
not militancy was involved. Whatever the "heated rhetoric ...
proclaiming women's power," in reality, women "have no power."
They were rarely orchestra conductors or heads of large music departments, for example.[70]

Nevertheless, at least some women were aggressively active in advancing their cause. At the festival mentioned above was heard "a gruesomely simple song attributed to a South Carolina woman who was hanged in 1933 for murdering and dismembering her husband." Did the presentation have a confrontational purpose or was it an expression in action of feminist rage? A year later Vivian Fine's cantata Meeting for Equal Rights, 1866 was presented, which denounced white males' domination over women. The next year came Jean Ivey's Testament of Eve, which offered "the composer's interpretation of the Garden of Eden events as symbolic of women's challenge to patriarchal authority. What fascinated Ms. Ivey was 'Eve chooses knowledge and growth, as opposed to remaining a pampered pet forever in the Garden.'"[71] In the same year, Kathleen Grandchamp of Minneapolis complained, in a letter sent to Musical America, about an earlier article praising "segregated boy choirs." She claimed that the Catholic Church was historically prejudiced against women, excluding them from choirs. During the Baroque period, "when high voices were urgently needed" in music "too difficult for boys: castrati were used ... as pretty a case as I know of male chauvinism cutting off its nose to spite its face." As if to prove her point, a Mark Fencke of Chicago sent a letter in rebuttal, calling Grandchamp's statement a "dictatorial piece of filthy feministic hogwash," the sort he expected from "dictatorial libbers.... People want to discriminate between the sexes because this is a natural desire."[72]

Musicians like Vivian Fine did experience provocation, not least of which was male condescension when their accomplishments were out of the ordinary. Fine mentions a performance of one of her orchestral works at Juilliard, after which "a male colleague said, 'That was nice orchestration. Did you do it yourself?' I'm certain he didn't intend to sound nasty, though it was a patronizing remark. But I don't think that prejudices against women composers can be isolated from attitudes toward women in general."[73] In like manner, Joan Tower says that when her Sequoia was performed by the New York Philharmonic under Mehta, some person found it difficult to accept the idea that it was a Joan, not a Bert or John, Tower who had written the piece. Later, when standing beside Zubin Mehta and Pinchas Zukerman, one annoying question she was forced to reply to was: "Whose wife are you?" The year was 1982.[74]

Grants for women oriented projects were not easily come
by. When Victoria Bond prepared to conduct an all-women
concert with the American Symphony Orchestra, in 1975, no
public or private funding was made available. She had to
cancel the concert. When, in the same year, Joan Tower won
a grant from the National Endowment for the Arts, she was
told by Miriam Gideon, then aged 69, that she had received
one also--"and it's my first!" Tower says: "I was absolutely
shocked that this composer had been around for such a long
time, and people knew her work, and yet it was her first
NEA grant! Then I looked at the situations of other women
who are a generation or two before me. And I saw that they
had hardly received awards or grants! Yet their male con-
temporaries had frequently gathered up the ribbons! I
thought, 'What is going on here?'"[75] It was not until 1969
that the first woman, Barbara Kolb, won the Prix de Rome;
and not until 1983 that the first woman, Ellen Taaffe Zwilich,
won the Pulitzer Prize.

Prior to the fifties, women in music meant singers or
instrumental soloists (normally playing harp, piano, or violin), though men far outnumbered women, won more frequent
engagements, and usually commanded higher fees if instrumental soloists. The great majority of musical women had to be
satisfied with amateur ranking, singing in choruses or playing in second-class orchestras for no pay.

Most competent women musicians who attempted to join
established orchestras that paid decent wages were denied positions. They were compelled to find a use for their talents
in their own orchestras. More than a dozen of them existed
in the United States during the 1930s, among them the Women's
Symphony of Chicago (actually established in 1925), the Philadelphia Women's Symphony, the Women's Symphony of Long
Beach, California, the Cleveland Women's Orchestra, and the
Orchestrette Classique of New York. Women conductors, like
Antonia Brico and Gertrude Hrdliczka, had to found their own
groups in order to practice their art.[76]

In 1942, only 31 women were to be found in major orchestras. By 1965, around 18 percent of the personnel in
33 major orchestras were women; by 1975, they numbered 25
percent. Sad to say, the Big Five (Boston, Chicago, New
York, Philadelphia, and Cleveland) still had only about 11
percent. On the other hand, even in 1954, community, college,

On Being a Musician

and other lesser orchestras had a women's membership of over 50 percent, in part owing to a willingness to work for less pay in ensembles with low budgets.[77]

   The women's movement did gradually extend its influence to arts organizations. Where once women were discriminated against in auditions for empty orchestra seats, soon blind auditioning, where applicants played hidden from view, became the norm, although many conductors insisted on testing finalists by having them play in the orchestra (where they could not hide!). Unfortunately, most major orchestras had non-American conductors, who usually held a strong anti-women bias. As one conductor once remarked, too many women in an orchestra made the stage "look like a kitchen." Zubin Mehta was quoted as saying, in 1970, that he did not like having women in the orchestra, although his Los Angeles Philharmonic had sixteen of them: "They are very good--they got their jobs in competition with men. I just don't think women should be in an orchestra. They become men. Men treat them as equals; they even change their pants in front of them. I think it's terrible." But the year was 1970, and Mehta found himself leafleted and picketed.[78]

   Apart from harpists, Elsa Hilger, a cellist, was apparently the first woman to hold a permanent seat in a major orchestra. She joined the Philadelphia Orchestra, under Stokowski, in 1934, and eventually held the position of associate solo cellist before her retirement in 1969. No women played in the Boston Symphony Orchestra until 1951, when Olivia Luetcke was hired as second harpist. The next year, Doriot Anthony Dwyer came on as first flutist. The New York Philharmonic acquired its first woman in 1966, the bass player Orin O'Brien--followed the next year by the cellist Evangeline Benedetti. By the 1980-81 concert season, forty percent of the positions in major, regional, and metropolitan orchestras were held by women--eighty percent of them were string players, eleven percent played woodwinds, four percent played brass instruments, and a few played percussion instruments.[79]

   The road of the woman conductor was strewn with obstacles. Antonia Brico, after studying conducting with Karl Muck, gave a concert with the Berlin Philharmonic in 1930, when she was 28 years old, then another that same year with the Los Angeles orchestra. Although she had made a strong impression on musicians like Artur Rubinstein and Bruno Walter, she could find no orchestra willing to accept her as a permanent conductor. Having no other recourse, she formed and conducted the Brico Symphony, which lived a hand-to-mouth existence. In order to give concerts in New York, for example, she had to do her own financing, with no assurance that she would come out debt free. Later, she located in Denver, where she conducted a semi-professional orchestra in five concerts a year. "How would you like to have just five concerts a year?" she asked, in 1974. "I don't get a chance to play my instrument--the orchestra." She was denied the opportunity to develop her considerable talents. Management agencies wanted no women conductors on their rosters. Arthur Judson told her that women subscribers, in particular, would stay away in droves if she conducted the New York Philharmonic. Mrs. Charles (Minnie) Guggenheimer, manager of the Lewisohn Stadium Concerts, told Brico that she found the idea of a woman conductor repulsive. Later, she would allow Brico into the Stadium, but only after some 4,000 people signed a petition requesting the action. When Antonia Brico was in her seventies, she produced a documentary film about herself, called <u>Antonia</u>, which clearly and persuasively presented the case for equal treatment of women in the arts. The critical acclaim granted the film helped to win her some major guest conducting engagements and to smooth the way for younger women conductors.[80]

Margaret Hillis got a conducting break in 1977, when Solti became sick in New York City and she replaced him as conductor of the Chicago Symphony. She has guest conducted throughout the United States, but is best known for her direction of the Chicago Symphony Chorus, the Elgin (Illinois) Symphony, and the Chicago Civic Symphony. She states that when she began her conducting studies in the fifties: "No master teacher would take a woman as a student because she had no future in conducting." Only after considerable effort was a master teacher willing to accept her as a student. In the eighties, attitudes toward women had changed: "If I were starting out now [1983], I would get to a master teacher. The women's movement had a lot to do with it. I think I probably had something to do with it, too. I've had students come to me and say, 'What's it like to be a woman conductor? I say, 'Master your craft and forget about being a 'woman conductor.'"[81]

Several women conductors have made names for themselves--Sarah Caldwell with the Opera Company of Boston,

Eve Queler with her Opera Orchestra of New York, and Victoria Bond and Judith Somogi, among others. None has found success easy to obtain. Writing in 1983 about the achievements of Eve Queler, Sheila Rizzo remarked: "There has been a great deal of speculation about why the Conlons, Tilson Thomases, and Russell Davieses are being overlooked in favor of the Marriners, Mutis, and von Dohnanhis. Since American conductors in general seem to be in such disfavor, it's no surprise to find that those who happen also to be women are up against even more formidable odds. Despite the gains made by the women's liberation movement in the last 10 years or so, women conductors, it seems, still have either to head their own groups, following the example of Antonia Brico, Sarah Caldwell, and Queler, or come in the back way, via choral conducting, the route taken by Margaret Hollis and Lorna Cooke De Varon. Queler has done better than most, but not quite well enough.... 'I will have made it when I have an appointment with a major orchestra,' she says firmly."[82]

One or two women have achieved fame not as performers. Nancy Hanks, to name one, was chairwoman of the NEA and the National Council on the Arts under Presidents Nixon, Ford, and Carter. She was also vice chairperson of the Rockefeller Fund, and board member of DuPont, Equitable Life Assurance, and Scholastics, Inc.; and regent of the Smithsonian Institution as well as trustee of Duke University. Of greatest importance to music was her knowledge of politics as a means of funneling money into the arts.[83]

When all is said, however, the democratic imperative to assess all people, including women, on their own merits and abilities is still weakly observed in the arts and remains a blot on the American historical record.

RACE AND ART MUSIC

An even greater blot on the historical record of the United States was the treatment of its non-white American minorities--native Indian, Asian, and African in origin. The tragic history of Afro-Americans is so familiar that it requires no retelling here. It has been an uninterrupted narration of democracy practiced in the breach, not of opportunity but humanity denied.

One can understand why so many black people, in the sixties, resented the tendency of rebelling white women and young white people to claim that they were in the same boat. Gladys Lesley Davis, wife of a bass player denied a position in the New York Philharmonic, said with bitterness: "I am one of those supposedly 'liberated women' (black) who, at this time [1971] is working seven days a week to help support our family.... I personally don't believe in Women's Lib for black women as we have always been liberated to work--many times at menial jobs. I would first like to be considered as a Human being in this society. I could not, now or ever, hold a job at the expense of my husband or any black man."84

As part of the rebellion of black Americans in the fifties and sixties, black musicians showed great concern about encouraging the talent of their young, exploring their musical heritage, and bringing their music to American audiences. They worried and with good reason, of course, about how they might find positions in the art-music world that would enable them and their families to make ends meet. Associations were organized, like the Society of Black Composers and the Afro-American Music Opportunities Association, for the purpose of survival, intellectual and emotional support, expressing and advancing a shared black viewpoint, and collective strength in furthering a mutual cause. Since its founding, in 1919, the National Association of Negro Musicians had tried to arouse Afro-Americans to greater activity in music, to develop taste, to find schooling for young people with talent, and to organize workshops, seminars, and concerts featuring black musical expression. Respected musical establishments with long histories of barring black Americans from employment were belabored to abolish their color line. In the postwar years, concerts increasingly were presented with integrated orchestras, like the Symphony of the New World, featuring black composers, conductors, and soloists.85

Reputable and dedicated black scholars appeared, like Eileen Southern, who wished to disseminate accurate knowledge about blacks in music and about black music, especially in those areas where little, no, or distorted information prevailed. She published The Music of Black Americans and Readings in Black American Music in 1971, and the Biographical Dictionary of Afro-American and African Musicians in 1982. In 1973, she began the journal Black Perspective in Music, where her problems included finding financial backing for the venture and she had mostly only the assistance of her husband in preparing the publication of each issue.[86]

Without question scarcely any Afro-Americans were active in American art music until the postwar years, and even then the number increased slowly, in spite of increased black militancy and the enactment of antidiscriminatory laws on all levels of government. In part, their absence was due to racial prejudice. This, however, was not the only explanation. Illustrating the complexity of the problem was the bias charge brought against the New York Philharmonic, in 1969. On 10 June 1969 a news item appeared in the Times stating that the Philharmonic faced a charge of hiring bias, brought by Earl Madison, a cellist, and J. Arthur Davis, a string bassist. Although Carlos Moseley, managing director of the orchestra denied the bias, the city's Commission on Human Rights noted that only one black person had ever been employed by the New York Philharmonic (W. Sanford Allen, a violinist hired in 1962), and a hearing was warranted. Robert Weltz, of the Commission shortly after observed that of the 500 musicians making up the five most important orchestras there were but two Afro-Americans. Rebutted a spokesman for the Philharmonic, to find qualified black musicians was difficult; indeed, in the last five years, of the 250 applicants for positions, only seven had been black.[87]

September 1969 saw the conductor Leonard Bernstein explaining that both musicians had been allowed to enter the finals without having passed the preliminaries, because they were black. Next, Martin Oppenheimer, the Philharmonic's lawyer, said few Afro-Americans were prepared to enter a career in art music, citing lack of opportunity for proper training, discrimination, economics, and studying with "too many bad teachers." Then Bernstein added that what was involved was a societal problem, that many black Americans were reluctant to put in long hard years of study and had deviant notions. It was true that no screen was used in the Philharmonic auditions, but screening was unsatisfactory since the judges had to spot defects like stiff bow arms.[88]

Eventually, the Commission on Human Rights did find instances of bias in the hiring of substitute and extra musicians. Of significance was the Philharmonic board's decision, in September 1970, to sponsor a one-week Orchestra Repertory Institute, open to blacks and other minorities. Moseley claimed the workshop was a result of the Philharmonic's own initiative and not owing to the adverse finding, although one cannot help wondering if the action would have taken place without the instigation of Madison and Davis. Shortly thereafter the orchestra announced an affirmative action plan to encourage musicians from racial minorities to apply for positions, which included a search for qualified instrumentalists, notifying minority groups of impending auditions for permanent positions, passing on information on the most advanced minority players to around 100 other American orchestras, and setting up scholarships for talented minority youngsters. Finally, in the summer of 1972, Donal Henahan said that the Philharmonic had three blacks on the board of directors and two in higher administration.[89]

Other attempts at discovering and encouraging talent among minority musicians soon followed. In 1979, Doris O'Connell, of the National Music Council, stated that the John F. Kennedy Center, of Washington, D.C., and a National Black Commission were sponsoring a National Black Music Colloquium and Competition, whose purpose it was to search for talented young pianists and string players and, after auditioning them, to give recognition and money prizes. The repertoire for the auditions would "draw from standard repertory and music of black composers."[90]

Efforts such as those of the Philharmonic and the Black Commission notwithstanding, increased orchestral employment for minority musicians moved at a tortoise pace. For instance, in May 1974, the seven-man Players' Committee (all white males) of the San Francisco Symphony, denied a contract renewal to Elayne Jones, a black-woman timpanist, and Ryohei Nakagawa, a Japanese man and principal bassoonist of the orchestra. Yet tenure was given to six others--all white males. The director, Seiji Ozawa, wanted to retain the two rejected musicians and opened the orchestra to charges of racism and sexism. A public scandal resulted. Not one of the 22 women in the orchestra had been on the Players' Committee. The fired musicians had repeatedly received critical praise, so it was not a matter of incompetence. Not once had any member of the orchestra mentioned dissatisfaction with their playing. A few people blamed a power play against Ozawa, who had wanted to demote four of the orchestra's principals, others pointed to insufficient communication on professional matters between director and orchestra members, still others thought it was

owing to jealousy and professional insecurity among the players. A vote of the entire orchestra was taken: 50 supported
the Players' Committee, 14 opposed it, and 30 abstained.[91]

Two years later, the National Urban League issued a
survey that found of the 5,000 players in 56 American orchestras, only 70 were from minorities. Among the "Big Five"
(New York, Boston, Philadelphia, Cleveland, and Chicago),
7 minority players were found.

To say these figures proved bias would not be entirely
fair. Another side of the minority-hiring problem was voiced
by Calvin Simmons in an article published in the New York
Times, 21 July 1980. That year, at the age of 29, Simmons
was appointed director (and only black member) of the Oakland Symphony Orchestra. The conductor was reported as
saying that although racial barriers persisted, they were
crumbling. One large obstacle still remained and that was
the lack of minority exposure to classical music, whether in
the home or school, which contributed in significant measure
to the dearth of minority musicians in the art-music world.[92]

Calvin Simmons was fortunate that other black conductors before him had made possible the advancement of his
career. Before the postwar years of black militancy, Afro-
American conductors had met with scorn in America. Dean
Dixon, to name one earlier conductor, was an exceptionally
fine musician, but found little American employment in the
thirties and forties. According to Ronald Smothers: "Throughout this time, Mr. Dixon was outspoken in the racial barriers
he faced in the United States in trying to establish himself as
a conductor. He ruefully told of the insults from one concert
manager after another, ranging, he said, from polite protes-
tations that there was little work for any conductors to ridiculous suggestions that he conduct in white face, wearing white
gloves." Like Everett Lee and George Byrd, two other capable black directors, he had to practice his art in Europe,
especially in Sweden and Germany. He guest conducted
throughout Europe, in Japan, and in Australia. But no invitations from the United States came his way until 1970, when
he was invited to conduct the New York Philharmonic in a
Central-Park summer concert. He died in 1976.[93]

At last, in 1968, Henry Lewis became director of the
New Jersey Symphony, at a time when its board decided to

transform it from a community to a "first-class professional
ensemble." He was the first Afro-American to head a metropolitan orchestra in the United States. By 1980, the orchestra's
board acquired five black members, and the orchestra's black
players went from one to eight. His youth concerts, family
programs, and low-price performances represented popular innovations. These and the regular concerts were soon drawing
large audiences, even though the orchestra under its new
conductor never compromised on quality in its programming.
What was of even greater moment to Lewis, over fifty percent
of these audiences consisted of black Americans. When LeRoi
Jones criticized the orchestra, saying it represented white
culture and was irrelevant to black lives, Lewis objected, insisting that black Americans were born into and had to be a
part of Western culture.[94]

At least two other Afro-American conductors have made
marks for themselves, Paul Freeman and James DePriest.
Both have done many conducting stints in the United States;
none is the permanent conductor of a major orchestra. Such
a goal is unrealistic however capable these musicians may be,
a black composer said to me in 1976, so long as "their white
brothers also can't make it to big conducting positions, most
everything going to those guys coming in from the outside."
Orchestra conductors from an Asian-American minority have
received negligible attention in musical circles, despite the
fact that several conductors born in Asia have made numerous
guest appearances with major American orchestras, and two--
the Japanese conductor Seiji Ozawa, and Indian conductor
Zubin Mehta--received appointments as permanent directors of
the Boston Symphony and New York Philharmonic, respectively.

Not numerous on the concert circuit, instrumental soloists originating from American minorities began making more
than token appearances in the seventies. The much praised
cellist Yo-Yo Ma, even though a Chinese born in Paris, is to
all purposes American. The spectacular Afro-American trum-
pet player Wynton Marsalis has been equally comfortable performing jazz and art-music works. The pianist Natalie Hinderas, had a jazz-musician father and a musically trained
mother. After her first appearance in New York, in 1954,
she "lived for many years on the fringes" of musical life.
In 1971, she "made a blazing debut with the Philadelphia Orchestra in four concerts, beginning on November 19." She
was "the first black female instrumental soloist ever to appear

on subscription concerts with the orchestra."[95] Since then
she has toured in Europe and Asia, conscientiously including
compositions by Afro-American composers on her programs.
André Watts, born to a black-American father and Hungarian
mother, was started on the piano by his mother and later
also won international fame as a piano virtuoso.

More frequently encountered are Afro-American singers,
some of whom have achieved star status, especially in opera.
Raoul Abdul maintains: "Opera is a natural form of expression for Black singers. The idea of human passion being expressed in song requires absolutely no special adjustment for
a Black audience. It responds to sung dialogue (recitative)
as easily as it does to the spoken word." Serving as an example is the worship service where the minister preaches in a
half-chanting and half-speaking manner, then breaks into song
when carried away with emotion.[96]

Anti-black discrimination was everywhere in evidence in
the first half of the century. Yet, the superb voices and successful concertizing of Roland Hayes, Paul Robeson, and Marian
Anderson, in spite of white-American opposition, helped a great
deal in making the road easier for young singers. Marian Anderson, for example, was a contralto who grew famous in Europe and
America during the thirties. Nevertheless, in 1939, the Daugh-
ters of the American Revolution refused to allow her to sing in
Washington's Constitution Hall, saying their segregationist bylaws forbad it! A national furor resulted. Eleanor Roosevelt
resigned from the DAR, and she and Harold Ickes, Secretary of
the Interior, arranged to have her sing at the Lincoln Memorial--
which she did before an immense audience numbering 75,000 persons. In 1955, Marian Anderson broke the unwritten anti-black
Metropolitan Opera taboo, by appearing as Ulrica in Un Ballo in
Maschera. Regrettably, she was by then past her prime. (Ca-
terina Jarboro was the first black woman to sing with a major
American opera company, the Chicago Opera, in 1933.)

It was left to younger black women to become preemin-
ent internationally for their operatic singing in addition to
their concert singing. Leontyne Price received her initial
break when Virgil Thomson, in 1952, asked her to sing in a
revival of Four Saints in Three Acts. This led to her singing the role of Bess in Porgy and Bess, both in the United
States and Europe. At the end of the fifties, she sang with
the San Francisco Opera and the most important opera companies of Europe, making the role of Aida especially her own.

At last, in 1961, she was invited to sing with the Metropolitan Opera. Grace Bumbry's first concert appearance was in London, in 1959. From there, she went to the Paris Opera, exciting great public interest when she appeared in Aida, and to Wagner's Bayreuth, where she sang Venus in Tannhauser. At last, in 1965, she was engaged for the Metropolitan Opera. A third singer, Jessye Norman, made her operatic debut in Berlin, in 1969, and received tremendous American admiration as a concert singer. However, it was not until 1983 that she appeared for the first time at the Metropolitan Opera. Obviously, the Metropolitan Opera Association was willing to take no chances with Afro-Americans, waiting until the most important European houses gave a stamp of approval before showing any interest at all.

Operatic stardom in the United States was an almost impossible achievement for Afro-American men. Simon Estes, who was prizewinner in Moscow's International Tchaikovsky Vocal Competition, in 1966, explains why: "There is racism in the music business. Certain opera companies have refused me because I'm black. I've been told to my face that although qualified in every other way for a role, the situation of a black male, even in white face, playing opposite a white female would not go down well with audiences and boards of directors. It's easier for black women than black men in opera.... George Shirley and I are the only two men with comparable status [in 1972]." Estes said that still influential was the "old plantation morality," where it had been all right for white males to make love to lower stationed black women but a prelude to a lynching if a black man had looked at a white woman. [97]

When Todd Duncan appeared with the New York City Opera, in 1945, in Pagliacci, he was not only the first Afro-American male to sing with that association, but also the first in the United States to sing in the role of a white male. George Shirley made his debut with the Metropolitan, in 1961; Simon Estes, in 1976. This should not be taken to mean the complete acceptance of black males in opera. None has received anything remotely close to the adulation granted his feminine counterparts. In the eighties, as in the fifties, the best advice for a black male interested in an operatic career is to leave the United States and go to Europe.

Afro-American composers have written competently in

every art-music style practiced in twentieth-century America.
Major composition prizes have come their way. Ulysses Kay
was granted the American Prix de Rome in 1949; Howard Swan-
sons' Short Symphony won the New York Critics Circle Award
for 1951; Olly Wilson topped the International Electronic Music
Competition held at Dartmouth College in 1968. Whatever their
style, they normally claim that some aspect of Afro-Americanism
has influenced their attitude and sound. The well known
writer on black musical culture Dominique-René de Lerma
maintains that their music "emerges from a variant sociology
with an aesthetic that can be quite different. To impose a
dictum that music is neither black nor white but only good
or bad, or to say that music is a universal language, is to
open the door for cultural imperialism. We might thereby miss
the dialects of the Renaissance or of the Orient. One could
hardly justify the stand that music is neither Baroque nor
Medieval, but only good or bad. Why should black culture
be philosophically subjected to the melting pot?" To quote
one Afro-American composer, Thomas Anderson, who has written his share of atonal and serial music, it is the composer's
duty "to unite musical diversity with the personal and thus
form an additional link within societies. My music, organized
through systematic sets which find adaptability in varying
contexts, draws upon sources which are expressed from my
contact with people. To date it has been influenced by Afro-
American music, art music, tradition, avant-garde, 'primitive
cultures'...."[98]

     One power base that has been denied Afro-American
art musicians has been the sustaining support of their black
communities. Whether owing to lack of money, cultural isolation from art music, or psychological unreadiness to participate in a white evolved culture, black attendance at concerts
and opera performances has been sparse. Henry Lewis's experience was the exception, not the rule. As Carl Cunningham, music editor of the Houston Post, stated in 1975, he saw
"almost total apathy on the part of the black community in
their poor attendance of musical events that rightfully merit
their interest and sometimes deserve their most vigorous support." Even when major attractions like the pianist André
Watts and the Alvin Ailey American Dance Theater have been
engaged for Houston, their sponsors have expressed dismay
at the "could-not-care-less attitude." Cunningham said it was
not a conscious boycott of serious music, just an "apathy,
which is shared to a lesser degree by the white segment ...

in a city where capacity audiences are sadly the exception to
the rule."[99] Unfortunately for black musicians, a similar
apathy has prevailed elsewhere. I have attended concerts in
Boston, New York, Philadelphia, Baltimore, Los Angeles, and
New Orleans where noted black musicians were featured. Even
when they performed music by black composers, they attracted
mostly a white audience.

Isaiah Jackson, who has been music director of the Flint
Symphony and associate director of the Rochester Philharmonic,
says even black Americans who do have excellent incomes do
not attend concerts. Yet, he noted that when he conducted
an orchestra in a Martin Luther King celebration, Afro-Americans
filled the hall. He therefore has tried to strengthen communication with the black community by selecting works appealing
to it, including those by black composers, that will register
on first hearing. Very successful was a concert in Cleveland,
where Olly Wilson's Voices was performed, Natalie Hinderas
appeared in the Grieg Piano Concerto, and the predominantly
black Shaw High School Chorus sang with the Cleveland Orchestra Chorus in selections from Copland's The Tender Land,
then in the Hallelujah chorus. He says he has tried to work
through the black community network, including churches,
clubs, service organizations, newspapers, and black-oriented
radio. When black Americans have been coaxed to attend, he
has found that it made sense to use black performers, choruses, etc. when possible, so that the audience would not be
turned off by music it would not ordinarily seek out and cannot respond to and could be turned on by performers toward
whom it would feel sympathetic.[100]

Despite what Jackson says about achieving increased
concert attendance, the Afro-American men and women belong-
ing to the regular concert- and opera-going public have numbered proportionally far less than the Afro-American musicians
who participate in the creation and performance of art music.
Attempts to enlarge that number have had mixed results at
best. Outreach programs have had small effect. School instruction has been desultory. Cultural reinforcement in the
home and community has remained weak. The identification
of art music with the white ruling class and black Uncle Tom-
ism has done little to help. Thus, a most important constituency for promoting the cause of black artists and the cultural interests in which they believe has failed to materialize.

Notes

1. Shirley Fleming, "The Case of the Disappearing Strings," High Fidelity (September 1964), pp. 43-46.
2. For a thorough study of the relation of music in America to late immigrants and their descendants, see Nicholas Tawa, A Sound of Strangers (Metuchen, N.J.: Scarecrow Press, 1982).
3. B. F. Martin, "Elmar Oliviera," Ovation (October 1984), p. 22.
4. Joe Goldberg, "To Be Young and a Concert Pianist," New York Times Magazine, 18 October 1981, p. 86.
5. Bernard Holland, "It Takes More Than Talent to Build a Musical Career," New York Times, 19 February 1984, section 2, p. 1.
6. Marianne Costantinou, "Musicians of the Future Discuss Life and Art," New York Times, 24 May 1981, section 2, p. 15.
7. Tim Page, "For Some Gifted Musicians Freelancing Offers Career," New York Times, 15 January 1984, p. 36.
8. The Schonberg reference is in Chasins, Music at the Crossroads, pp. 103-104; also see Edward Rothstein, "How Important Is The Music Debut?" New York Times, 2 January 1983, section 2, p. 15; and Richard Sennett, The Fall of Public Man (New York: Vintage, 1978), p. 288.
9. Rothstein, "How Important Is The Music Debut?" p. 1.
10. Helen Epstein, "Selling Tomorrow's Big Names Today," New York Times, 15 February 1976, section 2, p. 19.
11. Sennet, The Fall of Public Man, p. 288.
12. Goldberg, "To Be Young and a Concert Pianist," p. 90.
13. Richard Reeves, American Journey (New York: Simon & Schuster, 1982), p. 131; Schickel, Intimate Strangers, p. 251.
14. Marilyn Horne, with Jane Scovell, Marilyn Horne: My Life (New York: Atheneum, 1983), p. 91.
15. Frederick Dorian, Commitment to Culture (Pittsburgh: University of Pittsburgh Press, 1964), p. 467.
16. Beverly Sills, Bubbles (New York: Grosset & Dunlap, 1981), pp. 25, 34.
17. Kozma, "Music vs The Majority," Music Journal (March 1963), p. 50; C. D. Jackson, "The Quality of Life in this Technological Age," Music Journal (January 1964), p. 11.

18. Paul Moor, "Our Operatic Expatriates," High Fidelity (November 1960), p. 51.
19. Lipman, Music After Modernism, p. 226; Bill Zakariasen, "Marilyn Horne," Ovation (July 1983), pp. 12, 14.
20. Moor, "Our Operatic Expatriates," p. 52; also see
Eleanor Steber, in the Music Journal (April/May 1960), p. 9.
21. Henri Temianka, Facing the Music (New York:
McKay, 1973), pp. 26-27.
22. Chapin, Musical Chairs, p. 109; also see Judy
Bass, "Keys to Success," Boston (August 1983), p. 84.
23. Martin, "Elmar Oliviera," p. 22, 24.
24. Will Crutchfield, "The Philharmonic's Youthful Gam-
bit," New York Times, 21 October 1984, section 2, p. 27.
25. Paul Moor, "What Became of Joyce Flissler?" Musical America (May 1979), pp. 23-24; Chasins, Music at the
Crossroads, p. 103.
26. Byron Belt, "Ruth Laredo," Musical America (December 1974), p. 4.
27. Bass, "Keys to Success," pp. 84, 87; Chasins,
Music at the Crossroads, pp. 102, 106-09; Temianka, Facing
the Music, p. 26.
28. Zakarian, "Marilyn Horne," p. 14; Furlong, Season
with Solti, p. 33.
29. Erich Fromm, To Have or To Be? (New York:
Bantam, 1981), pp. 132-33, 135-36.
30. Goldberg, "To Be Young and a Concert Pianist,"
p. 88.
31. Philip Hart, in Musical America (October 1967),
p. 25; Andrew L. Pincus, "Malcolm Frager, Reflective Musician," New York Times, 24 February 1985, section 2, p. 28;
Harlow Robinson, in Musical America (February 1985), p. 26.
32. Bernard Holland, "Music: André Watts in Fisher
Hall Recital," New York Times, 24 February 1985, p. 46; John
Rockwell, "Music: The Concord String Quartet," New York
Times, 24 February 1985, p. 46.
33. For more information on this influence, see Nicholas
E. Tawa, Serenading the Reluctant Eagle (New York: Schirmer,
1984), Chapter 1.
34. Harvey and Georgeanna Whistler, "Guest Editorial,"
Music Journal (May 1968), p. 4; Mark Kramer, in Music Journal Annual (1968), p. 18; Harold Schonberg, "Why Have Programs Changed?" New York Times, 27 April 1980, section 2,
pp. 19-20; Harold Schonberg, "Earl Wild's 'Defiantly Kitsch'
Celebration," New York Times, 25 October 1981, section 2,
p. 21.

35. For a few of the comments on the performance of new American music, see the letter of Claudette Sorel, printed in Musical America (August 1959), p. 32; Ruth Slenczynska, in the Music Journal (September 1962), pp. 60–61, 93; Ned Rorem, Setting the Tone (New York: Coward-McCann, 1983), p. 223; Karen Monson, "Emanuel Ax," Ovation (April 1985), p. 10.

36. Bernard Holland, "When a Virtuoso and His Cello Take to the Road," New York Times, 24 May 1981, section 2, pp. 1, 10.

37. Holland, "It Takes More Than Talent to Build a Musical Career," p. 19.

38. Ibid., p. 19.

39. Holland, "When a Virtuoso and His Cello Take to the Road," p. 19; Waleson, "Paying the Piper," p. 844; Glenn Plaskin, Horowitz (New York: Morrow, 1983), pp. 265, 407, 437.

40. See the Music Journal (November 1976), p. 10.

41. Jacques Barzun, Human Freedom, rev. ed. (Philadelphia: Lippincott, 1964), p. 3.

42. Robert Cumming, "Total War," Music Journal Annual (1962), p. 9.

43. Joseph Levine, "The Vanishing Musician, " Music Journal (March 1962), p. 38; Baumol and Bowen, Performing Arts, pp. 107–08.

44. Baumol and Bowen, Performing Arts, p. 100.

45. Jeff McLaughlin, "Wresting a Living from the Arts," Boston Globe, 27 March 1983, pp. 1, 8; Lucy Kraus, "Being Called 'Concertmaster' Is All Right with Her," New York Times, 1 August 1982, section 2, p. 17; Joseph Dyer, "For Free-Lance Musicians, Boston Is On and Off Key," Boston Globe, 27 March 1983, section A, p. 1.

46. For a discussion of this turning away from the new and toward the old in music, see Laurence Dreyfus, "Early Music Defended Against Its Devotees," Musical Quarterly 69 (1983), 305.

47. John Rockwell, "Busy Activity on the 'Early Music' Front," New York Times, 16 November 1980, section 2, p. 17.

48. Ibid., pp. 17, 24; Richard Dyer, "Keeping Time," The Boston Globe Magazine, 22 May 1983, p. 50.

49. Rockwell, "Busy Activity on the 'Early Music' Front," p. 17.

50. Bernard Holland, "In Praise of Early Music," New York Times Magazine, 22 May 1983, p. 64.

51. Andrew Porter, A Musical Season (New York: Viking, 1974), p. 10. The comment appeared in the 7 October 1972 issue of the New Yorker.

52. Gilson, Painting and Reality, pp. 217-19.

53. Lorin Maazel, "Homogenized Art Is Tasteless," Music Journal (October 1962), pp. 36, 78.

54. Rose Heylbut, "Brainwash or Back Talk?" Music Journal Annual (1967), pp. 36-37, 58.

55. See the Music Journal (December 1969), p. 99.

56. B. F. Scherer, "Early Music Today," Music Journal (March 1978), pp. 14-15.

57. Schonberg, Facing the Music, p. 67.

58. Edward Strickland, review of Nonesuch 79036, Fanfare (January/February 1983), pp. 94-95.

59. Holland, "In Praise of Early Music," p. 82.

60. Ibid., pp. 72-73.

61. John Schneider, in Musical America (February 1985), p. 22.

62. Dreyfus, "Early Music Defended Against Its Devotees," pp. 297-303.

63. Heidi Waleson, "The Waverly Consort," Ovation (November 1983), p. 13.

64. Dyer, "Keeping Time," p. 64.

65. Marvin Harris, America Now: The Anthropology of a Changing Culture (New York: Simon & Schuster, 1981), pp. 88-89, 93-94; "Though Women Make Up More of the Work Force," New York Times, 1 January 1984, section 3, p. 15.

66. Reeves, American Journey, pp. 305, 310.

67. Fawcett and Thomas, The American Condition, pp. 100-02.

68. Allan Kozinn, "Electronic Music on Disks Reflects A Maturing Genre," New York Times, 5 June 1983, section 2, p. 25.

69. Laura Koplewitz, "Joan Tower: Building Bridges for New Music," Symphony Magazine (June/July 1983), p. 39; John Rockwell, in the New York Times, 21 February 1975, p. 13, and 27 March 1983, section 2, p. 25.

70. Nancy Van de Vate, letter in Musical America (August 1977), p. 2; John Rockwell, in the New York Times, 10 March 1975, p. 40; Donal Henahan, in the New York Times, 31 August 1975, section 2, p. 11; Jean Bowen, "Women in Music," Musical America (August 1974), p. 20.

71. John Rockwell, in the New York Times, 10 March 1975, p. 40; Andrew De Rhen, in Musical America (August

1976), pp. 26-27; Kathline Colvin, in the Music Journal (February 1977), p. 35.

72. See Musical America (March 1977), p. 2; (August 1977), p. 2.

73. Susan Galardi, "Premieres: The Composer Speaks," Musical America (February 1985), p. 18.

74. Koplewitz, "Joan Tower," p. 37.

75. Ibid., p. 39; news item in the New York Times, 10 September 1975, p. 33.

76. Quaintance Eaton, "Women Come Into Their Own in Our Orchestras," Musical America (February 1955), p. 179.

77. Ibid., p. 30; Barbara Jepson, "You've Come a Long Way: Women in Symphony Orchestras," Music Journal (December 1977), p. 13.

78. See the report by Judy Klemesrud, in the New York Times, 18 October 1970, section 2, p. 33; also the letter from "Members and Supporters of the Women Musicians' Collective," in the New York Times, 3 January 1971, section 2, p. 16; Phyllis Lehmann, "Women in Orchestras," Symphony Magazine (December 1982), p. 14; Jepson, "You've Come a Long Way," pp. 13-14.

79. See Ovation (April 1984), p. 6; Lehmann, "Women In Orchestras," pp. 11-13; Dickson, "Gentlemen, More Dolce Please!" p. 17; Seltzer, The Professional Symphony Orchestra in the United States, p. 165.

80. Grace Lichtenstein, "A Film Festival With No Stars or Prizes," New York Times, 15 September 1974, section 2, pp. 15-16; see also Donal Henahan's report, in the New York Times of 19 May 1975.

81. Heidi Waleson, "Orchestra Conducting Was What She Always Wanted," New York Times, 20 February 1983, section 2, pp. 21, 32.

82. Sheila Rizzo, "An Interview with Eve Queler," Fanfare (January/February 1983), p. 88.

83. See the tribute paid her by E. Atwill Gilman, in Symphony Magazine (February/March 1983), p. 35.

84. Hodgson, America in Our Time, p. 306; Gladys Lesley Davis, letter in the New York Times, 27 June 1971, section 2, p. 31.

85. Eileen Southern, The History of Black Americans (New York: Norton, 1971), p. 506; Raymond Ericson, "Black Visions," New York Times, 8 August 1971, section 2, p. 11; Raoul Abdul, Blacks in Classical Music (New York: Dodd, Mead, 1977), pp. 59, 68-69; Bernard Holland, "Concert: Black Composers," New York Times, 19 February 1984, p. 89.

86. Much of this information came from a talk with
Eileen Southern and her husband, who also works very hard
to put out the journal, in May 1985.
87. "Philharmonic Facing Charge of Hiring Bias," New
York Times, 100 June 1969, p. 50; Donal Henahan, "Philharmonic's Hiring Policy Defended," New York Times, 31 July
1969, p. 26.
88. "Bernstein Denies Bias by Philharmonic at Auditions," New York Times, 30 September 1969, p. 42.
89. Donal Henahan, "Philharmonic Plans Workshop, Its
First, To train minorities," New York Times, 27 August 1971,
p. 17; Musical America (September 1972), p. 18; Seltzer, The
Professional Symphony Orchestra in the United States, p. 421.
90. Doris O'Connell, letter in the Music Journal (May/
June 1979), p. 6.
91. Robert Commandy, "The Symphony Scandal," Musical America (September 1974), pp. 28-29.
92. Wayne King, "Oakland Conductor Shuns the Jazz-
and-Blues Groove," New York Times, 21 July 1980, section C,
p. 16.
93. Ronald Smothers, "His 'Maestro' Was Hard Won,"
New York Times, 5 November 1976, p. 22; news item in New
York Times, 15 October 1962, p. 29; Allen Hughes, "For
Black Conductors, A Future? Or Frustration?" New York
Times, 15 March 1970, section 2, p. 19.
94. Jack Hiemenz, "Henry Lewis," Musical America
(September 1972), pp. 4-5; Chasins, Music at the Crossroads,
pp. 214-15.
95. James Felton, in Musical America (February 1972),
p. 23.
96. Abdul, Blacks in Classical Music, pp. 143-44.
97. See Musical America (October 1972), p. 13.
98. Dominique-René de Lerma, letter in Musical America
(August 1975), p. 2; David Ewen, American Composers: A
Biographical Dictionary (New York: Putnam, 1982), s.v.
"Anderson, Thomas Jefferson."
99. Carl Cunningham, "How Black Is Black?" Musical
America (January 1975), pp. 24-26.
100. Isaiah Jackson, "A Common Chord," Symphony
Magazine (June/July 1983), pp. 33-35.

Chapter 5

MUSIC ASSOCIATIONS

A major portion of a music association's strength derives
from its sensitivity to, and concern for, the community to
which it caters and from the community's involvement in its
activities. To the extent that the audience drawn from the
community is sufficiently large and dependably attends performances and to the extent that well-wishers, who may come
only now and again to performances, think favorably of it and
approve its support financially and otherwise, the association
thrives. To the extent that the community contains spectators
passively viewing it from the sidelines, oblivious ones ignoring
it, and critics hostile ot its existence, the association lan-
guishes and may even die. Although these observations would
seem obvious, they have not usually guided many of the important arts organizations. Furthermore, those associations
that have taken them seriously are one moment up and another
down in their communal relationships, owing to difficulties of
accommodation to the constant changes affecting twentieth-
century American society.

To cite an example of artistic well-being, in 1964, the
inhabitants of Spartanburg, South Carolina, where reported
in the Music Journal as being deeply involved with, deriving
great value from, and having strong interest in art music and
the associations that brought this music to them. At that
time, Spartanburg's prominent citizens were working hard to
consult with and take seriously the desires of their neighbors.
The community's population numbered around 44,500. The
local Converse College numbered around 2,900 students. Despite this modest size, Spartanburg in cooperation with the
college had a very active musical life. Both worked to support a 70-member symphony orchestra, made up of townspeo-
ple, students, and college faculty, as well as an Opera Workshop, a Civic Concert Band, and a concert series that featured

visiting musicians. The town had also instituted a scholarship program in aid of its young talented musicians.[1]

In contrast, a close acquaintance of mine (an amateur
violist who asked that he and his city not be identified) told
me about his community of 155,000 inhabitants, which had a
symphony orchestra but nothing else musically. A narrowly
exclusive group alone determined the orchestra's policies,
among them a decision to exclude almost all local musicians
from the orchestra in favor of presumably more competent
but certainly more expensive players from places over 100
miles away. The group held to the opinion that compromising with majority views would lead to lesser artistic quality,
both in performance and programming. Except for the selling
of tickets, no attempt was made to involve the music public
of the city in the workings of the orchestra. This same
group also had controlled the Community Concerts series and
for the same reason. The larger community was not consulted
when it came to deciding who to bring in and what to program. By 1985, the concert series had foundered, attendance
at symphony concerts had dropped considerably, and money-
raising for the orchestra was meeting with increased resistance.
Now, in the fall of 1985, the orchestra was about to go under.
Meanwhile, despite the completion of a new Civic Center, the
city had little going on in any of the performing arts, save
for a resident theater company. Some stalwart music lovers
had taken to traveling to places an hour's distance away or
more in order to attend musical performances. Others relied
mostly on recordings and FM programming for their music.
The rest of the city could not care less about art music.

As Thomas Jefferson observed in a letter sent to Henry
Lee, on 10 August 1785, there are those civic leaders "who
identify themselves with the people, have confidence in them
as the most honest and safe, although not the most wise de-
pository of the public interests." Then wrote Jefferson, there
are those "who fear and distrust the people, and wish to draw
all powers from them into the hands of the higher classes."

The latter types, writes Herbert Tingsten, are basically
antidemocratic and doubtful "even of partial democratization."
They will given the general public a voice only when they
must and usually "after much opposition, unrest, and mis-
trust." Sometimes they give in after disaster looms. When
they give in they try to do so only in a minor way, granting

concessions in order to continue their influence and domination.[2] In art music, this minority group may include music
directors, managers, boards of trustees, well-heeled and
powerful financial contributors, and strongly opinionated cultural leaders--especially academics, prominent musicians, and
newspaper writers on cultural matters.

To reinforce their attempt to hold on to the cultural
reins, members of the minority group do advance one telling
argument. They claim that whatever the public's sentiments,
these are normally impossible to assess, or are expressed
murkily, and do not result from calmly reasoned and unmanip-
ulated thought. Therefore, the necessity frequently arises
for the smaller group, as representatives of the cultural community's best interest, to decide matters with little or no consultation of majority views. "Even when an opinion is available, decisions ... cannot always be expected to correspond
to the opinion of the majority," states Tingsten. Then he
adds a corollary observation of vital importance to understanding American society: "If there is a relatively high degree
of unity or community of values, however, this situation does
not present any danger to democracy."[3]

All this said, the presumably enlightened minority,
along with reaching decisions that are genuinely helpful to
their association, may also find itself acting in its own best
interest or in biased ways. Decisions may be reached for
reasons of self-aggrandizement, fashion, or status enhancement. However fastidious its taste, its musical preferences
may also be narrowly defined?

When persons or groups assume a public trust of any
kind, stated Jefferson, in 1807, they must consider themselves
public property and in need of public correction. Furthermore, several students of democracy have noted that no important democracy has ever been created immediately. One
must work toward it by repeatedly rectifying or changing the
"unreasonable and untenable" special positions of power
granted certain persons or groups. In short, "democratic
theory has been less notable as an ideology than as a critique
of ideologies and traditions."[4]

What Jefferson, Tingsten, and others seem to be saying
is that, granted its several shortcomings, the general music
public is not alone in harboring imperfections. Moreover, it

harbors wisdoms not possessed by any minority group that
considers itself socially and culturally superior. Furthermore, a viable democratic art culture comes into existence
gradually and after much trial and error. To be actively
sought out and cultivated is the commonality of values that
brings out the best in men and women and that is embodied
in the art music presented to them. The history of American
orchestra and opera associations is an extremely brief one and
the involvement of the public even briefer. Our arts culture
is still in the early stage where both minority and majority
must find a way to work together in order to correct an over-
whelming number of mistakes and inequities and to modify a
host of unreasonable and untenable special positions. For
their survival, these art-music associations must first discover, then be constantly ready to emend their raisons d'être
in a society that is skeptical of special privilege and hostile
to elitism. So important and bothersome is the question of
rule by the knowledgeable and the "best" or rule by the general public, it will be behind all of the discussions in this
chapter, whether openly stated or not.

Discovery of a music association's place in American
society is difficult at best. That place, even when found,
can never be fixed, but must continue to be fluid, in sympathy with the movements and alterations in society itself.
For example, in January 1957, the editors of Musical America
worried over the future of the New York Philharmonic. Many
of the adverse conditions they mentioned as then affecting the
ensemble have since been corrected or abated. Yet, several
still existed almost thirty years later and, what is more, were
affecting other orchestras as well. Also, in correcting old
problems, new ones were created. Finally, the America of the
eighties was vastly different from the America of the fifties--
several of the questions demanding solution in the earlier years
had no bearing in the later years, while serious problems had
arisen which could not have been anticipated earlier.

The editors, in 1957, found the Philharmonic suffering
from increased public apathy and a visible lack of interest
and esprit de corps among its personnel. It rarely scheduled
American music for performance. The orchestra was negligent
in rendering service to the community and in other activities
that might make its future life more certain. No strong
audience-building program, nor one to attract young people,
existed. Whatever the attempts at reaching boys and girls,

they were not integrated with any of the local school systems.
Nor was there a thoughtout plan in aid of cultural development from kindergarten through high school. The orchestra
was criticized for making no contributions to civic life. It
hardly ever participated in local celebrations and gala events
of community interest. It stuck to its own series of concerts,
decided on by itself, and caused people to feel that it was
not a part of their lives. As a final warning, the editors
said that because social life was becoming decentralized owing
to the flight of the population to the suburbs, the orchestra
could no longer afford to "sit smugly in its auditorium on
Manhattan island and wait for the suburbanites to battle the
long, weary miles to its door."[5]

Over the next two decades, the ensemble, like many
others, did try to change some of its ways, even as a fervent
populism infiltrated much of the general thinking about social
institutions and their functions. Unfortunately, the orchestra
seemed to gain little new strength from the changes it instituted. Efforts at reform, as pointed out in Chapter 1, stemmed
from no thorough research into and no profound knowledge
of the art-music audience and non-audience--why some people
came to concerts and why others did not.

In 1980, Samuel Lipman reported the New York Philharmonic as continuing to struggle for survival. His comments
on that struggle represent views held by the cultural minority
group to which I have been making reference. Reacting to
what he described as the excesses of cultural populism, Lipman spoke of his skepticism over the democratization of art
music. It was, he said, leading to a deterioration of artistic
principles. In order to retain what audience it had and, it
hoped, to increase that audience's size, the management of
the Philharmonic was scheduling mostly "solid hits" for performance and had chosen Zubin Mehta as a music director
because he would not rock the boat. Crippling was the striv-
ing to be "all things to all men," stated Lipman. The claims
made on the orchestra never ended. It had to please the
highly cultivated, instruct the uninformed, showcase contemporary compositions, present fine music from the past, nurture American players and composers, bring in artists--usually
European--who would excite subscribers, and somehow also
stimulate the masses. If it failed to do all of these things it
would be considered elitist and socially irrelevent. The burden
was too great.[6]

Similar stories were told of other major music associations, whether those of New York or other cities. Although most of these stories were told by critics oriented toward the cultural elite, they do testify to the continuing disquiet in art-music circles, however opinionated their explanations. In short, during the final years of the twentieth century, the place of art-music associations in American society was almost as insecure as it had been at the beginning of the century.

ORCHESTRA ASSOCIATIONS

From the above discussion, it is clear that the American professional symphony orchestra has changed fundamentally in the late-twentieth century and is not what it was in the thirties. What has it become?

Increasingly, the music association has been behaving like a large business corporation. No longer is its chief direction given mainly by musical people who appear to be singlemindedly intent on making fine music. No longer can it expect to command a faithful following, men and women who unquestioningly renew their annual subscriptions for the entire concert series. The orchestra has more and more become engaged in what seems activity to keep it economically viable, and managed by people who may or may not have strong musical backgrounds and inclinations but who do have experience in business administration and marketing. The management by committee has encouraged the music association to become an institution devoted mainly to the music not of living but dead composers. Geared to provide a fairly dependable service, an orchestra can give a correct rendition of the notes in a musical score. Commentators claim, however, that the rendition grows less and less unique, exciting, and differentiated from the renditions of other orchestras. Although a greater awareness of expenses and the need for their control has certainly come about, this increased monetary sophistication has not led to the closing of each season with a surplus. Considerable deficits are the norm, whose size tends to increase rather than diminish with the years.

One important transformation has occurred in the major American orchestras. Where once almost all the instrumentalists were foreign-born, in the postwar years, a large majority

of the personnel is American. Within this majority has grown
a militancy over working conditions. The art-music instrumentalists have learned that they must band together and
fight for improvements in working conditions and salaries.
Salaries have improved owing to the granting of fuller employment through a more extended concert season, and addition of a "pops" season, and an introduction of a summer
musical festival.

Regrettably, the professional association's musicians,
even as their work conditions have improved, are on occasion
ruled by a mentality of union-worker face-to-face with
management-bosses. The attempt to win concessions from
management, however justified, and with slight regard for the
the association's financial condition, have contributed to the
malaise. At the same time, conductors, especially those of
the most prominent orchestras, are here-today-gone-tomorrow
creatures with insufficient attention allotted to the ensembles
given into their care. They seem ever ready to vacate a position for greener pastures elsewhere. Therefore, the association's continuity from day to day and year to year increasingly
is supplied not by artistic but business types. They are professionals who busy themselves raising funds, winning grants,
soliciting media coverage, planning various strategies to woo
the wealthy and mighty, and advising on what music will enhance the bottom line. Worrisome to them is income that
neither grows nor is as dependable as it used to be.

With the eighties, government funds and grants seem
to be shrinking. Subscriptions are down and those that come
in are mostly for a mini-season. Nor is private and corporate
patronage what it was. Fewer people feel it to be their social
obligation to support an art-music association. The cachet
that once came with sponsorship and attendance at events of
high culture is less easily conferred. American orchestras,
hobbled by costs some 300 per cent or more higher than those
of their European counterparts, make fewer recordings. Conductors of American orchestras and soloists who are stars
remain unaffected, because they can jet fly anywhere in the
world and record with non-American ensembles. Meanwhile,
newspapers, general periodicals, and television and radio
broadcasting companies provide less and less information on
the activities of music associations. No matter how difficult
the process and uncertain the result, music associations find
that they must acquire the resilience to constantly reconstitute

themselves as they discover successful accommodations to contemporary conditions while preserving their artistic identity.

For some time it had been apparent that the myriad
problems of performing groups, whether financial, organiza-
tional, or vis à vis the community could more easily be coped
with through discussion, the sharing of information, and
jointly supported research. On 21 May 1942, Mrs. Leta G.
Snow, founder of the Kalamazoo Symphony, sponsored a meeting in Chicago, attended by representatives of twenty three
orchestras, to talk over problems that orchestras had in common. An outcome of the meeting was the establishment of the
American Symphony Orchestra League. A League newsletter,
the Inter-Orchestra Bulletin (later renamed Symphony News),
began life in 1948.

Helen M. Thompson was appointed as executive secretary. Immediately, she worked to increase membership, to
gather some (though not nearly enough) guidelines for inte-
grating concert life with the community, and to offer advice
on the establishment and maintenance of civic orchestras. Annual workshops for conductors, orchestra managers, and music critics were instituted. Surveys of members provided
information on subscription sales and the effect of ticket pricing. By 1971, of the estimated 1400 symphony orchestras in
the United States, a little over 350 were League members, including 28 major orchestras with annual budgets amounting to
millions of dollars each.[7]

A few music groups, like the Chicago, Philadelphia,
Cleveland, New York, and Boston orchestras, had international reputations and were ranked with the finest performing
groups anywhere in the world. Other admired ensembles, like
those in Los Angeles, Pittsburgh, and San Francisco, could
perform as well as, if not better than, most of their counterparts in Europe, despite the fact that in some instances full-
year employment was denied musicians, and governmental and
corporate financial aid was not usually substantial.[8] For a
country the size of the United States, said the Rockefeller
Panel Report on the future of the arts in America, there
should be at least fifty fully employed professional symphony
orchestras and numerous chamber groups emerging from them.
Nothing close to fifty existed.[9]

One partial explanation for this was that the reputations

of American orchestras were one thing; identities were another,
Were they truly American? For example, if one went by the
amount of music by Americans that was performed, scarcely
any orchestra seemed united in spirit and outlook with American culture. Again and again, French orchestras visiting
America played mostly French music; British orchestras
stressed their own country's music; and German and Austrian
orchestras did the same. In America, orchestras scheduled
native music grudgingly; when touring foreign countries,
mostly not at all. As a result, Europeans knew far more
about American literature, poetry, and paintings, then they
did about American art music. The excuse once given, that
American composers had produced scarcely any works of significance, is without question untenable in the late-twentieth
century.

Nor did there seem to be much native support for the
propagation of America's art-music culture. In 1981, the
composer John Harbison expressed the frustration of most
American composers, when he said, while visiting Rome, that:
"Italians don't know much about us and we know a great deal
about them. I went over with a fairly typical consciousness
of Dallapiccola, Petrassi, Berio, Nono, Donatoni, and even
younger ones like Sciarrino. But conversations with Italian
composers reveal their knowledge of American [art] music to
be very sketchy. Our scores do not reach them. We print
fewer pieces. We don't export our music as a cultural product
the way they do. When our orchestras tour they rarely bring
our own music; when European orchestras travel they invariably bring theirs.[10]

Even in the United States, the music performed by
American orchestras continued to be overwhelmingly European.
Annual surveys taken by the American Symphony Orchestra
League showed that of the total number of works performed,
usually less than five percent were by Americans. A woefully
small percentage of music lovers could recognize the name of
an American art composer, let alone recognize his music.
Without the necessary public or private means to defray expenses, it was impossible for orchestras to underwrite the rehearsal time required to prepare unfamiliar music. Nor did
they dare hazard the loss of subscribers, which they feared
might easily ensue with the presentation of strange and possibly repugnant American compositions--or so the given wisdom
among conductors and boards of trustees went. Furthermore,

even with the music of the most prominent American composers, if a new work was performed by one orchestra, it was
rarely performed again by that orchestra or performed at all
by any other orchestra.   To cite one instance, Elliot Carter's
important Concerto for Piano was premiered in Boston in 1967
but waited until 1975 to receive a New York performance.[11]
This curious reluctance to play any American music prevailed
even as more and more orchestras enlarged their seasons and
produced greater numbers of compositions annually.

Mentioned earlier was the increase in the salaries of
players (though, in most instances, not even to the level that
ordinary artisans were getting).   Television and FM radio stations were making concerts available to millions of additional
listeners.   Yet, as Baumol and Bowen indicated in 1966, and
which continued to be true twenty years later, players expressed boredom and unhappiness over the "predominantly
conventional repertoire" they had to perform continuously and
"the necessity of subjugating one's own musical ideas to those
of the conductor," who was likely to be foreign born, especially if the music director of a major orchestra.[12]   Owing to
their persistent demands, players were allowed to negotiate
over issues like wages, rehearsal schedules, royalties from
broadcasts and recordings, and auditions of candidates for
open positions.   Programming, however, was usually off-limits,
and suggestions about policy in relation to the community and
American music were not solicited.[13]

I do not mean to say that all players would have pushed
hard for native works, especially those that departed most
from the triadic tradition.   Nevertheless, with the passage
of time, a growing percentage of orchestra members were also
to be found, who were dedicated to the performance of unfamiliar and contemporary American works, some of quite radical nature.   Presumably their spirit of adventure, if allowed
input into decisions on orchestra programming, could have
leavened the deadness prevalent in this area.

During the years that we are investigating, instrumentalists operated within an American econo-cultural system
where, in too many instances, they found themselves in ad-
versarial relationships with the managements of professional
symphony orchestras.   To be sure, this was not always true.
But in most professional ensembles, union rules wrung from
higher-ups defined inner orchestral dealings.   As an inevitable

outgrowth of our capitalistic system, instrumental players
were regarded as a part of labor, providing services for
wages. The determination of wages was the result of private
decisions within the association--the least management could
get away with, the most workers could exact. The supply
of musical workers was much larger than the demand. Music
associations constantly found money in short supply. A competitive market situation resulted that on balance served to
keep wages and musicians' spirits depressed.

There was a crying need for the comradely give-and-
take that might work for mutual benefit and the benefit of
American culture. Regrettably, when the internal doings of
an orchestra made the news in a big way, as often as not they
were reports of strikes (or the threat of strikes), and the
cancellation of performances. Wages were adjusted and players' working conditions changed. Eventually concerts resumed
and, usually, ticket prices were boosted.

Of the approximately 1400 orchestras active in the United
States, only around half a hundred could be defined as made
up of mostly professional instrumentalists. The rest were in
large part, or entirely, low-budget amateur ensembles supported by a non-metropolitan community or jointly by a community and a local college or university. In large measure,
these groups were active in geographic areas not in conven-
ient proximity to the large cities where the professional ensembles resided. A season consisted of five to ten concerts,
rarely more. However few the concerts, they were a means
of aesthetic release and gratification for thousands of men and
women, players and concertgoers, whose avocation was music.
Because they lived in small cities and towns, these concertgoers might otherwise have heard little live orchestral music.
By the early sixties, around two million adults were playing
one of the bowed string instruments; three million, one of the
brass instruments; more than three million, one of the woodwinds. Out of this amateur pool were drawn orchestra players with abilities ranging from admirable to adequate.[14]

The Norwalk, Connecticut, Symphony Orchestra, in the
mid-sixties, was regarded as an exceptionally fine performing
group and one that scheduled a great deal of American music.
It rehearsed and gave concerts, typically, in the high-school
auditorium and numbered among its players, a lawyer, a phys-
icist, a 15-year-old schoolboy, a minister, a judge, and an

airline pilot--plus businessmen, physicians, dentists, house-
wives, college students, and school teachers.[15]

Another ensemble, the Boston Philharmonic, directed by
Benjamin Zander, was an orchestra operating under the awesome shadow of the Boston Symphony Orchestra. In 1983,
some retired professional instrumentalists and conservatory
students were members; but the first oboist worked in a book
store, the first bassoonist was an astronomer-physicist, one
violinist was a mental-health worker and another a psycho-
therapist. Members also included lawyers, physicians, house-
wives, and a professional clown. They gave compellingly expressive performances, especially of Mahler's symphonies, not
for pay but for the love of music.[16] More than once have I
come away from a Philharmonic concert feeling I had attended
a performance that could easily rival one given by a major
orchestra.

To be sure, not all of the orchestras came up to this
mark of excellence. Depending on the quality of the local
talent, they played with whatever competence they could mus-
ter or stumbled along as best they could. Max Kaplan, who
has studied and written about the general musical audience,
observes that without doubt the performances of most amateur
orchestras were less than perfect. However, their audiences
were unlike those found in New York City. (His main experience was with the audience of Champaign-Urbana, Illinois.)
In attendance were "friends, civic patriots, and, here and ther
there, extra-familial consumers of art. An audience to a community symphony, even to one which does a very creditable
job, adjusts its expectations, and is pleased to get more; they
[sic] have often been drummed up by members of the orchestra itself; the concern of community promoters is usually short-
timed, that is, planning at most for the next season."[17]

After weighing the evidence, I must conclude that amateur players, whether active as orchestra or chamber players,
have always made up an important part of the dependable
audience for concerts by professionals. On the other hand,
if not engaged in their own music making, they occasionally
become indifferent concertgoers. To cite one out of many
examples, Walter Hendrickson, manager of the Jacksonville,
Illinois, Symphony Orchestra, wrote in 1968 of knowing amateur musicians who gave up playing and concert attendance,
saying it was because they were too busy. However, upon

investigation, he found that the real cause was the lack of
a community ensemble in which to play. Indeed, he discovered a direct correlation between amateur musicians engaged
in one or more performing groups, lovers of music, and concertgoers. He mentioned a musically inactive trombonist, Joe
Barber, who "once enjoyed listening to music, but somehow
nowadays ... doesn't even go to a concert." In contrast, a
violist, Susan Jones, a mother of four children and a social
worker, played in the community orchestra. "She still takes
her place in the first chair of the viola section. She is also
a steady listener to music, attending concerts by professional
musicians whenever she can, and she is bringing up her four
children to be a string quartet." Both Barber and Jones had
had considerable music training.[18]

Democratic action, social equality, and snobbery kept
in abeyance normally characterized amateur orchestras, as
compared with the completely professional orchestras. Conductors and managements had to accept the conditions of their
tenture. Players remained loyal and attended rehearsals not
because they were paid to do so, nor because the conductor
was a musician of top rank. Paul Schmid, music director of
both a community and a youth orchestra, writes that the conductor had to offer them good music, usually music that had
withstood the test of time, including playable and potentially
enjoyable contemporary compositions. But, "a good conductor
'sells' good music and never interposes himself between his
'goods' and the orchestra. He is dispensable, the music is
not." He sets basic goals, proposes materials, determines
what artistic level the group should aim for, and feels out
the collective personality of players who usually come from
disparate backgrounds. He must recognize that the orchestra
members are constantly appraising his worth as a person and
musician and responding accordingly. They attend rehearsals
for recreation, for exercising an affection for music--and because they want to be there. He warns that the music director must respect his amateur musicians: "To assume that people don't know the difference between good and bad music is
foolish. To belittle these amateur players because they make
their living in some other way is small-minded. The chances
are that the conductor's own accomplishments have been exceeded by several of these people in their respective fields.
They came to him out of love, and play for relaxation."[19]

OPERA ASSOCIATIONS

At the beginning of the sixties, two visitors from Soviet Russia, Tikhon Khrennikov and Dmitri Shostakovich, came to observe the musical activities in the United States. They were amazed at how few professional singers and instrumentalists could make a living from opera performance and at how cur- tailed were most opera-performing seasons: "Considering the richness of concert life, we were astonished to see that there was an unbelievably small number of opera houses."[20]

In 1965, during the height of the "Cultural Explosion," around 24 opera companies subscribed in varying degrees to the international star system as a basis for the engagement of singers. About 53 companies, professional and semi- professional, did not adhere to a star system. Scarcely any of these 78 organizations presented anything resembling a full season. Additionally, some 320 colleges and universities spon- sored opera workshops and produced at least two operas an- nually. Finally, 31 summer music festivals presented operas to the public.[21]

Obviously, the people of the United States had made an exceedingly modest commitment to opera, not at all in ac- cord with the country's size, and inadequate when measured by European standards. Therefore, when the Rockefeller re- port on the performing arts came out in 1965, it urged as a national objective the establishment of at least six professional regional companies to serve metropolitan areas not ready to support opera on a year-round basis.[21] Other objectives mentioned by writers on music were the encouragement of new opera-company formation beyond these minimal six and the fos- tering of American opera compositions, old and new.

True, since 1883, the Metropolitan Opera Company of New York had operated as a fully professional performing group with claim to being America's outstanding national operatic insti- tution and to setting the highest operatic standards for the nation, if not the world. Around a thousand men and women belonged to the company, whose main effort centered on a New York season of almost seven months. Yet from the Met- ropolitan's birth, its orientation has been more international than national. It paid out large sums to attract foreign sing- ers, conductors, and managers. The criteria for hiring them resided as much in the stimulative excitement which their

appearances generated as in the outstanding musical abilities
they boasted.

The Metropolitan mounted next to no American operas.
Until recently, it gave few breaks to young American singers
and discouraged the existence of other opera companies that
might compete with it. At times spectacle was placed before
musical values. Taking a chance on the new was not generally
a part of its agenda. Unfortunately, it is one institution in
the United States that can be singled out as contributing
greatly to the far-flung American impression that art music
is elitist and connected with upper-class social activities.

For twenty-two of the postwar years, 1950-1972, an
Austrian, Rudolf Bing, was the Metropolitan's general manager.
He played no small part in defining its policies. About discovering American talent, Bing said America gave too much
attention to the training of singers and called the Metropolitan
Opera auditions, which sought to uncover able vocalists, "a
bore of little productivity for the company." About the touring Metropolitan Opera National Company that was approved
by the Board against Bing's wishes, he said it "was an expression of the typical American weakness for doing something
--anything--for education and the young.... I was never
pleased with the idea of a young touring company that bore
the name of the Metropolitan Opera. That name was part of
what we paid our leading soloists [most of them foreign born]
--it brought them television dates and recording contracts and
invitations to endorse products for advertisers.... Now the
name was to be used for a group of unknown singers in productions designed to be hung in whatever auditorium space
might be available in smaller cities around the country."23

Bing fought to exclude the New York City Opera Company from Lincoln Center, where the Metropolitan resided.
"A low-priced popular house" like the New York City Opera,
he insisted, would harm opera both through the sort of indiscriminate audience it would attract and the sort of inferior
productions it would mount: "I thought it was simply wrong
to house two opera companies operating in different systems
on the same square. It would upset the box-office--people
could see _Traviata_ for $15 at the Met or $6 only one and a
half minutes away. And later people would say they had seen
a shocking _Traviata_ 'at Lincoln Center.'" The absence of
democratic sentiments is obvious here, as it also is in his

approval of "boxes and their anterooms for the richest patrons"
as opposed to "a 'popular' house with only tiers of seats above
the orchestra level."[24]

A large number of voices were raised which were critical
of the Metropolitan's aloofness from the commonality of Americans. Indeed, the Metropolitan under Bing reinforced its
already established reputation for social exclusiveness and
for demanding uncritical respect. "Every hint of criticism is
shouted down with the cry that the opera house is a temple
dedicated to art which must preserve its sanctity ... away
from the dirty finger-prints of the lowly mob, the common man
who can't possibly understand or appreciate art," once wrote
Richard Barri, who advocated the cultivation of larger audiences for opera. Barri spoke up against the Met's neglect
of new music and its extravagant productions subsidized by
public and private funds, which benefited few people other
than those able to afford the astronomical ticket prices.[25]

Similar comments were made by Winthrop Sergeant, while
he was music critic for the New Yorker. He also said that
however expensive the productions, they were generally poor
and without musical merit. Moreover, the "star" system fostered by the Met's management attracted, not cultivated operagoers, but an immature audience made up of claques for various soloists, whose attendance resembled a "quasi-sexual
rite." No improvement of taste, no education of novice listeners, and no increased love for music were engendered.
Schuyler Chapin, who followed Bing as manager of the Met,
admitted to the astronomical fees exacted by some thirty or
forty international stars and to acquiescing in whatever these
singers demanded because the special audience that the Met
had cultivated expected their appearance on the New York
stage.[26]

American singers, of course, lost out, especially before
and during the Bing regime. Beverly Sills says that it was
twenty years after a debut at the New York City Opera, six
years of singing at La Scala and five years at Covent Garden,
and at the ripe age of 46 [!], that she made her first appearance at the Met in 1975. Phyllis Curtin says that Bing ap-
preciated her only as a luncheon companion, and even when
she finally sang at the Met, she made few appearances. Complaints from American singers were constant about how little
they were paid if engaged for the Met, and how apt they

were to be "displaced time and time again by foreign imports"
not always of superior quality.

Matters did improve in the eighties. By 1985 it was
no longer a rarity to find American singers taking leading
roles at the Metropolitan. Nevertheless, the music director
of the Met, James Levine (a native American), was still com-
plaining of the need to hire superstars five years in advance,
and of how this need forestalled "our ability to use our artistic imagination spontaneously to engage an artist who bursts
suddenly on the scene, or to revive a work that turns out to
be more popular than we expected."[27] He could also have
added that the Met, despite its intermittent appearance on
public television, continued to neglect the cultivation of the
larger non-New York audience for opera, except when soliciting contributions to pay off its deficits. Money continued
to flow into costly productions which provided spectacle but
detracted from the music's impact.

It is of significance that when a cultural committee of
the People's Republic of China wanted to invite representatives of an American music association to its shores "for a
series of master classes and meetings with officials and to
learn how a people's opera company worked," it believed "the
New York City Opera deserved this designation better than
the Met, and therefore was closer to an imitable model for
them."[28]

The New York City Opera began life in 1944. Beverly
Sills was asked to become its general director in 1979. From
its birth, this opera company, far more than the Metropolitan,
has deserved to be regarded as the national opera of the United
States. Annually, the company presented two seasons lasting
around three months each. Orchestra and singing cast were
entirely professional. Instead of international stars, the singers were usually young and comparatively unknown but quite
accomplished Americans. Instead of giving the audience a
diet of safe, often repeated, musical dramas, its repertory
included music that was chancy because unfamiliar, new, or
native. Among the contemporary American operas that the
New York City Opera mounted were Beeson's Lizzie Borden,
Blitzstein's Regina, Dello Joio's The Triumph of St. Joan,
Floyd's Susannah and The Passion of Jonathan Wade, Giannini's The Servant of Two Masters, Hoiby's Natalia Petrovna
and Summer and Smoke, Moore's The Ballad of Baby Doe,

The Wings of the Dove, and Carrie Nation, Rorem's Miss Julie,
Weisgall's Nine Rivers from Jordan, and Ward's Pantaloon
and The Crucible. Instead of operas always sung in their
original language, it experimented with operas in English
translations so that viewers could better understand the
drama. Under Sills, the New York City Opera actively sought
to telecast its productions for the benefit of American opera
lovers distant from Lincoln Center. In the eighties, it tried
flashing English subtitles of untranslated operas (the dialogue
itself or condensed summaries of the action) above the pro-
scenium--a practice that met with strongly favorable response
from the audience.[29]

I have attended its performances of operas in their original language, but subtitled (like Donizetti's Lucia di Lam-
mermoor), and operas in translation (like Mozart's The Magic
Flute), and come away delighted with the singing, grateful
for the subtitles, and impressed by the clearly understandable
articulation of words in English. When compared with the
attitudes and actions of the Metropolitan, the New York City
Opera's greater commitment to fostering American talent, mounting American oepras, and responding sympathetically and prag-
matically to operagoers' needs is admirable. With less prestige
and more limited financial resources than the Met, it has had
to exercise imagination and flexibility in the pursuit of excellence. If, as does happen, a production fails to storm the
music public with its perfection, so also can a far more expensive production of the Metropolitan fail.

Most major American cities have some sort of resident
opera company. None gives as extended a season as the two
New York opera associations. Frequently in the news are
the opera companies in San Francisco, Chicago, and Boston.
All three engage more or less prominent soloists for their
productions. Of the three, the Boston Opera Company, under Sarah Caldwell's direction, has been most apt to deviate
from the standard repertoire and the conventional way of doing things.

Of great interest has been the "grass roots" opera movement that grew in the postwar period, which tried to modify
or do away with the star system and to reach American audiences with well-staged works sung in English. In 1957, John
Crosby presented his first outdoor Santa Fe Opera Festival.
His objective was a regional music theater comprised of instrumentalists and singers working cooperatively and harmoniously

together.   Operas in English, operas by Americans, and operas distinct from the warhorses were performed.   Sought
out were young, talented singers with acting ability.   Sherrill
Milnes and Judith Blagen were two outstanding singers brought
to public attention at Santa Fe.   In 1960, the Santa Fe Opera
Apprentice Program was begun, which gave opera novices
a small salary while they studied singing and acting, gained
experience in opera performance, and sang in the chorus or
appeared in minor roles. [30]

Santa Fe Opera was instrumental in fostering other regional operatic endeavors.   For example, after working as
assistants to Crosby at Santa Fe, David Gockley went to Houston, Richard Goddes to Saint Louis, and Edward Purrington
to Tulsa.   Often in the face of local conservative opposition,
the three directors espoused principles learned at Santa Fe.
Also, former apprentices at Santa Fe have gone to scores
of opera companies in American and Europe.   Others have become administrators of, or instructors in, opera programs
offered at several universities and conservatories of music. [31]
In short, the involvement of the Santa Fe Opera in and with
American culture has been vastly significant.

By 1978, Dick Netzer, of New York University, was
boasting of the relatively new and exciting phenomenon of
resident and fully professional regional opera companies spring-
ing up throughout the United States.   Especially pleasing to
him was the stress placed on high standards and "innovation
in the form of new operas or the performance of older ones
that are seldom seen and heard."   He cited the Baltimore
Opera Company as an example of such an opera company.   Its
orchestra was the Baltimore Symphony.   Each year it mounted
three operas, for nine presentations, to sold-out houses and
hoped within three years to increase its presentations to
twenty annually.   To be commended was the association's establishment of a touring opera group that visited Maryland
schools over a five week period each year, staging operas
with singers backed by an audio tape of the orchestra, in
order to diminish costs, and a video tape of the conductor,
in order to increase students' interest. [32]

Richard Edelman, in 1966, described the North Shore
Friends of Opera, in Flushing, New York, which he directed,
as a thriving grass roots opera company established in 1961.
Performances were given in English.   No large expensive

theater building and no costly star system operated to limit experimentation and bar promising young American singers. The result, he claimed, was an "aesthetically cohesive" company that dispelled the notion of opera being "highbrow and esoteric." Paul Hume, in 1984, wrote in praise of the Washington Opera Company, whose 14 week season and 72 performances were exceeded only by the Metropolitan, New York City, and San Francisco companies. Among the contemporary works it had done were six by Menotti, two by Ginastera, two by Stravinsky, and one each by Barber and Hoiby.[33]

All of the regional opera associations operate on a shoestring. Because musical theater is costly to produce--money having to be spent on scenery, costumes, orchestra players, dancers, choral singers, and vocal soloists--deficits can pile up and threaten a company's existence. Miscalculations can be fatal. To give an illustration, in 1983, the Boston Lyric Opera, under John Balme, won praise for its performance of Wagner's Ring, in Boston and New York City, and proved that uncelebrated native singers were quite capable of handling exacting Wagnerian roles. But costs were excessive. The money from ticket sales was insufficient to cover the bills. No Maecenas offered to bail out the group. Therefore, future productions had to be cancelled and the association went through two arduous years trying to bail itself out of its difficulties.[34]

Opera companies did seek ways to cut costs. One approach was the sharing of expenses through two or more companies agreeing to do a specific opera and having one designer think in terms of a production suited to their several houses. As early as 1958, Paul Collaer, in La Musique Moderne, had suggested this sort of collaboration. Houston and San Diego were among the first American companies to experiment with the idea. In an article on the New York City Opera, John Rockwell, in 1984, said that this company had kept down costs by co-producing Akhenaton with Houston Grand Opera. Also, the sets used for Lakme and The Rake's Progress were rented from the Chicago Lyric Opera and the San Francisco Opera, respectively. He added that the Gramma Fisher Foundation was actively encouraging such cooperation by funding productions meant to be shared. When Opera America was founded in 1970, it was intended to be an umbrella organization in aid of cooperative efforts among member companies to share scenery, costumes, and scores. In addition, it was

meant to function as a referral agency for singers seeking positions and also as a sponsor of national auditions for vocalists, who were asked to perform before the directors of opera
companies. [35]

Despite the problems of expense and of retaining the
goodwill of America opera audiences not noted for their curiosity about unfamiliar works, regional opera companies, like
Santa Fe, Houston, Kansas City, and St. Paul, and various
school opera organizations, like New York's Juilliard, Florida
State University, and University of Kansas, have dared present more than just a few operas by contemporary American
composers. However, not all of these American operas have
featured the effective theater, effective melody, and effective
libretto in understandable English that opera audiences seem to
demand. Moreover, the small number of American theater works
that do have a potential for wide appeal are usually performed
for a very limited time and by one or two companies. Only
a couple of them have become musical staples. One thinks of
Menotti's Amahl and the Night Visitors, written in 1951, for
the National Broadcasting Company, and Mollicone's The Face
on the Barroom Floor, written in 1978, for the Central City
(Colorado) Opera House, each of which has received several
hundred performances. Nevertheless, the United States can
point to at least six additional composers (Pasatieri, Hoiby,
Beeson, Ward, Floyd, and Moore) who have each composed
more than one attractive operatic work in the postwar period.
Their contributions to musical theater have been successfully
mounted before a variety of audiences. Pasatieri's operas,
for example, have been premiered by opera companies in As-
pen, Houston, Seattle, Detroit, and New York (City Opera,
Juilliard, and Brooklyn College). Like most of the more successful new operas, Pasatieri's remain in a conservative idiom
--tonal, triadic, lyric and not overly dissonant. [36]

MUSIC DIRECTORS

The music director today is supposed to wear several
hats. Gone are the days when a Stokowski could tell the
board of the Philadelphia Orchestra to leave all musical decisions, including how many hours were needed to properly
rehearse a program, to him; he would leave the problem of
finding subscribers and the money to finance his music-making
to the board.

In the postwar years the music director is asked to be
an administrator, sharing the executive duties necessary for
the management of a music association. The director is also
expected to symbolize the association to the public, when
granting interviews, participating in social events, and helping to raise funds. The director is supposed to help originate
and carry out ways for meeting the necessary obligations the
association owes the community to which it caters. In the music association itself, the director must decide on the qualifi-
cations of musicians hired as replacements and must keep on
top of potential problems between management and musicians.
The director is the principal planner of musical programming,
and must rehearse and maintain a disciplined ensemble capable
of satisfactorily executing some of the world's greatest musical
literature. The task is a difficult one.

Are music directors of the necessary mold being produced, directors who in turn produce performances of the
highest artistic excellence? One of America's most successful
postwar conductors, Lorin Maazel, thought not. In 1985, he
singled out one grave limitation, which served to limit their
musical contributions: "I can say that the intellectual level
of today's conductor does not live up to what it was 50 years
ago. Today's conductors are not well-cultured, not well-read,
and not interested in a variety of sister arts that interested
musicians of old.... Nine out of 10 of today's conductors
probably never heard of Thomas Mann. That is depressing,
and it can be heard in their music-making. They're looking
for the fast buck and trying to fulfill the needs of the local
organization and to meet the challenge of pushing ahead in
the rat-race of music-making. Unfortunately, a lot of values
have gotten lost along the way."[37]

In the same year, further flaws in music directing were
mentioned by William Crutchfield. Looking over the decades
of postwar conducting, he concluded that no longer was a
distinct orchestral or conducting style valued, citing statements by Riccardo Muti, Leonard Bernstein, Seiji Ozawa, and
Daniel Barenboim to this effect. They subscribed to the late-
twentieth century aesthetic idea, commonplace amongst musicians abreast of the times, that the performer had to be true
to the composer's intentions alone, as explicated in the score,
while personally remaining neutral. On their minds were the
excesses in the idiosyncratically emotional interpretations of
past conductors.[38] (To be sure, an individualist like Leonard
Bernstein was more apt to observe the idea in the breach.)

Regrettably, the dangers in carrying out such an approach were a sterile impersonality and a lack of emotional conviction and expressive communication--dangers already mentioned in connection with non-symphonic performance. Forgotten in this approach was the obvious fact that scores never completely embody composers' intentions. As mediators between the music and the contemporary audience, directors, in maintaining their neutrality, might fail to make the necessary expressive connections which would make the sound meaningful to today's listeners. In the 1985-1986 season, I attended decidedly cool Boston performances of two Mozart piano concertos, Schubert's Symphony No. 9 ("The Great"), Handel's Messiah, and Bach's St. Matthew Passion, all led by well-known conductors. During the intermissions, complaints were voiced around me and people could be seen heading for the exit doors.

Two other factors affecting the way an orchestra sounds, wrote Crutchfield, are the failure of one conductor to be constantly working with the players over an entire season and the limitations on rehearsal time in the preparation of even the most difficult score for performance--detriments less apparent in the music-making of the thirties and before. Seymour Rosen, managing director of Carnegie Hall, was quoted as saying: "One of our biggest problems today is the era of the guest conductor and the music director who isn't." Ozawa in Boston, and Mehta in New York were present only during a little over one-half the home season; Muti in Philadelphia, only thirteen weeks. "They are not orchestra builders," continued Rosen, "they are career builders," dashing back and forth between America and Europe, sometimes combining directorships of two orchestras, plus a summer festival or an opera house. The result, he said, was sound that is homogenized and without personal reference. Vienna, Philadelphia, and Chicago--the orchestras were beginning to sound alike. Prevalent, concluded Rosen, was a "consensual international style that won't rock the boat when strange orchestras and conductors face each other in dizzying succession."[39]

Prevalent, also, was a reluctance to study any new works, since too much time would be taken away from busy traveling schedules. Besides, it required less effort to achieve a success with a work familiar to orchestras and audiences in various cities and countries. John von Rhein states that the jet-setting conductor's repertoire is one "easily pulled out of

an overnight bag and exploited over and over again all over
the world." Harold Schonberg adds that "the new glamour-
boy conductors" see to it they are booked solid and have
neither the time or inclination to try much that is unusual,
unless it promises a great deal of publicity for them. Careers
come first.[40]

When the Boston Globe, in January 1986, published
Thomas Morris's announcement of his impending resignation
as general manager of the Boston Symphony Orchestra, it
quoted him as strongly hinting that the orchestra needed
but lacked artistic leadership. His comments, though impli-
cating Seiji Ozawa, could apply to almost any music director
heading a major music association, orchestral or operatic, in
the United States. Morris pointed out the music association's
need for unquestioned leadership in some performance area.
He saw little imagination and orderliness expended on programming, no consistent rescheduling of older commissioned
works, and no present interest in commissioning new works
or having a composer in residence. He saw the value of a
contemporary two-week long music symposium held annually,
where the Symphony would read through at least ten new compositions. Why weren't more sincere attempts made at cooperation and coordination of the orchestra's activities with those
of the community's other music organizations? All of this was
possible, Morris insisted, given genuine artistic leadership.
And this sort of leadership could not come from management.[41]

In order to free themselves to travel where they wished,
music directors like Ozawa lined up guest conductors to take
over the preponderance of the concert season. The Hungarian-
born George Solti has been an outstanding postwar music director and was appointed as head of the Chicago Symphony
in 1969. Few other contemporary conductors equaled him in
ability. Yet, as William Furlong pointed out in 1974, Solti
conducted the Chicago orchestra only 13 weeks a year, which
enabled him to "keep one foot in Europe and the other in the
United States; one arm in opera, the other in symphonic music. And it makes him, at an estimated $10,000 a week, one
of the highest paid wage-earners in the United States." Sixty
percent of the Chicago season was directed by guest conductors, mostly "international jetters," who "are not much interested in learning new scores."[42]

In 1980, Riccardo Muti, a talented Italian conductor, was

named to head the Philadelphia Orchestra. No sooner was he
in place than he announced that his aim was "to bring in guest
conductors who are strong and can bring special qualities to
their music." He then went on to name several European conductors whose services he wished to enlist, but named not a
single American. [43]

Back in 1961, W. McNeil Lowry complained that orchestra
boards and managers preferred a European name and accent,
"for social and box-office prestige." Moreover, European conductors had been given the chance to gain wide experience
with a varied repertoire, owing to a sort of conductors' "farm"
system. No such opportunity existed here for American conductors. [44]

In the sixties and seventies, a number of apprenticeship
programs for conductors were supported by foundation grants
and funds from the N. E. A. Some fortunate Americans became assistant conductors of major orchestras. Leonard Bernstein won the directorship of the New York Philharmonic in
1958 and by the eighties had achieved outstanding international
recognition. At the same time, he had prepared the way for
younger talented Americans, like Lorin Maazel, James Levine,
and Michael Tilson Thomas. By the end of the seventies,
more than a few Americans with a special aptitude for orchestral leadership could be found. Yet, in 1980, Alan Rich was
still able to say that the American-born conductor continued
to be up against the "old snobbery that attaches automatic
cultural cachets to European manner and accent. Of the ten
orchestras generally regarded as America's finest ... none is
currently being led by an American." The art-music association was a bit of exotica in the American community and its
conductor was expected to participate in the city's social
whirl. "This is where the premium on exoticism stems from;
exotic art demands exotic practitioners. More than one conductor has acceded to a major American podium purely on his
ability to hold a teacup elegantly in high society." [45] (An ex-
aggerated statement, to be sure, but one containing more than
a kernel of truth.)

Three years later, Irving Kolodin spoke at the annual
conference of the American Symphony Orchestra League and
denounced the recent appointment of four foreigners as directors of major American orchestras, while Americans of equal
or greater talent were ignored. Said Kolodin, there seemed

to be an invisible sign reading: AMERICANS NEED NOT AP-
PLY, when it came to the top conducting jobs. William Schuman and Leonard Bernstein voiced similar criticisms. As
Schuman said: "We do not ask for any special consideration
for our American conductors, except that they not be discriminated against in their own country. And the evidence
that they are is inescapable."[46]

At the end of 1985, Gunther Schuller saw the picture
as unchanged. Foreign conductors continued to win the
plums. Lay boards, he said, did not know who was good.
They were influenced by extravagant promotions, press releases, hearsay evidence, deceptions, agents, and other persuasive individuals. Then the new conductor arrived from
abroad and refused to be responsible for developing one orchestra and for staying in place. He wanted to be able to
conduct "all over the map."[47]

These foreign conductors arrived with little or no knowledge of or curiosity about American music or culture. When
Riccardo Muti, in 1980, was recognized as the heir presump-
tive to the Philadelphia Orchestra, he said in a New York
Times interview that he had never conducted an American
work in his life and, what is more, doubted that he ever
would.[48] When, in the fall of 1981, it was announced that
Seiji Ozawa and the Boston Symphony were setting off on a
world tour, it was also admitted that Ozawa wanted to play
no American works on the trip.

Georg Solti was honest enough to admit that he did not
schedule American music with the Chicago Orchestra because
he conducted it poorly. Pierre Boulez, when conductor of the
New York Philharmonic, avoided American works or gave them
short shrift when he did perform them simply because he de-
spised most American composers and their music. Sergui
Celibidache came, in the 1983-1984 season, to lecture at the
Curtis Institute and to conduct its orchestra, appointed by
John de Lancie, who had never heard him conduct. "I am
not an admirer of American culture," Celibidache immediately
announced. "I am an admirer of the American potential. It
is a God-blessed country, but no culture. You have tech-
nically the greatest orchestras, the best players in the world.
But no music, no music whatever."[49] Celibidache was a Ru-
manian-born and German-trained musician whose pronounce-
ments on artistic matters rested more on authoritarian than

democratic values. He had a conviction that the American
democracy existed in a cultural wasteland. Celibidache probably should not have been brought to the United States. It
is typical of the attitudes of art-music's controlling group that
he was.

Presumably, music directors born and brought up in the
United States would have shown greater understanding of and
sympathy for American democratic culture. In this regard,
an excellent precedent had already been set by Howard Hanson, American composer and conductor, during his forty years
of leading the Eastman-Rochester ensemble. Annual festivals
of American music, and the performance of at least 1500 different compositions by some 700 native composers took place
during those years.[50]

Prior to the fifties scarcely any American conductors
were allowed to occupy positions of prominence. One recalls
Henry Hadley's leadership of the Seattle and the San Francisco orchestras in the twenties; Howard Barlow's, of the
CBS Symphony from 1927 to 1943; and Arthur Fiedler's, of
the Boston Pops, from 1930 until 1979. One also recalls Al-
fred Wallenstein's formation of the Wallenstein Sinfonietta in
1933 and directorship of the Los Angeles Philharmonic from
1943 to 1956.

Just after the end of World War II, in 1947, Thor Johnson became head of the Cincinnati Symphony. In 1949, Walter
Hendl took over the Dallas Symphony and Howard Mitchell,
the Washington National Symphony. Yet, as Roger Dettmer
points out, when all three vacated their positions, "it was
not for greater glory but because they weren't asked to stay
on longer; none was replaced by another American."[51]

When Leonard Bernstein was appointed head of the New
York Philharmonic, in 1958, the action was recognized as
groundbreaking. He, in turn, appointed two native Americans as assistant conductors, Thomas Schippers and Seymour
Lipkin. Within ten years, almost 80 percent of the orchestra
consisted of native-born instrumentalists. In addition, he
made it his business to increase greatly the number of American soloists who performed with the Philharmonic. Works by
himself, Samuel Barber, Aaron Copland, David Diamond,
George Gershwin, Charles Ives, and Walter Piston, among
others, were programmed. Transoceanic tours with the orchestra

invariably showcased American compositions. Bernstein inaugurated "Preview" evenings where he talked to audiences about works which he then had the orchestra perform. Free community concerts, children's concerts, and television lectures cum performance also ensued.[52]

Assuredly Bernstein became America's greatest nativeborn conductor, one whose genius was recognized internationally. He gave concerts and made recordings with the New York Philharmonic and various foreign orchestras. Some, like the performances and recordings of Beethoven's nine symphonies, with the Vienna Philharmonic, were numbered among the most outstanding from the postwar years. His appearances guaranteed full houses; his recordings had ready buyers. Yet, during his entire career, both his capabilities as a composer and music director underwent constant attack by professional American music critics--not an unusual experience for American music directors. Leon Botstein, for example, saw tragedy in his career. Botstein, in 1983, denigrated Bernstein as a champion of contemporary composers, described him as a self-aggrandizer, a poor conductor, a most ordinary interpreter of musical literature, and one responsible for relaxed discipline and sloppy playing in the orchestras he led.[53] Although he does not say so, Botstein seemed to question Bernstein's rapport with audiences and, by transfer, with musical literature, detecting chicanery in the relationships. He was decidedly unhappy about the conductor's flamboyant and outgoing personality, which he saw as compromising integrity. He was uncomfortable with the reaching out to a larger audience by non-traditional means and blind to the artistic leadership displayed.

On the other hand, younger American conductors do not hesitate to say how indebted they are to Bernstein, artistically and otherwise. As the conductor Leonard Slatkin admits: "Leonard Bernstein was a tremendous influence on me. No one of my generation could have escaped that. I resent some of the things that people say and write about him now [1983]--how could anyone forget how much that man has done?"[54]

After Bernstein, several American conductors achieved wide recognition as conductors, among them Robert Shaw, Lorin Maazel, Thomas Schippers, Leonard Slatkin, Jorge Mester, David Zinman, James Levine, and Michael Tilson Thomas.

André Previn, though born in Berlin, came to the United
States when ten years of age and is generally accepted as
an American conductor. Roger Dettmer claims that American
conductors are much less inclined to "jet from podium to podium with a large itinerary but a small repertoire." They are
more committed to the artistic leadership of a single orchestra.
Nevertheless, America's most prominent orchestras shun their
services.[55]

Contemplating the spurning of American conductors,
however competent, Leonard Slatkin speaks of his resentment
at being a token young American conductor to the New York
Philharmonic, while Pierre Boulez was music director. Years
later, after his own reputation had grown considerably, it
still made him angry when an American orchestra engaged
"a lesser European instead of a better-qualified American."
Although "an accent charms the pants off of everybody,"
he said, he hoped the pattern of rejecting Americans was
changing. American conductors deserved better.[56]

An American conductor found it difficult to get started.
Not only was there having to contend with the prejudices of
the powerful in music circles, but also with the lack of opportunity for gaining conducting experience. "No group, nor
orchestra," said Lukas Foss, "will put up with a student conductor, least of all a student group. In order to be allowed
to stand up there and learn how to conduct, you have to
know how to conduct. That means: you have to pretend
that you can do it as you learn how to do it. I'm afraid I
did just that, at age 17 at Tanglewood."[57]

Even after having training and some experience, the
American, unlike the European, conductor did not find the
directing of lesser orchestras preparing the way to higher
positions. Erich Leinsdorf, a most successful European conductor in America, once wrote about this problem. He saw
a "vast difference between the provinces in Europe and in
America. In Europe, cities such as Ulm, Aachen, and Ons-
brück are still the stepping stones to Berlin, Munich, or
Vienna, while the smaller towns in the United States are completely unmarked dead ends." In addition, he said: "If a
conductor's career in America is seen as a stepladder to the
so called Big Five (Boston, Chicago, Cleveland, New York,
and Philadelphia), the last fifty years have witnessed only
three instances when any of the 'five' took their new musical
director from an American provincial organization."[58]

Like American singers, American conductors have often
had to go to Europe in order to hone their skills, gain reputations, and, if fortunate, win major posts--Previn with the
London Symphony and Maazel with the Deutsche Oper and the
London New Philharmonia, to name two. Although the Rockefeller Foundation, the Ford Foundation, Exxon, and the National Endowment for the Arts have sponsored apprenticeship
programs and residencies for American conductors, the lack
of American places to gain continuing experience and the still
prevalent prejudice against them from those who guide the
fortunes of music associations has frustrated their ambitions.

Not all American conductors get what they merit, writes
Alan Rich. Two conductors sponsored by Exxon, for example,
were placed with the Saint Paul Chamber Orchestra. Both
conducted many concerts, proved their competence, and won
popularity with audiences. Nevertheless, when the St. Paul
conductorship opened up, the board's appointee was neither
of these, nor anyone with a reputation for imaginative programming. Indeed, he was not even a conductor but an Is-
raeli violinist, Pinchas Zukerman. A similar occurrence happened in Denver. After Carl Toplow built himself an enormous
following, writes Rich, he found that the board of trustees
scorned him when the position became empty and hired instead an Italian, Gaetano Delogu.[59]

Every such denial of equal opportunity to America's own
conductors demonstrates a further reason for art music's remaining alien to American society.

AN INCIPIENT COMMUNALITY

When the first years of the eighties saw the size of
audiences shrinking, the American Symphony Orchestra League
voiced great concern and, in 1984, put out a handbook on educational programs for its members, along with the warning
that orchestra associations had "a monumental task in front
of them. They have a community largely unaware of their
product and unconcerned about their existence."[60]

Attempts at experimental programming and bridging the
gap between art-music groups and the public had already
taken place before 1984, to be sure. The hope for some lasting success, however, was rarely realized. In part, this was

owing to the continuing perception of art music as having
slight connection with American democratic society; in part,
to the superficial, unthought-out Band-Aid approach, without
follow-through, to a great deal of the experimentation. Critics asked: what of permanence was really accomplished, for
instance, when Robert Shaw and the Atlanta Symphony led
their audience in a sing-along of Bach's St. John Passion; or
when the Baltimore Symphony employed Donald Sultner-Welles,
a photosynthesist, to show slides illustrating Handel's Water
Music and Eric Knight's Concertino for Camera and Orchestra?
Then again, what was behind the thinking when the Elkhart
(Indiana) Symphony elected, in 1979, to entertain its audience
both visually and aurally: "The musicians arrived in Napol-
eonic Empire costumes ... and performed some of Beethoven's
liveliest chamber music in an appropriately set and staged
Viennese aristocratic salon. The entire performance was
viewed from behind a scrim, giving the effect of a misty,
romantic memory, as well as the passage of time."[61] Was it
a thing of the moment or a part of a thoroughly considered
long-range plan?

    Greater respect can be given the Lancaster (Pennsyl-
vania) Symphony. Its conductor, Stephen Gunzenhauser,
announced, in 1982, that he and the orchestra were attempting to honor at least one American composer each year. Gunzenhauser, music director of both the Delaware and Lancaster
Symphony Orchestras, also said that when he took over the
Delaware Symphony, in 1978, he found it to be "a 'minor'
league orchestra on the verge of bankruptcy," with only 700
subscribers and no artistic leadership. Cultured and sophisticated listeners went to nearby Philadelphia for their live
music. He found the orchestra's management giving tickets
away in order to "paper" the hall. Immediately on taking
over, he talked to business people on marketing the orchestra. he met with the musician's union and evolved a plan to
reaudition the players and replace those who were incompetent
with better players, giving preference to local musicians. An
ongoing commitment to innovative programming and a willingness to engage in a variety of regional, children's, and pops
concerts helped turn the situation around. By 1982, a waiting list for subscriptions existed.[62]

    Praise also could be rendered the Midland-Odessa (Texas)
Symphony which, since 1977, had tried to be more widely accessible in the area it served. A chamber group, formed

from its members, was performing "in banks, shopping centers, dress shops, at Christmas parties, and in the lobby of
the community theater." The result, writes Shirley Fleming,
was the building up of the orchestra's core of supporters.[63]

Affiliated Artists, formed in 1966, had as its goals the
promotion of its artists (dancers, actors, and musicians) and
the increase of audience-support for the arts. Its members
were sent out to perform and talk about their art to every
description of audience, whether at old people's homes, public schools, hospitals, etc. By 1979, there were over 385
artistic residencies in communities throughout the country.
The basic residency lasted eight weeks, in which time an artist made about eighty to one hundred informal appearances.
These artists tried to establish rapport by talking about how
they worked, rehearsed, studied, and drove themselves hard
to grow as artists, and about why what they did was of value
to the public. The programs of Affiliated Artists might include "a dancer in a factory. An actor in a firehouse." In
other instances: "a conductor leading a major orchestra ...
in a suburban shopping mall. One of opera's new generation
singing a major role in an international house at night. And
sharing the experience with a rotary club the next morning."
Corporations and foundations funded the programs. Colleges,
local arts councils, opera companies, orchestras, and various
civic groups sponsored the artists. Another organization,
Young Audiences, also tried to bridge the gap between artist
and public, a public consisting of school-age children, trying
out special approaches, instructing artists on how to be ver-
bally communicative, and seeking better ways to inform the
young about art music.[64] Of course, when corporations and
foundations decided to direct their funds elsewhere, as was
often the case, programs like those of Affiliated Artists and
Young Audiences shrank or ceased.

The handbook published in 1984, Orchestra Education
Programs: A Handbook and Directory of Education and Outreach Programs, mentioned earlier, does list a tremendous
assortment of programs sponsored by music associations, which
were meant to involve listeners from the youngest to the old-
est. The cited goals of these associations were the greater
appreciation of symphonic music, the development of future
audiences, and the promoting of the music association in its
community. Three quarters of the listed orchestras claimed
that they helped prepare young people to attend children's

concerts by putting together and sending out beforehand
teacher's manuals, recorded excerpts and commentaries, and
other information to the schools involved. Worrisome, nevertheless, was the fact that the music directors of ninety-one
percent of the major orchestras did not bother to participate
in these educational activities, leaving them to subordinates
to plan and carry out. They were too busy with other affairs or, because so many of them were foreign born, were
unable to communicate in the English language.[65]

Several commentators have spoken of the inadequate
planning that went into efforts to involve the community and
of the fragmentary nature of actions whose chief purpose was
more propagandistic than educational. Nor were there many
critical evaluations made that summed up the effectiveness of
educational activities and suggested modifications in them.[66]

In the final analysis, the association's sensitivity to the
community and communal involvement in the music-making of
the association remained tenuous. Attendance at performances
did not always grow as hoped. Support, financial and otherwise, had not increased. Music associations were deriving
scarcely any new strength from their communities. Seen from
this perspective, art music's permanent bonding with the larger
American society was still in the future.

On the other hand, more than a few associations are
alert to their problems and willing to try and try again to
break down isolation and bridge whatever gaps exist between
them and their communities. When one effort fails to produce
results, another effort is mounted. Discovering ways to navi-
gate in the uncharted waters of our democratic system is not
something easily accomplished. What is most heartening is the
number of associations that will not give up. They may eventually succeed.

Notes

1. Music Journal (May 1964), p. 30.
2. Herbert Tingsten, The Problem of Democracy (Totowa, N.J.: Bedminster Press, 1965), p. 80.
3. Ibid., p. 112.
4. Ibid., pp. 81-82.
5. "Future of the Philharmonic," Musical America (1
January 1957), pp. 4-5.

6.   Lipman, The House of Music, p. 143.

7.   Hart, Orpheus in the New World, pp. 121-123, 126, 131; Music Journal (February 1966), p. 94; Symphony Magazine (December 1982), p. 42.

8.   Roger Dettmer, "The State of U.S. Conductors," Fanfare (September/October 1982), p. 85.

9.   The Performing Arts: Problems and Prospects, p. 50.

10. Joan Peyser, "Harbison's Continuing Ascent," New York Times, 16 August 1981, section 2, p. 20.

11. Surveys published in Musical America (September 1950), p. 6; (October 1951), p. 4; (July 1952), p. 6; (June 1961), p. 59; (January 1965), p. 76. Also see, Harold C. Schonberg, "Beethoven and Rogers," Musical Journal Annual (1968), pp. 23, 97; Donal Henahan, in New York Times, 9 March 1975, section 2, p. 21; Laura Koplewitz, "From Pen to Podium with New Music," Symphony Magazine (February/March 1982), p. 9; Janet Tassel, "Pros and Concerts," Boston Magazine (October 1983), p. 119.

12. Baumol and Bowen, Performing Arts, pp. 122-123; John W. English, Criticizing the Critics (New York: Hastings House, 1979), p. 31; Philip Hart, "The Symphonic Strike Season," Saturday Review, 26 September 1970, pp. 47-48; program notes of the Boston Symphony, 19 August 1983.

13. Seltzer, The Professional Symphony Orchestra in the United States, pp. 101-103; Hart, "The Symphony Strike Season," pp. 48-49; Donal Henahan, "How Should Conductors Be Judged?" New York Times, section 2, p. 19; Louis Snyder, Community of Sound: Boston Symphony and Its World of Players (Boston: Beacon, 1979), pp. 19-23.

14. Baumol and Bowen, Performing Arts, p. 39; Music Journal Annual (1962), pp. 82, 168, and (1965), p. 100; The Performing Arts, p. 14.

15. Joseph R. Boldt, Jr., "Pioneer 'Home Town,'" Music Journal (February 1966), p. 68.

16. Tassel, "Pros and Concerts," p. 114.

17. Kaplan, "Sociology of the Musical Audience," p. 61.

18. Walter B. Hendrickson, "Speak Up for the Amateur!" Music Journal (April 1968), p. 34.

19. Paul B. Schmid, "Conducting an Amateur Orchestra," Symphony Magazine (June/July 1984), p. 10.

20. Tikhov Khrennikov and Dmitri Shostakovich, "Impressions of American Music," Music Journal (March 1960), p. 11.

21. Owen Anderson, in the Music Journal (October 1965), p. 4.

22. The Performing Arts, p. 50.

23. Rudolf Bing, 5000 Nights at the Opera (Garden City, N.Y.: Doubleday, 1972), pp. 310-211, 349.

24. Ibid., pp. 294, 298.

25. Barri, "Opera for the People," pp. 16-17.

26. See Winthrop Sargeant, in the New Yorker, 19 June 1971, p. 83; Chapin, Musical Chairs, pp. 412-413.

27. See, respectively, Sills, Bubbles, pp. 210-211; Phyllis Curtin, "Pioneering for New Music," Music Journal (October 1961), p. 86; Dyer, "Keeping Time," p. 35; Winthrop Sargeant, in the New Yorker, 2 May 1964, p. 178; James Levine, in the New York Times, 1 January 1984, section 2, p. 1.

28. Harvey E. Phillips, "Epilogue," to Sills, Bubbles, p. 269.

29. Ibid., p. 264; John Rockwell, "Subtitles Win at City Opera," New York Times, 23 October 1983, section 2, pp. 21, 24.

30. John Moriarty, "A Boon for Opera: The Santa Fe Apprentice," Music Journal (October 1964), pp. 28-29; Winthrop Sargeant, "Musical Events: Desert Airs," New Yorker, 4 September 1971, p. 82.

31. Moriarty, "A Boon for Opera," pp. 66-67; Scott Heumann, "Grassroots Opera," Horizon (January/February 1982), p. 62-68; Bernard Holland, "The Crosby System," New York Times, 31 July 1983, section 2, p. 17.

32. Dick Netzer, The Subsidized Muse: Public Support for the Arts in the United States (Cambridge, England: Cambridge University Press, 1978), p. 123.

33. Ricahrd Edelman, "New Directions for Opera," Music Journal (June 1966), pp. 29-30; Paul Hume, "A Tale of Two Cities' Opera Companies" Ovation (September 1984), pp. 8-9.

34. Dudley Clendinen, "Here Comes the 'Ring' on a Shoestring," New York Times, 7 August 1983, section 2, p. 17.

35. Netzer, The Subsidized Muse, pp. 124-125; Sills, Bubbles, p. 189; John Rockwell, "City Opera Tries a Bold New Tack," New York Times, 4 March 1984, section 2, p. 19.

36. For an optimistic overview of the state of regional opera in the mid-eighties, see Edward Rothstein, "Opera Is Thriving in the United States" New York Times, 19 February 1984, section 2, pp. 19, 25.

37. Mortimer H. Frank, "Conversations with Lorin Maazel," Fanfare (January/February 1985), pp. 111-112.

38. William Crutchfield, "Orchestras in the Age of Jet-Set Sound," New York Times, 6 January 1985, section 2, p. 1.

39. Ibid., p. 19. On the same subject, see John von Rhein, "The Unpredictable Carlos Kleiber," in Ovation (September 1983), p. 10.

40. Rhein, "The Unpredictable Carlos Kleiber," p. 10; Harold C. Schonberg, in the New York Times, (18 January 1970), section 2, p. 17.

41. Margo Miller, "Marquee," Boston Globe, 5 January 1986, section B, p. 7.

42. Furlong, Season with Solti, pp. 35, 37, 42.

43. Daniel Webster, "Ricardo Muti," Ovations (February 1983), p. 10.

44. W. McNeil Lowry, "Music and the Ford Foundation," Music Journal (April 1961), p. 50.

45. Alan Rich, "The Training of Conductors," Horizon (January 1980), p. 60.

46. Raymond Ericson, "Notes: American Conductors," New York Times, 29 June 1983, section 2, pp. 17, 22.

47. Jane Tassel, "Gunther Schuller," Ovation (November 1985), p. 26.

48. Allan Kozinn, "Samuel Barber: The Last Interview and the Legacy," High Fidelity (June 1981), p. 45.

49. Robert Baxter, "Sergiu Celibidache at Curtis," Symphony Magazine (June/July 1984), pp. 77-78, 80.

50. Baker's Biographical Dictionary of Musicians, 7th ed., s.v. "Hanson, Howard."

51. Dettmer, "The State of U.S. Conductors," p. 86.

52. Howard Shanet, Philharmonic: A History of New York's Orchestra (Garden City, N.Y.: Doubleday, 1975), pp. 327-328, 335, 338-339, 344-349.

53. Leon Botstein, "The Tragedy of Leonard Bernstein," Harper's (May 1983), pp. 58-59.

54. See the Boston Globe, 17 July 1983, section A, p. 53.

55. Dettmer, "The State of U.S. Conductors," pp. 89, 92.

56. Boston Globe, 17 July 1983, section A, p. 53.

57. Lukas Foss, "To a Young Conductor," Ovation (April 1984), p. 15; see also, John Rockwell, in the New York Times, 27 January 1980, section 2, pp. 1, 19.

58. Erich Leinsdorf, Cadenza (Boston: Houghton Mifflin, 1976), p. 143.

59. Rich, The Training of Conductors, p. 61.

60.   Charles B. Fowler, "Reaching the Kids: How Symphonies Do It," Musical America (February 1985), p. 12.
61.   All of these activities were reported in Symphony News (June 1979), p. 68.
62.   Stephen Gunzenhauser, "Are American Conductors Really Victims of Discrimination?" Ovation (May 1982), pp. 7, 36.
63.   Shirley Fleming, "The Thouvenal String Quartet," Musical America (March 1981), pp. 6-7.
64.   Vera Giannini, "Sherrill Milnes," Ovation (February 1982), p. 13; Symphony News (October 1979), pp. 11, 13-14; Netzer, The Subsidized Muse, pp. 137-139, 151-152.
65.   For a discussion of the handbook, see Charles B. Fowler, "Reaching the Kids: How Symphonies Do It," Musical America (February 1985), pp. 11-13, 15.
66.   For one commentary, see Hart, Orpheus in the New World, pp. 427-428.

Chapter 6

BUSINESSPEOPLE AND THE MARKETING OF ART MUSIC

The cultural problems that critics attribute to democracy, claimed to result from majority rule, constitute an oversimplification. An important thread that has run through American history has been the impact of the American capitalistic economic system on the course society has taken. In terms of art music, we have seen performances influenced by enterprisers who operate under competitive conditions to produce, distribute, and sell cultural "goods." Such a system cannot help but seek out the most gainful, as well as the most meritorious, artistic goods. It understands that before there can be a commitment to cultural education for the public good, one must provide for the economic health of a music association. Only then can one show concern for a richer national life. This chapter, in particular, centers on the influence of economics on the nature and communication of America's art music.

First to be noted is the fact that art music in the United States is produced largely by enterprises whose directions are usually guided by private decisions. Frederick Dorian, in Commitment to Culture, insists that these enterprises now make up a "gigantic entertainment industry," which is convincing audiences "that art serves merely to relax, to divert, to amuse." The creation of "aesthetic pleasure and enchantment" is not placed first on the industry's agenda.[1]

Dorian's contention is not proven. Surely, art-music enterprises do not consciously aim "merely to relax." When asked, the people engaged in these enterprises insist that they are honest brokers mediating between the needs of their association and those of the public.

Nevertheless, board members and administrative personnel

of music associations, concert management organizations, recording companies, radio and television networks, publishing firms, corporate foundations, and governmental arts councils as often as not must behave like members of economic councils and have a great deal to say about the production, distribution, and utilization of art-music commodities. They help decide what musicians and musical compositions can successfully compete in the cultural marketplace, determinations made in part through examining attendance at performances and sales of recordings, and also through the way monetary contributions come from public, private, and corporate donors. The size of donors' contributions is of especial importance in defraying potential losses when unfamiliar musicians or new, potentially off-putting, and difficult-to-play works are performed.

One notes how the appeal to corporations for funding must often augment the argument of the high intrinsic value of art music by resorting to terms redolent of commercial thinking. Oil, automotive, and tobacco firms are promised great social prestige, an improved company image, and a worthwhile tax-deduction. David Rockefeller, when chairman of the Chase Manhattan Bank, urged his fellow corporate heads to take the arts seriously, not only out of love for music and painting but as a matter of good business: "From an economic standpoint, such involvement [in the arts] can mean direct and tangible benefits. It can provide a company with extensive publicity and advertising, a brighter public relation, and an improved corporate image." He continues: "It can build better customer relations, a readier acceptance of company products, and a superior appraisal of their quality. Promotion of the arts can improve the morale of employees and help attract qualified personnel." Rockefeller is quoted in a book by Suzi Gablik, who states that corporate sponsorship of the arts normally is highest when the arts yield the "greatest public-relations dividends through their popular and sensational appeal.... Under the new cultural style, the success of an exhibition [or performance] is measured--in Hollywood terms-- by media coverage and box office. Attendance figures become the great yardsticks for everything."[2]

Because an uncertain worth was attached to the essential nature of art music, in times when the public wisdom saw sponsorship as urgently needed in other areas (health-research and social-welfare programs, for example), and when art music offered lower prestige value, then businesspeople might

be tempted to decrease their arts funding. For this reason,
in the eighties, even as attendance at performances dropped
and the expenses of concerts rose, the inflow of money to
aid music institutions seemed to level off.

BOARDS OF TRUSTEES

The ideal role of music-association trustees was enun-
ciated in 1982 by Peter Kermani, head of the Albany Symphony
Orchestra's board and newly elected president of the American
Symphony Orchestra League. Trustees, he said, should establish and supervise artistic policy. However, they should
not interfere with program planning and selection, except after
they have scrupulously examined a situation and found that
their policy had been put in jeopardy with consequent injury
to their music association. They can state as policy, for example, that emphasis should be given to the most serious compositions of the past--symphonies, concertos, and symphonic
poems; or that the finest available soloists be engaged; or
that the performance of American music be given special consideration.

Why should trustees make artistic policy? Kermani answered in terms of the enlightened eighties, because it is
presumed that they know their community and have a responsibility to art. He regretted that he also had to admit to the
lack of announced policy in many associations and an ignorance
of the communities in which they operated. He called for reform. The status quo was untenable. Audiences needed to
hear fresh compositions; composers needed to get an "honest
public reaction" in order to "refine and improve" what they
produced. Boards in general had to establish an American
repertoire of fine quality that was constantly put before the
public. Think of the long term, he urged, not the short
term with its threat of canceled subscriptions and private
contributions: "New subscribers and contributions will be attracted to take the place of the ones who leave." Of paramount importance was the underlining of "quality, imagination,
and integrity of purpose.... We must broaden our audience.
We must give quality performances. We must establish an
American repertoire. To prosper. To survive. To have a
real future."[3]

Kermani's worry about the state of art music in the late

twentieth century in large part had to do with those flawed
boards of trustees who were inflicting harm on American music associations. Occasionally a board included a token trustee representative of some local constituency, which was not
necessarily made up preponderantly of art-music lovers but
was politically active and therefore required appeasement.
However, for the most part board members continued to be
those men and women who donated to or raised large sums
for a music association. In the past, the money raised had
come almost entirely from a few people of vast wealth; now,
a substantial amount of it also had to come from thousands
of more modestly situated music lovers.

Erich Leinsdorf observes that the boards of New-York
based music associations were "dominated by old families and
old money, with a proportional representation of 'Our Crowd'
members. The Cleveland board was mostly made up of immigrants who had made within their lifetimes huge fortunes they
now wished to share in a way peculiarly and solely American:
by supporting something worthy, of which they knew little
or nothing but which had always loomed as the 'Good Life.'"[4]

Bankers, business tycoons, and women of great wealth,
some with a keen knowledge of and curiosity about music,
others with narrow tastes and limited imaginations have usually
set what policies there were for orchestras and opera companies. These policies could work against the best interests of
the music group if the latter types predominated, as they
frequently did.[5] One is reminded of the words of Theodore
Roosevelt, in a letter he sent to Sir Edward Grey, in 1913:
"There is absolutely nothing to be said for government by a
plutocracy, for government by men very powerful in certain
lines and gifted with 'the money touch.' but with ideals which
in their essence are merely those of so many pawn-brokers."

On 11 November 1985, I had dinner with a friend who
has been prominent in Lincoln Center arts circles and who has
had to work closely with Lincoln Center board members. I
said that Schuyler Chapin had referred to him and some of
his problems, in the book Musical Chairs. I then asked what
he thought of Chapin's mention of Anthony Bliss, former president of the Metropolitan Opera board and trustee of Lincoln
Center. Chapin said that Bliss saw the Center not as a home
for the arts but as a real-estate project. I also asked about
Chapin's mention of John D. Rockefeller III, head of the

fund-raising drive for the Center, as not much of a music
lover but a person who felt an obligation to do his part for
the arts.[6] My friend's reaction was one of sorrow over
wealthy New York trustees who knew nothing about the nature of the audiences that came to Lincoln Center. He commented: "They think everybody has extra money to spend
and don't hesitate to raise prices for performances." What
my friend experienced in the autumn of 1985 was the pricing
still higher of the high-priced seats. They continued to sell
well, since the buyers were well-to-do and had discretionary
income. On the other hand, the inexpensive seats, also
priced higher, now sold poorly, since the people who usually
occupied them had a marginal surplus of money and raising
admission fees priced the performances out of their reach.

The best intentioned of the trustees as often as not
were cautious individuals worried over the economic shortfalls
that could beset their association. They might wish, by their
light, to play it safe and recommend the programming of "blue-
chip" compositions from the past. Thus they would please
conservative donors, who were also big givers. They spoke
against scheduling second-rate compositions while at the same
time believing that the music performed, although perceived
as first-class, should offer at least some promising financial
expectations. They went along with the hiring of foreign-
born music directors. By so doing they hoped to improve the
commercial prospects of their association. Sergui Comissiana,
a Rumanian conductor who was made head of the Baltimore
Symphony in 1969, says that he found it difficult to schedule
contemporary works owing to his commercially-minded board.
Moreover, his success as a conductor was not based on the
excellence of the orchestra under his care or his sensitive
interpretation of musical literature, but rather on the size of
the box-office receipts and the growth of the subscription
list. Comissiana's remarks are echoed in a comment made by
the violinist Rafael Druian, in 1986, that one of America's
leading orchestras, in need of replacing its conductor, "is
not looking for a music director, it's looking for someone to
sell tickets."[7]

On the one hand, some trustees delegated the burden
of policy-making to their association's management, because
they lacked the time and the expertise to deal with the many
complex problems that arose. On the other hand, other trustees, without foreseeing the outcome of their actions, insisted

on taking full control of affairs--with adverse consequences.
A cautionary tale is provided by the activities, in the seventies, of the board of Civic Music Association, which directed
the fortunes of the Rochester Philharmonic. The board members were conservative and cost-conscious to the extreme.
In November 1971, the musicians of the orchestra gave a vote
of no confidence in the conductor, Samuel Jones, who had
been hired by the trustees despite the protests of the musicians. Instead of considering the vote seriously, the board
gave Jones a new contract and fired several instrumentalists
who had criticized Jones, three of them first-chair players.
The players immediately charged the board with trying to
frighten them into submission and refused to ratify a new
work contract. The controversy quickly became public.

When Mrs. Francis Wilkins and the executive committee
of the board threatened to stop the orchestra's operations,
several liberal board members commenced an active fight
against the executive committee, charging it with indifference
both to its responsibilities to the public and the orchestra's
personnel. The upshot of the struggle was the formation of
a "New Approach" committee, which included Rochester's mayor,
the composer-conductor Howard Hanson, and an official from
the New York Philharmonic, Helen Thompson. Its charge was
to study and make recommendations on how to resolve the situation.

In August 1972, the report came in. Recommended was
the search for a music director and assistant dedicated to artistic excellence, and the active participation of the orchestra
members in planning for the future. Recommended also was a
revision of the bylaws "to more adequately reflect ... the organization as a community cultural institution dependent on
broad-based public support." Diehard trustees fought the
implementation of the report and obstructed the campaign to
hold new elections to the board, until a court order warned
them to cease and desist. At the end, more progressive
candidates, all professional or amateur musicians, were elected,
conservative trustees not up for reelection resigned, and the
fired musicians were reinstated. However, it would take
years before the damage to the orchestra--artistic, political,
financial, and psychological--could be repaired.[8]

If trustees as a whole could boast a love for a broad
spectrum of music, some exoneration of their actions, however

mistaken, might be advanced. Unfortunately, the evidence
points in another direction. In general, they continue to be
conservative people of wealth, descended from old families or
parvenus wishing to improve their social positions. They
favor older traditional music or exhibit unformed tastes. They
are still impressed by musical celebrities, especially if foreign-
born.[9]

An embarrassing obtuseness characterizes the thinking
of a few of them. Howard Hanson mentions a board president
of "a greater symphony orchestra" who told his newly appointed music director that he understood the man also composed music, an activity he would not object to so long as
the director composed music on his own time." Janet Tassel
describes the death of the excellent old Boston Civic Symphony, owing to the board's firing of the conductor, Benjamin
Zander, because he was too adventurous in his programming,
played too much Mahler, and neglected the tried-and-true.
Astoundingly, one trustee thought the composer Mahler was
"Mailer" and another trustee pulled Zander apart for not playing more "Chopin symphonies." Finally, Ralph Black, writing
in Symphony Magazine and elsewhere, says that most board
members have no idea of what they are supposed to do, rarely
work from an agenda, have problems understanding financial
reports, give ineffective or detrimental advice to the music
director and general manager, and do not really know what
is going on within the association: "When we see them in the
Board meeting we dance the minuet-of-good-manners in status-
quo-time and say nothing."[10]

There is an obverse side to the coin. Alvin Toffler
claims that the old type of board member is slowly giving way
to the informed, activist type of individual, full of fresh energy, enthusiasm, and ideas, who acknowledges the responsibility of art institutions to the community. Harry Dickson
maintains that the board of the Boston Symphony Orchestra
radically changed its thinking in the late sixties and invariably consults the players in matters of musical policy. Perhaps this is true to some degree; however, in several of its
actions during the eighties, it seemed less enlightened.[11]

Edward Arian writes about the 1981 crisis of the San
Diego Symphony, which forced reforms and resulted in a
new, "aggressive, hardworking board leadership; a highly
competent and professional staff; growing community involvement

and commitment; growing artistic quality; a suitable hall; and the potential for an adequate endowment fund."[12]

What is certain is that major stumbling blocks to the acceptance of art associations as viable institutions within an American context can be the boards meant to guide their fortunes. Needed are members who passionately love music and who have a real concern for their association's place in the community. We hope that what Toffler, Dickson, and Arian indicate as the direction of the future will truly come about.

THE MANAGERS OF MUSIC ASSOCIATIONS

The bureaucratic structure of music associations usually includes a salaried general manager or president, appointed by the board of trustees, who presides over several under-managers responsible for artistic, personnel, marketing, financial, and developmental matters. In the June 1979 issue of Symphony News, Ralph Black outlined the duties of a music association's general manager. Coming first was the administration of the board's policy. The manager also prepared and presented the proposed budget to the board, and saw to the carrying out of whatever budget decisions were reached. He had to see to the smooth operation of his ensemble by acting as an intermediary between the musicians, conductor, and board. He had to make certain that the physical plant was kept in good order and that all necessary tools were provided the performers. Working with the music director, the manager helped plan and schedule rehearsals and performances at home and during tours. The contracts of the association's musicians and of guest artists requred negotiation. Publicity and promotion came within his province. So also did the cultivation and utilization of volunteers, and the hiring and supervision of office workers, stagehands, and other non-musical personnel. Tickets had to be sold; money raised from donors; grants applied for--these were additional duties. In the postwar era, the functions of the general manager became so complex that the American Symphony Orchestra League established a training program for managers.

Obviously, the position of manager does carry great power, which is that much greater when the board fails to set policy. The possible impact of managerial decisions on

artistic matters is demonstrated by an action of the former
manager of the Boston Symphony Orchestra, Thomas Perry.
He decided that the instruments of the Baldwin Piano Company should be endorsed by the orchestra and employed both
at Boston's Symphony Hall and at Tanglewood. The reason
for his decision, he said, was because the piano firm made
annual contributions to the orchestra, supplied around 70 pianos and a piano tuner gratis to the Music Center at Tanglewood every summer, and made free loans of Baldwin pianos
for use by the orchestra and its conductors. In order to insure a continuation of these benefits, Perry threw his weight
behind the selection of pianists to appear with the orchestra
who declared a preference for playing on Baldwin pianos.
Perry's actions illustrate the remark of Margo Miller: "It's
a truism in the music management business these days [1986]
that in the era of the jet-setting absentee music director ...
an orchestra's general manager really runs the show."[13]

As the Perry example makes clear, it is the general
manager and subordinates who engage in cost-benefit analyses
and define the factors to be considered when making economic
decisions that affect artistic planning and programming. It is
they who recommend to the board an initial investment in one
or more courses of action that ultimately involve the public
sector and therefore necessitate a consideration of social costs
and benefits. When Bruce Crawford was appointed general
manager of the Metropolitan Opera, he said: "My responsibility will be to report to the board. In turn, eight department heads will report to me--departments like marketing,
television, public relations, and so forth." Together they
managed a budget in excess of $75 million, he said, and ar-
rived at financial decisions that could not help but involve
artistic matters. A case in point was the management's decision to cut back on tours to other cities unless operating
costs were guaranteed beforehand.[14]

Like the boards that appoint them, managers of music
associations lean toward conservatism, and are chary about the
new and untried--whether in the music played, the guest artists
who are engaged, or the activities of their organization in
relation to the community. They avoid controversy, particularly if it may threaten ticket sales or money donations. Certainly the notorious Vanessa Redgrave affair of 1982 illustrates
these guides to artistic decisions. If the test for a successful democratic culture is its ability to accommodate differences

and respect minority opinion, then the manager and board
of the Boston Symphony failed to meet the test. Moreover,
they established that when the chips are down, art does not
always transcend politics.

The orchestra had contracted for Redgrave's appearance
in Stravinsky's Oedipus Rex, at a time when her support of
the Palestine Liberation Organization was no secret. Suddenly,
her appearance was cancelled. William Bernell, the artistic
administrator, said he feared somebody might be killed, citing
as precedent the 1972 bombing of the Sol Hurok offices by the
Jewish Defense League, in which a woman was murdered.
Thomas W. Morris, the general manager at that time, said he
was concerned with the orchestra's ability to put on the production, owing to telephone threats from the Jewish Defense
League to disrupt the performance. Yet, Morris never returned the call of Arthur Bernstein, founder of the Massachusetts League, in order to discuss the matter. Nor did he
consult with the Boston Police prior to canceling the performance. Then the hidden reasons for the cancellation came to
light. Members of the Jewish community had objected to Redgrave's appearance, and Irving Rabb, a trustee, had told
Morris to try to get out of the commitment. Rabb feared that
her engagement "would be a devastating thing from the point
of view of fund-raising. There were a number of people who
are Jewish who would withhold their money if she performed."
Morris agreed: "If we went ahead, it very well might affect
fund raising." A couple of letters to newspapers suggested
that since Jewish philanthropists contributed heavily to the
arts, they had a right to say what artists should and should
not appear. One letter, in the Boston Globe of 14 November
1984, demanded that Redgrave be expelled from the United
States.

Nevertheless, during the court trial that ensued, the
board and management of the Boston Symphony suggested with
some insouciance that considerations neither of politics nor
money were involved. Stated Morris: "We did not take her
politics into account in the cancellation." The music director,
Seiji Ozawa, testified that music was a "very sensitive and
fragile art," an escape from the world of hate, and "should
not mix with any political issue."

At the end, the jurors found that Redgrave should receive $100,000 plus the contract fee of $27,500. At the same

time, the jurors made public a letter they had sent to the
presiding judge, stating they were convinced that politics got
Redgrave fired and "that there was indeed an abrogation of
Ms. Redgrave's civil rights by the BSO." However, "we
could find no way to express" that belief "within the confines
of the verdict question." John Reinstein, an attorney with
the Civil Liberties Union, saw no difference between the orchestra canceling because it disliked her political views or
canceling because financial donors disliked her views. "The
orchestra is still making the decision." Lastly, an editorial
in the Boston Globe concluded that manager and board had
compromised the orchestra's integrity and had come "perilously
close to abrogating" the orchestra's "own artistic freedom. If
the BSO capitulated to threats, insisting to the end that it
made the correct decision in refusing to defend the right of
Redgrave to perform on artistic principles alone, what hope
is there? This tawdry chapter in the orchestra's history
must never be repeated.... Artistic freedom and integrity
must be guaranteed in a democracy, or politics will have no
meaning at all."[15]

In addition to managers of performing groups, there
are those who manage a roster of individual artists and small
chamber ensembles, like the huge Columbia Artists Management
and its subsidiary, Community Concerts, and the solo management of Sol Hurok (who died in 1974). There are also concert
managers who arrange for performances in local halls and towns
across the country. Finally, there are community arts-council
managers, and also campus concert-series administrators, who
are organized as the Association of College and University
Concert Managers.[16]

Ideally, the concert manager seeks out gifted musicians
and presents them to far-flung audiences. He or she is supposed to call public attention to the musicians, negotiate and
schedule their concerts, arrange recording sessions, and offer
advice to advance their careers. Yet, as indicated in an earlier chapter, when I discussed the launching of artistic careers, the reality in most instances fails to correspond with
the ideal. The requirements of the marketplace and the necessity to show a profit (at the least, to avoid monetary loss)
perforce dominates managerial actions. Scarcely a manager
can afford to act purely in response to the obligation to nurture a promising musician. They must see to remaining sol-
vent. One concert manager says that the players he represents

had better do as he advises, which may include a bit of compromising of artistic integrity, or he will not represent them.
Another manager says he likes the people he agrees to represent to have appeared on television, or in some way to loom
large in the public eye, in order to ensure large audiences.
Still another manager refuses to allow any artist on his roster
to play any twentieth-century music, declaring that subscribers really do not want to hear it. Most managers insist that
their instrumentalists and singers take part in the social activities attendant upon concert appearances, but few of them
stipulate that the presenters must give hot meals to performers, rather than the ubiquitous finger-food and cookies char-
acteristic of after-concert receptions. For all managers, the
profit-and-loss sheet determines the value of a player. They
are, after all, businessmen. They need to keep their risks
low.[17]

Concert managers tend to behave like sales representatives, "carrying a variety of product lines" and "having more
than one musician to sell," writes Barbara Jepson. Especially
the large management firms treat musicians like commodities:
"Artists say there is an unofficial pecking order inside the
biggest firms, with favoritism shown to top money-makers
rather than to newcomers or middle-level performers who need
more assistance." Not to make money meant that you were
handled by underlings or were completely forgotten. Pianist
André-Michel Schub, for example, says his former manager
and the staff at Columbia Artists ignored him, scarcely knew
what he was doing, and failed to attend his concerts. Even
when he entered the Van Cliburn Competition, which he fortunately won, nobody from Columbia Artists showed up.[18]

In a farflung nation like the United States, managers
provide an essential service. It is unfortunate, therefore,
that they find necessary a dilution of their mission of providing the best talent to a widespread constituency, owing to the
exigencies of the profit-and-loss column. To a certain extent,
the latter affords a useful check-and-balance to the former.
The problem is to keep it from dominating the thinking of
managers.

THE FINANCING OF MUSIC

The role of the arts in the American civilization is often

debated.   The debate usually focuses on the question of why
the arts should receive financial support.   For some time now,
it has been the fashion with some prominent postwar musicians
and musical aesthetes to maintain that art is created for art's
sake, carries its own vindication, and tries to attain no social
object.   Owing to such an argument they have not been able
to take that further step and show how such art can benefit
the community and therefore should receive funding from the
community or private corporations.

Alvin Toffler advances certain hypotheses on art's benefits about whose validity one must decide.   An argument goes
that art should be supported because it is "a social lubricant."
Its value is therapeutic, because art aids self-expression, releases antisocial passions and civilizes people.   The justification
is problematical and of doubtful validity.   A second argument,
that art educates although not in the mundane sense, has a
greater validity since music can take a person outside the
range of his ordinary experiences and widen "the individual's
conception of the alternatives available to him."[19]   This justification for support is a telling one because it fits comfort-
ably into the concept of American democracy.

Again, many listeners testify to music being a mystical
and profound experience, one that bypasses the usual processes of communication and evokes the indescribable.   The
kinship with religious experience is obvious.   Although Toffler hesitates to accept this hypothesis, enough psychologists
have observed and written about the importance of this sort
of aesthetic experience to make the testimony convincing.[20]
Regrettably, it is too personal and subjective an experience
to prove music's right to support.   Toffler would agree, however, that art music does contribute to the diversity in society, its "richness and variation" adding "to the richness
and variation in society," and therefore should be promoted.[21]
Here is a far more effective reason for financing art music.

The explanations for governmental funding have not
centered only on the music itself.   Promoting cultural exchange programs with other countries is thought to win us
friends abroad.   Hence the need to find money to send American "music ambassadors"--performing groups, composers, and
music students--abroad.   When we viewed the European tradition
of public support for the arts, and the high valuation placed
on art music, it seemed incumbent upon American civilization

to behave likewise. After World War II, the United States
did not wish to appear wanting in areas that defined the
quality of its cultural development for others. In addition,
Gary Larson writes, the citizens of the United States accepted,
and even cherished, the democratic thought "calling for a
chicken in every pot and fine art in every home." Governmental support was a means for increasing cultural possibilities in America and making them a greater reality not just
in the large cities but in the hinterlands. [22]

The long and short of it is the inability of art-music
institutions to support themselves, however well managed they
might be. A major orchestra employs some 500 people, and
an opera company like the Metropolitan even more. The performance industry is labor-intensive, over 60 percent of expenditures going to personnel. And the constant rise of wages
is never matched by the equivalent rise in income. The star
system, which includes orchestra conductors, instrumental
soloists, and singers, adds prohibitively to the expenditures.
As Baumol and Bowen suggest: "In the performing arts, crisis is apparently a way of life. One reads constantly of dis-
appointing seasons, of disastrous rises in costs, of emergency·
fund drives and desperate pleas for assistance.... Even the
venerable Metropolitan Opera has several times threatened to
suspend a season." In 1975, Thomas Scherman's Little Orchestra Society did suspend all operations owing to the rise
of costs, the high fees of stars, and the reduction in contributions by donors suffering from inflation. [23]

Management can reduce costs by shrinking orchestras
or letting operatic sets and costumes get shabby, but the
quality of the performance deteriorates and audiences cease
to come. Ticket prices can increase, but audiences may refuse to pay the extra tariff. After all, music is not a necessity for survival, and for many men and women radio, television, and motion pictures provide less expensive alternatives.
Besides, a moral dilemma arises--is it proper for a democratic
society to exclude more and more of the less affluent and reduce the performing arts "to a vestigial state, with a very
small number of theaters and orchestras catering to an exclusive group of persons?" [24]

With the eighties came more stringent financial controls.
Attempts were made to eliminate luxuries, like "lavish cast
parties" and "flights on the Concorde," to conduct more

efficient rehearsals, and to encourage greater cooperation and,
when possible, a sharing of expenses between arts groups.
"Imagination" and "an inventive use of limited resources" have
increasingly replaced "wanton waste" and "outrageous excess,"
like the constant reliance on "super stars with super fees."[25]
Sad to say, more stringent financial controls have also made
managements less eager to schedule new or little known mu-
suc, since that would necessitate extra rehearsal time and
possibly produce lower attendance figures. A similar caution
has worked against untried and unglamorous performers. The
best intentioned music directors and managers know that somewhere money must be found to cover the inevitably greater
expense or loss of audience that may result from the abandonment of beaten pathways.

Money is raised through black-tie benefit performances,
first-night suppers, special dinners and other select evening
events for trustees and wealthy benefactors, gala entertainments, radio marathons, soliciting pledges over the phone, and
selling goods and services normally through auctions.[26] The
chances of giving public offense sometimes are high. If the
approach was too hard a sell, the results were negative. For
example, the Metropolitan miscalculated, in 1953, when the
management melodramatically halted a performance of Tristan
und Isolde that was being broadcast. Milton Cross then announced over the air and through the loudspeakers in the
auditorium that a "problem" had arisen and he and others
were trying to find out what happened. Shortly, the "problem" proved a hoax, when the interruption led to an appeal
for funds. The angered audience jeered loudly at the appeal;
the radio listeners sent, not money, but irate letters.[27]

If the money-raising events ballyhooed the wealthy and
were reported as activities appropriate to the society pages,
it was likely that offense would be taken. Bernard Taper
writes that part of the fund-raising scene involves a great
deal of "hoopla on behalf of the arts one reads about in the
society pages--and which probably offend as many untapped
and potential sources of funds and allegiance to the arts as
they attract." This, writes Taper, is a remainder from private-
patronage days and can turn off business corporations as new
sources for funds.[28]

Where money comes from, other than ticket sales, varies
from music association to music association. The less major

the group, the more it relies on the small donations received
from humble members of its audience; the more major the group,
the more it expects to come in from wealthy donors and corporations. The sources for funding the New York City Opera
Association (America's second most prominent opera company)
were investigated in the eighties. It was found that 55 percent involved individual donations, 18 percent foundation
grants, 17 percent corporation giving, and 10 percent governmental contributions. Although individual donations loom large
here and in other statistics on funding, the mistake has been
to assume that most of it came from a few affluent donors.
When Baumol and Bowen issued the results of their investigation of the performing arts, in 1966, they found that 23 percent of the orchestra audience gave money regularly and 25
percent occasionally; also, that 17 percent of the opera audience gave regularly and 27 percent occasionally. In addition,
they observed that nine times as much money was contributed
by the lesser income groups as came from the higher income
group.[29] This certainly speaks well for the ordinary members
of the audience.

     What counted most, nevertheless, was the large sum a
wealthy contributor might give. As the orchestra conductor
Eugene Ormandy had to admit, it was the taste of such a person that associations respected. He or she would expect to
hear a great deal of the conservative music they liked and
only a little of the unfamiliar or contemporary dissonant music that could at best only be tolerated. The commoners, who
made up the majority of the audience, were given much less
heed. Oftentimes, the taste of the wealthy giver was attributed also to them, whether justified or not. It was a way of
strengthening positions already occupied. And the youngest
auditors, who would have been most receptive to new or dissonant music but who were least able to donate money, were
given scarcely any heed at all. That art-music associations,
save for the few that specialized in unconventional and contemporary music, turned off many young people and thus discouraged the development of future audiences was not merely
a matter of conjecture.[30]

     In 1967, corporations contributed about $22 million to
the arts; in 1979, about $436 million. In 1981, the contribu-
tion ominously shrank to $350 million. This figure represented
about 12 percent of the total contributions to all nonprofit arts
and cultural organizations.[31] The spurs to corporate giving

were the governmental codes that permitted the deduction of
such contributions from profits and the expectations of economic benefit. Most of this money came from a few of the
largest corporations. Business firms, in general, gave very
little to the arts. Furthermore, three quarters of the money
given music associations reached only about 3 percent of the
total number--those most prestigious or prominent, like the
Metropolitan Opera and the Chicago Symphony. Fortunate
were a few music associations in whose communities the head-
quarters of large corporations were located. They were apt
to receive a large portion of whatever funds such corporations
normally gave to the arts.

Corporations gave with the expectation of some return,
not the least of which was publicity by way of added media
news coverage and acknowledgements in advertisements of performances and in concert programs. An enhanced corporate
image was assumed to come when donations won the good will
of the community. The music association might offer lower
ticket prices or free admission to the employees, or special
privileges to important officials and clients, of corporate donors. Heidi Waleson notes that tours often are directed toward
cities where corporate sponsors had an interest. When the
McKesson Company helped underwrite the domestic tour of the
San Francisco Symphony, in 1983, it specified that the ensemble had to visit Salt Lake City and Hartford, where Mc-
Kesson had subordinate offices. In return for a donation from
Scott Paper, the Philadelphia Orchestra included Turin, where
the company had an interest, as part of a European tour.
The cultivation of corproations for donations of this sort is
obvious in the statement of Richard Hoffert, director of development for the Saint Louis Symphony. He speaks of re-
searching home corporations and also figuring out "what corporations are in the cities where you want to go," and then
crossing back "to see whether they are in your home town.
We're lucky in that we have nine or ten major international
corporations headquartered here, and by cross-referencing
we can come up with companies that have never given to the
symphony that we might be able to tap."[32]

When a corporation senses less economic benefits coming
from sponsorship of the arts, then its contributions may decrease. For example, Exxon Corporation has been a big giver
to music associations and an underwriter of other ambitious
arts activities like concert and opera performances over public

television and the Exxon/Arts Endowment Conductors Program, which places gifted conductors in full-time residencies with orchestras and opera companies. Yet, in the eighties it began to shift millions of dollars away from the arts and into health and social welfare activities. At the same time, Mobil Oil Corporation, another big giver, earmarked some of its arts money not for music associations but for bringing performances of all sorts to schoolchildren and the handicapped. The Reagan Administration's taking over of the federal government and its active endeavor to cut governmental contributions in all cultural, health, and social-welfare areas further exacerbated matters in the eighties. The political leadership then urged business corporations to channel more money into the social-welfare sector. "Whatever the sincerity of big business's motives," writes Sandra Salmans, "giving to the arts can always be considered a luxury."[33]

Disquieting to a lover of the arts is a corporate officer's letter that Bernard Taper quotes: "Our giving to the arts has been based on who is asking and how good a friend they are and how cheaply we can get out of it.... I think the value of the arts is very marginal in coping with our great urban problems. Usually it is the art 'owned' by the upper middle class which we are asked to support--for example, the Symphony or the Opera. These are hard to duck although we try. At the other end of the system are the few art activities actively centered in the ghetto and doing worthwhile work on a limited budget. Here it is not really art that is fostered but, hopefully, a sense of dignity and the feeling that someone does care and that it's possible to participate in civilization.

"I have a simplistic formula:

1. Let the upper classes pay for their own delectation.

2. Let the middle and affluent working class get their 'art' from television which they are going to watch anyway.

3. Let's go into the ghetto with every program that is constructive and meanwhile recognize that art programs are near the bottom of the priority list."[34]

Foundations, that is to say organizations endowed by corporations or wealthy private donors to act philanthropically for humanitarian and cultural purposes, are steered by the same veering winds that affect the direct corporate givers. The altogether too few officers responsible for distributing and administering grants may have slight knowledge of the arts and no time to acquire that knowledge. For this reason, they become unduly affected by current fashions in the music world. In addition, they turn to advisors for help, who are usually people from the arts world itself. Because these last are also the beneficiaries, they can make many suspect judgments. Lastly, owing to the changeableness of general social trends, priorities from one decade to another are not necessarily the same.

Robert Brustein, in 1974, warned of other failings of private foundations when they decided where to put their cultural dollar. He described one small foundation which tried to "quantify subjective criteria" by weighing "quality of leadership, quality of planning, quality of community impact, quality of fiscal management, quality of audience development," standards that were "sociological, educational, and administrative, since they were more easily measured." Artistic standards and values formed no part of the considerations.[35]

With the sixties, and coincident with the Cultural Explosion, came a substantial investment in the arts. The foremost giver to art music was the Ford Foundation, followed by the Rockefeller Foundation, and then the Avalon Foundation, the Mellon Trust, the Mayer Foundation, and the Old Dominion Foundation.[36] Normally, grants from foundations necessitated the raising of matching money from other donors. Nor were the grants intended for the long run. The money was meant to seed infant ventures and experimental programs, including the launching of American conductors, instrumentalists, singers, and musical compositions. W. McNeil Lowry, then the Ford Foundation's Director of Humanities and the Arts, explained in 1963 that foundations regarded themselves as "catalysts rather than reformers." They tried to make things happen. Although they studied and tried to understand the arts world, they did not see themselves as permanent backers of any artistic enterprise, nor as critics of art works.[37]

Frequently, foundations felt that their seed money did not produce the anticipated results. During 1963, the Ford Foundation gave close to a million dollars to the Metropolitan, New York City, Chicago Lyric, and San Francisco Operas to

mount eighteen American operas, expecting the action would
encourage local support and the production of other new
operas. Experts were consulted who knew a great deal about
contemporary musical trends but little about opera audiences.
Unfortunately, the audiences did not take to the commissioned
operas on first hearing, nor had provision been made for repeated performances of them. Instead, in Milton Goldin's
words: "New experts were needed. A new term was coined--
'Foundation music'--to describe those unique works by which
no audiences felt benefited, stimulated, or emotionally affected,
but which had been brought into existence by the students
and friends of renowned experts."[38]

Later, the Ford Foundation gave matching grants to
certain orchestras, in order to firm the financial ground under them. Again the results were ambiguous. The orchestras
acted to guarantee year-round employment for its instrumentalists, but at the same time had to turn to new ways and means
for employment during the months when heretofor they had
suspended or reduced performances. One result was a heavy
outlay of funds in summer-festival centers, like the Blossom
Music Center for the Cleveland Orchestra and the Meadow
Brook Festival for the Detroit Symphony Orchestra.[39] Another was an increase in "pops" concerts. A few orchestras
tried touring. In several instances, orchestras found themselves locked into a new situation that only increased their
deficits.

Under the best of circumstances, foundation funds for
the arts must be spread thinly. With the eighties, they were
spread thinner still. With less and less funds coming in, arts
organizations faced a potentially disastrous future. Three
foundations--Ford, Mellon, and Rockefeller--were concerned
over the danger and the limited way they could respond to it.
They contributed $9 million dollars to a National Arts Stabili-
zation Fund that offered grants as incentives to reduce deficits and install sound budget practices. If an arts group
acted to halve its deficit, the fund took responsibility for the
remaining debts. Also, the fund offered to provide a working
reserve from which an arts group might borrow.[40]

Whenever people in the arts seek governmental aid, political contention arises that eludes resolution. One recalls
the sarcasm of Representative Howard W. Smith's in opposition to any federal aid to the arts, which he inserted into the

1963 <u>Congressional Record</u>: "What are the arts? And here is where I display my ignorance. I do not know. What does it include? What is it about? I suppose fiddle players would be in the arts, and the painting of pictures would be in the arts. It was suggested that poker playing was an artful occupation. Is this going to subsidize poker players that get in trouble?"[41]

Politicians unsympathetic to the arts were given ammunition by cultural populists in music, like Tom Lehrer, who said the arts were "essentially dead, and nobody really" cared "about them any more.... The symphony's only real role now is in making recordings, and the theater ... has practically been replaced by the movies. These things concern only a small minority, and I am no more disturbed by their decline than I would be by the demise of polo." Or by conservative academics involved with music, like Jacques Barzun, who said tax payers insisted on their simple preferences and wished no pioneering in the arts by means of governmental subsidy. "Not wanting it, a self-governing people cannot be asked to pay for it, directly or indirectly."[42]

Other critics defined art music as entertainment for the few, which the many should not be forced to support. Like all entertainment, it should be tested on the entertainment market. If enough wanted to buy it, fine. Otherwise it should die. Still others maintained art music represented a foreign, not an American, cultural tradition and therefore could make no claims on American public money. Besides, more pressing problems demanded all the resources of government--among them, military defense, care of the aged, and housing and jobs for the poor.

Yet, in the face of opposition, public subsidy of the arts did increase in the postwar years. In addition to the arguments for financial support already given, several with direct connection to democratic imperatives are cited by Richard Hoggart, in a discussion of the relation of the arts to politics ("Culture and Its Ministers").[43] He comments on how difficult it is for a working-class youngster to go beyond the narrow choices possible to him or her in a home without books and artistic interests, where television is the constant companion, or in a school whose values and instructional offerings dismiss or begrudgingly recognize the performing arts. "On the basis of all this--on the argument for the <u>possible</u>

liberating power of the arts, and on the fact that all societies, if left to their own devices, tend to limit rather than liberate --one can found the case for public intervention in favor of cultural development." Hoggart writes about realizing potentials, increasing choice, and breaking out of a "masses" concept, so that an individual becomes more than a "market-research consumer's profile" (which, Hoggart claims, tends to be self-fulfilling). Government should step in to make more and different "intellectual and imaginative experiences" available and to counteract the "market" domination of culture. Also, it should underwrite socio-cultural experimentation and risk-taking. Emphasis, he states, should be given to helping increase the arts audience, so that "artists get their support obliquely, from sufficiently large, free, critical, and responsive publics."

At the beginning of World War II, the federal government had dismantled its massive support for the arts under the Works Progress Administration.[44] In the fifties, spurred by the Cold War, the United States funded cultural tours of foreign countries by performing and creative artists and groups, alongside tours by sports groups. From 1955 to 1961, a little over $16 million was spent for this purpose.

From the fifties into the seventies, mostly Democrats urged an increase in funding for the arts. They optimistically viewed the dissemination of culture "as the crowning achievement of America's social and political democracy," and a "rite of passage for American civilization, to counterbalance the nation's emphasis on science and technology."[45] Indirect aid from state and local governments increased, especially where liberal Democrats were in control. Allied with them were normally conservative and influential business figures who found themselves involved, as trustees and prominent donors, with the financial health of one art institution or another. Tax-exempt arts property and donors' gifts, and free use of public auditoriums soon prevailed. In one or two instances, local taxes aided local art institutions. With the eighties, state lotteries and monies also provided financial assistance to art groups. The poorer states, of course, gave only token assistance. Wealthier states gave much more. Alaska, for example, has immense monetary surpluses, owing to revenues derived from its vast natural resources. As a result, Anchorage, with a population of around 200,000, can boast a regular symphony orchestra, a youth orchestra, an opera company,

and a civic ballet. Around 15 percent of the budgets for
these groups comes from the sale of tickets. The rest comes
from the largess of the city and state, as well as from grants
provided by the National Endowment for the Arts.[46]

In the mid-eighties, all states had arts councils which
received money from the National Endowment for the Arts and
from in-state appropriations. However, the sums appropriated
were usually piddling, rarely coming close to or exceeding $1
million, As Netzer observes: "In most of the United States,
the alleged intensity of local pride in the orchestra, opera
company, art museum, or resident theater company does not
manifest itself in initiative on the part of state or local politicians to commit state or local funds to the institution's support. For the most part, local pride is compatible with letting
NEA bear the burden of providing public funds for the support of the primary institutions."[47]

With John F. Kennedy's election to the Presidency came
the first strong drive to meet nation-wide cultural needs, in
despite of conservative, usually Republican, opposition. When
Lyndon Bains Johnson assumed the Presidency, after Kennedy's
assassination, he worked to persuade Congress of the necessity for arts funding. Johnson held that artistic achievement
and this achievement's availability to all citizens were "among
the hall-marks of a Great Society," and ways for winning "respect and admiration for the Nation's high qualities as a leader
in the realm of ideas and of the spirit." At last, in 1965, was
created what later was known as the National Endowment for
the Arts, with $2.5 million dollars appropriated for the arts.[48]
The appropriation increased in later years. In 1970, about
$2.5 million went to music alone; in 1980, over $13.5 million;
in 1984, over $15 million. None of these sums, it should be
noted, were very large when compared with the resources of
the country. Arts agencies set up by the states, nonprofit
performing groups, and musicians perceived as exceptionally
talented received grants, but only when they were requested.
A staff and an advisory panel of professional musicians decided on the merits of the requests.

The artist-dominated panel usually acted in aid of music
groups and artistic individuals with slight consideration given
to music education and audience development. Indeed, as late
as 1978, advisors Theodore Bikel and Hal Prince were contending that the mandate had to do with fostering professional

excellence in the arts and had nothing to do with audiences:
"We (the Endowment) are not in the business of developing
audiences. We are in the business of developing artists,"
said Prince.[49]

General criticism arose about the uneven distribution of
NEA grants. Complaints increased about the seeming favoritism
in NEA decisions. For example, Nancy van de Vate writes
that in 1975 the NEA gave fellowships to 128 composers and
9 librettists. Only six grants went to persons in the thirteen
southern states, although many strong applications had come
in from Texas, Florida, Tennessee, among others. Midwestern
composers received seven of the grants. Yet, sixty grants
went to people in New York. The explanation given by the
NEA was that composers living in the Northeast had more performance opportunities and had submitted strong applications.
Nevertheless, on closer examination, one found that the symphony orchestras of New York, Philadelphia, and Boston did
not do more contemporary American works than, say, the orchestras of Houston, Atlanta, Louisville, and Oklahoma City.
In addition, well-known composers from places like Muncie,
Indiana, were denied NEA assistance, while less-known and
less-performed composers of the Northeast, especially if connected with a university, got the lion's share. Apparently,
the artistic panels advising the NEA were biased and not
representative of all sections of the country.[50]

The direction of the funding commenced to change in
the fall of 1979. Grants went to provide low-priced admission in the summer season (Atlanta), free summer concerts
and pre-concert discussions (Boston), family concerts (Seattle
and Syracuse), children's and in-school concerts (Buffalo),
performances for the aged (Chicago), travel to neighboring
communities (Cleveland), music for the handicapped (Dallas),
inner-city musical activities (Detroit), and informal brown-bag
concerts (Dayton). More and more money started to go to
smaller localities, to educational programs, and to getting art
music out to the ordinary citizen.

Unfortunately, many people in the arts continued to be
blind to the issues involved. In 1984, for instance, managers
of cultural institutions, executives from foundations, and performers met to investigate public policy with regard to funding for the arts. They concluded, among other things, that
the Federal Government deserved severe criticism for its

increased catering to mass taste. Walter Goodman, reporting
on the meeting, states: "It was the old elitism vs. populism
dispute. Government assistance to the arts requires some
democratic rationale. How can an aesthetic experience for the
well-fed be weighted against food stamps? And if tax funds
are to be allocated to the arts, why should they go to avant-
garde works instead of to those that attract more of the citizenry?"[51] The arts conference of 1984 had provided no answers.

Ronald Reagan's election to the Presidency and the increased strength of conservative Republicans in the eighties
brought on an effort to reduce arts appropriations by 30 percent. At the same time, the ceilings that voters of the eighties forced several states to place over taxes depleted revenues
and discouraged further funding for the arts. The shortfall,
political conservatives insisted, had to be covered by the
private sector. Fortunately for the arts, the conservatives
were checked by congressional liberals committed to arts support. A change in the political wind, on the other hand,
could blow away the entire support-apparatus.

Fear of political interference in the arts, so prevalent
in the fifties and sixties, has proved largely false, at least
in the expected area of artistic decisions. Moreover, much
of whatever political interference has taken place was intended
to redress the balance between the potentially exclusive creative imperatives of artists and the needs of a nationwide music
public.

Local, state, and national politicians in the late-twentieth
century feel that they need a democratic mandate for support
of art music. It is difficult to find. Some politicians maintain, rightly or wrongly, that the art composers and performers have only themselves to blame, ever bent as they are on
excusing their excesses, if avant-garde artists, or their timidity, if traditionalists. On the one hand, art music is identified with contemporary compositions that the public simply
cannot buy; on the other, with a restricted traditional repertoire that can weary listeners with its unimaginative sameness.
To illustrate the first criticism, in 1983, Francis Hodsoll,
chairman of the NEA, hesitated about approving certain "musical" projects, among them a "Brooklyn Bridge Sound Sculp-
ture," by Bell Fontana, to place 6 to 18 microphones below
the bridge's road surface, in order "to capture the 'singing'

tones produced by the vibrating metal structure." Another project was the "Dance of Machines," by the Snake Theater/ Nightfire Division, in Sausalito, California, where cranes and heavy construction machines would be made to "dance at a large construction site in a performance featuring video productions and original music." Hodsoll said music projects like these raised a basic question about where does art end and what sort of audience was addressed. At the end, he did fund them, persuaded of their "serious intentions" by his artistic advisors. Nevertheless, he was attacked by various art groups for holding up these projects and repressing artistic expression that was not to his liking.[52]

Also noticed by politicians is the way intellectuals and creative people from disciplines other than music adhere to different cultural values. They hear writers, painters, sculptors, dancers, sociologists, and political scientists extolling musics other than art as being of equal or greater value. Without consensus in the art and intellectual world and fewer allies elsewhere, art music may suffer even as politicians see its sway weakening.

ANCILLARY MUSICAL ENTERPRISES: PUBLISHERS AND RECORD COMPANIES

My subject here is business ventures utilizing or marketing music, which are involved with a degree of risk-taking in the pursuit of profit. In certain instances the risk-taking centers not on monetary profit but on the retention of a large enough consumer group so as to convince private and public financial donors of their viability. Men and women presumed to be knowledgeable about the cultural market evolve methodical schemes for satisfying consumer demand, while also identifying, anticipating, and interpreting the nature of this demand. They are employed by enterprises, whether profit-seeking or non-profit, that are linked to the publishing and recording of music, and to music's dissemination through the medium of motion pictures, radio, and television.

American publishers have an interest in three sorts of commercial venture. First, there is the issuance of musical scores and parts, for study or performance. If not copyright, the music costs them nothing in royalties; if also with a sufficiently large following, profits may be anticipated.

Costs and the risk of failure are minimized. If the music is
new, royalties must be paid to composers and a following of
respectable size usually does not materialize. Therefore costs
are higher and loss is more than just a threat. Second, there
is the publication of books on prominent composers and performers of the past, on the musical stars of the day, and on
the one or two contemporary composers exciting current interest. Although royalties must be paid to authors (except
when the reprint of an older book is involved), market demand
is more easily estimated and the amount of potential profit
more accurately gauged than that for new music. Third,
there are the books meant for study, consultation, and education. These comprise reference materials, musical criticism
and aesthetics, score analyses, letters by and about musicians,
and texts designed for classroom teaching.[53] To have a book
adopted as a text is often a publisher's primary objective,
since it means the sale of not one copy but many copies at a
time in several classrooms and over a period of perhaps five
to ten years.

During the seventies and through the year 1980, as
editor of the Sonneck-Society Newsletter, I was constantly
investigating and reporting on the publication of books on
music. My findings were in substantial agreement with those
contained in an article written in 1968, by Patrick Smith.[54]
For one, a decreasing number of books on art music were being published from year to year, and what was published had
an unconscionably higher and higher price tag. Publishers
argued that the music examples in the books were costly to
prepare and proofread, and that a large readership was discouraged by the ungraceful styles of most writers on music.
Further handicaps were the use of a technical terminology beyond the understanding of lay people, and the few retail outlets willing to carry and display books on music. Even as the
population of the United States increased and the Cultural Explosion was discussed, no increased interest in music books
had taken place. The sale of 1000 copies of a work was normal, they said, and the 5000, exceptional. To cover expenses
and the dearth of customers, prices had to be high.

Also true was the fact that overpricing turned many
potential customers away. As the years went by, several
large publishers grew more anxious to increase the volume of
sales beyond the 5,000 figure mentioned above. They were prone
to refuse excellent book-manuscripts if unlikely to generate

large sales, and quickly remaindered books that sold modestly,
however steadily. They were most reluctant to accept a work
that expressed an unusual viewpoint, fearing damnation by
orthodox reviewers, many of them academic musicologists to
whom American music and socio-historical musical studies, for
example, were anathema. This became more and more the
state of things as smaller publishing firms were swallowed up
by huge conglomerates.

Volume sales were possible in textbooks. Quite a few
publishers began to confine their music publications to this
area. In 1983, I received a visit from a music editor employed
by a publishing house noted for the number of music titles it
put out. The purpose of his visit was to get my reaction to
a textbook intended for introductory-music courses. What he
told me of his company's policy in the eighties could easily
apply to most of the publishing world. I learned that the music division could no longer act as independently as before.
It was told to concentrate on textbooks or general books with
potential for classroom use. Furthermore, the authors had to
be well-known; preferably, as the editor said, an "'in' figure"
writing in a "come-hither style." Scholarly credentials were
less important than the writer's perceived ability to generate
interest among buyers. The marketing division now had the
ultimate say on the worthiness of a manuscript. If too original and by an unknown author, it meant rejection: "There
was nothing surefire there." Even when a promising general
book came out, strict budgeting allowed next to no advertising ("after all, it wasn't as if it would be a bestseller!").
Publicizing the book had to be done through reviews. If no
reviews or adverse reviews, the publication was cast aside.

Non-profit university presses, by the late seventies,
found themselves subject to constraints like those of commercial publishers. University administrators grew reluctant to
pick up their presses' deficits. In addition, subsidies to the
presses from their universities shrank. Perforce, market considerations were given more attention by the editors. Several
university presses no longer would publish music books, saying their successful marketing necessitated special expertise
that they did not have. Other presses for the first time required that authors of possibly marginally profitable books
help shoulder expenses or find a subvention from a foundation or governmental cultural agency.

Limitations like those imposed upon the publication of books on music affected the publication of the music itself. Rudolph Tauhert, when president of G. Schirmer in 1966, said that G. Schirmer's success with music compositions was owing to acknowledging and meeting the wants of students and educators who played a particular instrument or were busy with school bands, orchestras, and choruses. The firm published 1800 music volumes for the piano alone, primarily to satisfy the demands of novice and veteran pianists. Its editors dedicated themselves to "catering to the needs of teachers and students," Tauhert said. When "deciding whether we should publish a particular piece of music, the educator is never shunted aside." He admits: "We ask ourselves, 'is it needed' and, at the same time, 'will it sell.'"[55]

The music publisher Arnold Broido states that the budgets of publishing houses became strained as costs climbed and the audience for art music grew smaller in relation to the total population. Income from sales and rentals to performing groups, and from fees charged for recording, television and movie use, and foreign rights was not what it used to be. Many stores stocking art-music scores and parts had gone out of business. Fewer outlets, fewer sales. Out of necessity, publishers had turned more and more to the educational market, if only to meet expenses.[56]

Contemporary art composers have been affected by the fallout from such a policy. They complain about no publication of their compositions or, if accepted by a publisher, the delays in publishing, the failure to promote their music, the inferior quality of the printing, and the absence of editing.[57] When, however, composers have tried to remedy the situation by taking publication matters into their own hands, the result has been mostly discouraging. For example, Nicolas Roussakis and Francis Thorne, officers of the American Composer's Alliance, once essayed the issuance of special editions of new works. A chastened Roussakis describes the result: "These turned out to be a white elephant for the Alliance. We went to great lengths to see that the scores were beautifully engraved, quality editions, carefully edited and maintaining the highest standard in every possible way.... The problem was that the works were often very difficult; even though all the flutists who could play Harvey Sollberger's flute piece bought a copy, that accounted for maybe a dozen or so sales. That was the end of the edition."[58]

Only the rare art composer who was currently in fashion internationally and had a considerable following could succeed through self-publication, unassisted by a commercial publisher. This was the case with Philip Glass in the eighties. He formed his own publishing company in order to retain not a percentage but all of the profits from print, mechanical, movie, video, and performance rights. He was sufficiently popular to gain thousands of dollars from the venture.[59]

The viewpoint of the commercial publisher is expressed by Arthur Cohn of Carl Fischer, who states: "We just brought out a symphony at the end of last year [1981] by a well-known composer: a 150-page score, and the costs were close to $7,500 just to get it out. Now maybe, over the next twenty-five years, there might be sufficient income from performances of that score to wipe that red ink off the books, but I doubt it."[60] Publishers' reluctance was fueled by the avoidance of contemporary music by most professional and amateur musicians, owing to a dislike of the posttriadic idioms, the technical difficulties that had to be surmounted in order to perform the usual twentieth-century composition, and incuriosity about those contemporary works that audiences might more readily enjoy.

Opposed to the publisher's viewpoint is that of the American composer Ralph Shapey. He says that when he tried to have a publisher accept his works, Peters and then Boosey and Hawkes turned him down. Finally, after an important article about his music was printed in the New York Times, Arnold Broido, President of Presser, asked to see him. "Finally I got a so-called publisher," states Shapey. "I say 'so-called' because they don't publish." He explains: "You know what publishers are like today [1980]; there's no sense in being with one. The only reason for being with a publisher is distribution. Most of my music is on rental, from Presser; everything is at Presser, all of my music. A couple of things they finally put out as publications, but I don't think of them as publications: They take my manuscript, and Xerox it or whatever, and stick a lousy cover on it. They call that publication; I don't. But there's nothing you can do about that."[61]

The hesitation of commercial publishers when offered scores that few customers would buy or rent is understandable, as is the paring of expenses when scores were accepted.

Again, the only way out for composers writing marginally
profitable or unprofitable scores has been through subven-
tions from private and public donors, and these have not
been easy to find. Nor do subvention-sponsored publications
increase the list of customers.

The making of disc and tape recordings of music was
another possible way for reaching a widespread music-loving
public. Professional musicians and performance groups saw
recordings as a means for increasing their public recognition,
enhancing their reputation, and, above all, making extra
money. When one examines the Schwann Catalogue, obvious
is the rarity of contemporary and less familiar compositions
amongst the recordings of most prominent American soloists,
chamber groups, and orchestras. To find recordings of American music, one must usually turn to less known musicians and
ensembles or to specialists.

The first long–playing discs came out in 1948. Stereo
became a reality in 1958. Cassette-tape recordings gradually
improved in quality through the sixties. Then, in the eighties, came the compact disc. An immense recorded repertoire,
including very long compositoins, was soon available to customers. Harold Schonberg underlines the significance of this
postwar change in the way music reaches the public, calling
it "the single most important musical development of our time."
He continues: "Within two decades after 1948 virtually the
entire repertory was on records ... a repertory that extended from the early Renaissance to the latest concoction of
John Cage or Pierre Boulez. The music lover had a whole
world free to explore, and many did."[62]

The last sentence requires qualification. In the late-
twentieth century, much of the public's knowledge of contemporary and American music had to come through recordings,
since this music was not well-represented in concerts. Unfortunately, most people would remain unaware that such music existed on recordings. In addition, the increased purchase of music for listening in the home meant that many listeners would neglect concerts they might otherwise have attended. The bulk of sales inevitably comprised the familiar
and the well liked. As early as the sixties, writers on music
were observing that 90 percent of the art music listed in the
Schwann Record and Tape Guide were works written before the
year 1900. These sold relatively well. In contrast, the 10 percent

representing unknown and more recent works sold poorly on
the whole.[63]

Furthermore, Schonberg's explorers of any art music,
whether it was old or new, through recordings began to decrease. Up until 1960, the estimate was that 12 percent of
total record sales comprised art music. By the mid-seventies,
such sales were down to 3 to 5 percent, with "only a sliver"
of this being contemporary art music, according to Allan Kozinn. Where a recording of a popular rock singer might sell
close to ten-million copies, a sought-after recording of a highly
admired artist was fortunate to achieve a sale of 15,000 copies. In most instances sales were less, not more, than this
figure.[64]

To add to the woes of the art-music recording industry,
the seventies witnessed the sale of thousands of cassette-tape
machines, thus making possible the wholesale taping of art
music from FM broadcasts. Guenter Hensler, speaking for
the Polygram group of recording companies, says that by
1980 the problem had become a serious one. Hurt most was
that part of the repertoire that sold poorly: "Where we would
have planned to sell 3-4-5,000 records, we will be able to sell
1,000. This will just make it impossible for us to do some of
the more esoteric things."[65]

Beginning with the sixties, American companies like
RCA and CBS almost abandoned the recording of art music,
except for some standard repertoire done by artists exciting
immediate and intense interest. Contracts with major American
performing groups were canceled. If a recording of an art
work were desired, companies found it cheaper to engage a
foreign ensemble, since wage scales and other production costs
were much lower than they were in America. Curiously, the
promotion of what art music they still had on recordings became nil. American workmanship grew slipshod and the quality of the recorded sound deteriorated. (Columbia's Michael
Kellman states: "There's a limit to how much attention a
profit-making corporation, that must answer to stockholders,
is going to spend on something that is only 5% of their business.") Not surprisingly, the number of retail outlets offering such music for sale shrank. Nor did the retail outlets
that continued in business desire to carry a title longer than
a few months before remaindering it, a policy that valued
quick turnover and failed to take into account the longer time
period during which art-music albums were sold.[66]

RCA Red Seal's Vice President, Thomas Shepard, sums
up the attitude of the record industry at the beginning of
the eighties.   He says that for record companies, art has to
turn into "an attempt at commerce."   Salesman tout "a piece
of product" to retail stores not concerned with art.   The bottom line for a profit-oriented record company, like RCA, was
"can this piece of product sell through?"   One recording ses-
sion for an orchestra costs around $15,000.   Two or three
sessions are generally necessary to do an album, at a cost of
$45,000.   Engineering, studio use, travel, and paying a con-
ductor can add $20,000 more.   Just to get a return, at one-
dollar profit per record, requires the sale of 65,000 recordings.   "But the likelihood is that it will sell a minimum of
3,000 and a general maximum, let's say, of 25,000.   If you
really have something terrific and you sell 35,000 to 50,000,
in classical terms you've got a hit."   An album by a Rampal
and Bolling might sell several hundred thousand copies.   However, the reality was that normally a company had to look at
a loss.[67]

By default, what few recordings of American performers
were made came usually through the efforts of European companies.   Deutsche Gramophon was soon recording both the
Boston Symphony and the Chicago Orchestra; Philips, the
San Francisco Symphony; London, the Detroit and Cleveland
orchestras.   Successful as had been the Boston Camerata while
with Turnabout and Nonesuch, the group had to eventually
resort to European companies, which in the eighties were "far
more likely to issue the group's discs than" were "the hard-
pressed (and unimaginative) American companies, with the
paradoxical result that the Camerata today sells more records
in Europe than in America."[68]

No strong desire to record American ensembles existed.
By the eighties, the preponderance of art-music recordings
offered for sale on the American market were being produced
by non-American firms and featured the performances of foreign musicians.

As for recorded music by American composers, it had
never figured largely in the catalogues of RCA and CBS.
Guided by Goddard Lieberson, CBS for a while did shake off
its lethargy and record a respectable number of contemporary
American works.   Regrettably, the mid-seventies brought an
end to this activity.   These CBS recordings nothwithstanding,

American music has had to depend on smaller, more specialized companies for recorded representation. More often than not, private and public grants have subsidized the recordings.

During the fifties and sixties, especially, the Louisville Orchestra, directed by Robert Whitney and Jorge Mester and aided principally by the Rockefeller Foundation, was able to commission and record new American works, issued on its own label. Nonesuch Records, under the leadership of Teresa Sterne, engaged in similar activity, until Ms. Sterne was dismissed by the cost-conscious parent firm, Warner Communications. To Karl Krueger and the Society for the Preservation of the American Musical Heritage, which he founded in 1958, we owe a spate of recordings of compositions from the American past.

Oliver Daniel, Otto Luening, and Douglas Moore founded the non-profit Composers Recordings, Inc., in 1954. By the end of 1984, the CRI label had been responsible for around 500 recordings, containing over 1500 works by more than 600 composers born after 1910.[69] New World Records began life in 1976 with money from the Rockefeller Foundation, its purpose being to put together an anthology of American music, in all its varieties, then to distribute it without charge to various cultural and educational institutions, American and foreign. New World Records has continued with annual releases of newly recorded productions of American compositions.

Some individual composers and composers' groups have formed their own firms. Since 1963, for example, Alan Hovhaness has issued his own music under the Poseidon label. Minni Johnson, wife of Robert Ashley, started Lovely Music in 1977 in order to record the compositions of her husband and those of a few likeminded composers, among them Pauline Oliveros, David Tudor, and Roger Reynolds. Northeastern Records commenced as a showcase for Northeastern University's own faculty and students but was soon paying attention to American composers, particularly those from the Boston area. In 1983, one of its directors, Lynn Joiner was quoted as saying: "There's no point in our going up against major labels doing major repertory. We are interested in filling in the nooks and crannies in the catalogue, in seeking out exciting music from all periods, with a special focus on Americana, and particularly on New England."[70]

David Moore has written in praise of specialist companies
who serve "the cause of specific composers, genres, styles,
and repertoire that would not be covered in such depth by a
more commercial or state-supported enterprise." He cites
"such projects as Leonarda's coverage of women composers,
Opus One's collection of maverick American composers, and
Painted Smiles's concentration on little-known show songs....
Not least among the specialist group is Paul Kapp's Serenus,
which not only records but publishes music by those composers in whom Kapp has confidence."[71]

Many of these smaller companies are shoestring operations kept alive through the dedication of a few individuals
and the off-and-on financial aid of a few donors. Their modest budgets limit staff support and the ability to advertise.
Record reviews in magazines must alert the public to their
offerings. Because hardly any retail outlets carry their recordings, they usually depend on mail-order sales to sustain
them. Their contribution to our awareness of America's musical riches has been of inestimable value.

ANCILLARY MUSICAL ENTERPRISES:
RADIO AND TELEVISION

American commercial AM radio stations did broadcast
recorded art music during the thirties and forties, but reluctantly and desultorily. Regrettable to say, a great deal
of whatever art-music programming existed was the result of
a need to convince the federal government that because radio
stations gave the appearance of operating for the public good,
they deserved broadcasting licenses. Some commitment to live
performances over the air was also evident, especially as
heard in the weekly concerts of the New York Philharmonic.
The NBC network, the CBS network, and station WOR even
boasted in-house orchestras.[72]

After the war came two major developments, television
and FM broadcasting. The commercial broadcasting networks
now neglected radio and drastically reduced their efforts on
behalf of art music in order to exploit the mass-market possibilities of television. This meant the winning over of as large
a viewing audience as possible, since popularity ratings determined advertising revenues. Around the same time, the
Federal Communications Commission increased the number of

radio frequencies available for broadcast and permitted a proliferation of new stations, large numbers of them local, uncon-
nected with the national networks, and thus responsible for
their own programming. At the onset of the seventies, about
750 TV stations, 4250 AM stations, and 2000 FM stations were
in operation. Because frequency modulation allowed decreased
ambient noise and musical distortion when compared with am-
plitude modulation, FM broadcasting became the favored means
for sending art music over the airwaves.

In the mid-sixties, the Carnegie Commission on Educational Television called for the creation of a Corporation for
Public Television. Soon, radio was added to the proposal.
The call was answered in 1968, when the non-profit Corporation for Public Broadcasting began life, in order to counterbalance the trend toward greater commercialization, with the
creation of totally public-oriented broadcasting stations. Over
200 of them had come into existence by 1972. National Public
Radio was incorporated in 1969 to acquire, produce, and distribute art-music and other non-commercial programming to
member stations. Higher-education institutions and some city
governments established their own FM stations. In addition,
there appeared a new phenomenon--the commercial FM station
with programming devoted to art music. Such stations were
not costly to start-up and maintain and required less staff
than did television stations. An FM broadcaster could readily
define the local interest in the specialties offered, and listeners knew what to expect when they tuned in. A surprising
amount of loyalty from art-music audiences for favorite stations resulted.

At the close of the seventies, of the 900 odd radio stations broadcasting art music, 45 percent were commercial stations. Most of the music broadcast was in the form of recordings. However, because of the improvement in the quality of
taped music, from 15 to 25 percent of airtime was given over
to live-on-tape concert and operatic performances.[73] By the
eighties, New York's stations WNCN and WQXR, who played
art music all day and night, estimated their combined listenership averaged 85,000 for any given hour. When the Metropolitan Opera performances were sent over the air nationally,
around seven million opera lovers at a time usually tuned in.[74]
These were dazzlingly large numbers of listeners when compared with the thousand or two men and women who could attend a sold-out performance of the same music.

The large quantities of art music aired by FM stations, however, did not always lead to constantly varied and adventurous programming. The managers of these stations mostly chose not to lead but to follow general taste. Educating their listeners or exposing them to unfamiliar or potentially offensive music was not accepted as part of their mandate. Even those station managers who spoke in favor of education and of programming less familiar repertoire usually neglected to replace words with deeds. Especially neglected were all American compositions and those 20th-century European works composed in posttriadic idioms, despite the fact that much of this music was available in one or another recorded format. Featured were the select works of the past that paralleled the programming of most established performing groups and soloists.

Moreover, music lovers could rarely tell beforehand what titles were scheduled for broadcast. Sunday newspapers in the largest cities gave sketchy summaries of the following week's offerings, provided the stations volunteered copy. With some stations, one had to subscribe to a national magazine (for example, Ovation) in order to be informed of scheduled broadcasts (the information usually bound up with the magazine). Other stations insisted on a minimal "voluntary" contribution before they would send out information on what they intended to play. Often programs were changed without warning or a general statements, like "Concert by the Boston Symphony," helped to lower expectations. Also, the music lover had to grow accustomed to irritating advertisements, if tuned in to a commercial station, or to the suspension of programming in order to solicit funds, if tuned in to a non-profit station. These were not actions calculated to increase listenership.[75]

In the summer of 1978, representatives of around sixty stations, half of them non-profit broadcasters, met for a Music Personnel Conference. The men and women in attendance at the conference admitted to their timid programming, explaining that they feared to alienate their listeners. American composers attending the conference insisted that listeners had greater curiosity and openmindedness than was credited to them. Suggested was a station's featuring the works of local and visiting composers. The composer Joan La Barbara remarked: "I can only suggest that for each irate new music hater there must be ten people starving for information about

what is happening now, what kind of music is being produced
by our culture, affected by present day politics and civilization."[76] Few stations elected to prove or disprove her statement.

In many instances, boldness in musical offerings only
meant scheduling untried or unusual music in time periods
when most listeners might not be tuned in--late at night, very
early in the morning, or at best in a slack daylight hour. In
its May 1979 issue, Musical America published a letter from
Katie Sloan, Program and Music Director of the University of
Oregon's Station KWAX-FM. She complained of radio's endemic
"ghetto-izing" of music. Her former station manager, for example, had allowed her to schedule 20th-century music only
after 10 p.m., never as part of the station's main programming. Fortunately, she now could present two new-music
programs, each of them one-hour long. Yes, she did get some
complaints. In the normal run of things, such complaints
were impossible to avoid, she insisted, and did not typify
most listeners' attitudes.

In 1982, John Beck, director of New York City's WNYC-
FM, made a major commitment to programming twentieth-century
music, although much of it was not of the extreme, avant-
garde type. Two-thirds of the mix consisted of accessible,
one-third of difficult, music. No formal announcement of the
new policy was made, since he expected that the phrase "20th-
century music" could "create palpitations in the heart of the
most stalwart classical music lover, curable only by a swift
turn of the dial." The average listener, Beck claimed, thought
of "20th-century music in terms of difficult-sounding pieces."
This problem was perceptual: "There's an enormous repertory
of other things--by Samuel Barber, Walter Piston, Peter Mennin, Leonard Bernstein, just to start a long list--that are well
worth hearing. But these works, many of which are gracious,
approachable and simply beautiful, have been lost because of
the chasm of alienation between composers and listeners. Somebody has got to take the initiative in order to change people's
perceptions." When WNYC first tested the receptivity to modern music, in 1981, with Tim Page's daily afternoon program,
a great deal of negative reaction was expected. Predictably,
the station's programming was criticized, depending on the
critic's point-of-view, as overly conservative, far-out, eclectic,
or narrow. The management of WNYC was ready to "move back
if there really" was not "an audience." Nevertheless, the program "quickly became reasonably popular."[77]

The growth of television was phenomenal during the postwar period--from 1946, when only around 7,000 black-and-white sets were in American homes, to the 1980s, when virtually every home possessed one or more sets, most of them with color. Television stations were expensive to operate; therefore the percentage that were non-profit and operating solely in the public interest remained extremely low. Commercial stations, a majority of them linked to powerful national networks (like NBC, CBS, and ABC) dominated the field. A pernicious ratings system constantly sampled and responded to mass preferences in entertainment, with little consideration given to the cultural tastes of America's several minorities, some of them sizeable ones. Art music, save for that heard in staged opera and dance, did not lend itself to video presentation, unless a visually sensational element was involved in the performance. Besides, the minority, however educated or affluent, that would watch art-music performances insured a loss of advertising revenue, since such monies went to the programs delivering the largest possible number of viewers. Put on the Chicago Symphony or the Juilliard Quartet and the Neilsen popularity rating plummeted; put on a segment of a sexually suggestive and violent crime series and the rating soared, so said one complainant.

In the sixties and seventies, observers of the American cultural scene grew pessimistic about American taste as represetned on television. Broadcasters insisted that the blame for the low quality of television shows lay not with them but the public. Programs had to be of inferior character because public taste and public interest were so degraded. "If education, parents, the government, intellectuals, and critics would do their job better, broadcasting would soon be fine," they explained.

Some critics decided that television only reflected what was wrong with American society: "The notion that anything goes for a fast buck, tolerance and enjoyment of brutality gratuitously thrown on the screen, non-think--these and like characteristics are not peculiar to television, for all that it aids and abets them. They are part of the temper of the people."[78] The view that "anyone who would bother to listen to TV music was a moron" did not faze Steven Gottlieb when he produced the recorded album of "Television's Greatest Hits," 65 theme songs aired between 1947 and 1986. "It reeks of television," Gottlieb said. People in 1986 would love the

album not just because of nostalgia but because the music was
"emotive" and the themes were designed to be "hooks," that
is to say addictive.[79]

Culture is thought to be stuffy, said Claus Adams,
cellist of the Juilliard Quartet, in 1972. Although he spoke
of a growing interest in chamber music amongst students at
colleges and universities, evident in recent tours of the quartet, television people refused to believe him: "On a recent
television talk show, the two selections we were asked to play
were cut to one. Then we were not interviewed for fear we
might not have anything to say. Possibly someone in the television audience might switch the dial."[80] Obviously, the musical artist was granted low status and regarded as having
passing interest for television viewers, who inhabited not the
arty but the "real" world.

As early as 1965, Harry Skornia was warning that television people could easily "rig it" to prove that the public did
not want cultural programming. Put the New York Philharmonic, for example, in a poor time slot and of course ratings
would drop. He distrusted the ratings system anyway. A
high number of viewers refused to be polled. Other viewers
were excluded from polls because they were considered "too
highbrow" and their preferences would "distort" the figures.
The problem with giving the public what it wants is that nobody could be sure of what it wants, he said. Moreover, the
public is not an entity but made up of many disparate house-
holds. No accurate or clear method for ascertaining its wants
existed and no one inquired about the public's needs.

"Ratings," he continued, "tend to equate wholly different forms: slapstick and religion, sacred music and singing
commercials, madonnas and bathing beauties. All are lumped
together. Instead of lifting people to the level of art, art is
lowered and vulgarized to the supposed level of the mob--the
digits revealed by ratings. Yet this process does not reflect
what people want. No one person has such homogenized
tastes. The American seems to be becoming more unable to
demonstrate the individuality which democracy requires."[81]

Demonstrable problems affecting television transmission
of art music included the poor sound sent over the airwaves,
sound which was further degraded by the inferior amplifiers
and speakers in the television sets manufactured during the

years under discussion, only partly compensated by simultan-
eous broadcast over FM. It discouraged the most serious music lovers, unless they were willing, in the eighties, to spend
extra hundreds of dollars for high-fidelity stereo t.v. sets from
taking advantage of the new trend toward stereo broadcasting. In addition, though a large minority numbering in the
millions, the middle-class television audience for art music,
on the whole, was not as ardently interested in the form as
was the audience taking the trouble to attend performances.
How did one immediately engage viewers attention so that the
program would not be flicked off? Opera on television undoubtedly had a built in advantage, compared to other kinds
of televised musical performance. Opera companies were
scarce in America; tickets for entry, expensive. Televised
opera was free; the visual experience of scenery, costumes,
and stage action could be captivating. Concerts given by a
photogenic personality like Leonard Bernstein conducting the
New York Philharmonic or the Vienna Philharmonic did also
succeed. Excellent examples are provided by his Omnibus
telecasts of 1954-1955, during which he lectured on music,
showed how a composer went about structuring a work, then
conducted the composition under consideration. On the other
hand, scores of televised concerts given by other fine conductors leading excellent orchestras failed.[82]

The camera might stay in one position for an entire
concert, but where so as to prevent boredom? Or it might
float from orchestra, to individual players, to conductor, and
to audience. This discarding of a viewpoint from a particular
seat in a particular row was not correlated to the volume and
direction of sound, which remained the same, resulting in dis-
crepancies between what one saw and heard. Or it might resort to visuals external to the concert itself. If done with
care and taste, this last could be effective.

Each approach contained a danger. In 1983, Donal Henahan, of the New York Times, wrote that during his thirty
years of viewing, no television concert had really excited him.
Nor had it excited viewers whose letters he had received.
For example, a Washington viewer, Steven Herman, wrote to
him after watching Mehta and the New York Philharmonic perform Beethoven's Ninth Symphony, saying: "The emphasis of
the TV show was clearly not on giving the people in their
homes an opportunity to attend the concert and enjoy Beethoven's great symphony. Rather, the emphasis was singlemindedly and obsessively revealed to be the conductor and

showing off how many camera angles they could find and use
on the stage of Avery Fisher Hall. Thus, here was Mehta
smiling; here was Mehta being gripping; here was Mehta being intense; and most of all here was Mehta sweating. There
were more closeups of Zubin Mehta during this performance
than of Bergman and Bogart in all of 'Casablanca.'... Jump,
zoom, and then jump again. God forbid that the camera might
just stay still for a while. I finally closed my eyes. Next
time I will have the TV set off."[83]

    Art music in television broadcast need not prove boring.
Around 1960 I had charge of an unsponsored weekly program
on a Springfield, Mass., commercial station. Involved was my
selecting and playing of art-music recordings after introductory remarks. Visuals were employed constantly. Projections
of the record jacket with title and graphic, dancing, movie
clips, paintings, literary quotations, photographs, etc. accompanied the sound if suitable. However, every camera shot
was planned to be a visual illustration of musical meaning,
placed on screen in order to bring home the composition to
the viewer. Changes in camera shots took place in appropriate divisions of the music--sectional divisions and movements
--and in a thought-out and carefully timed sequence, always
aimed at adding further meaning to the auditory experience.
The program became popular. Record stores, especially
around Christmas, reported that they were selling out of the
music played on the program and requested advance warning
of what would be done next. Yet, no sponsorship of the program ensued. Since I was appearing gratis and the hours con-
sumed in preparation were many, I eventually ceased hosting
the program. Yet, the lesson to be learned is that given
serious thought and a preparation of visuals in harmony with
the musical composition (not just a registration of a conductor's facial joy and agony, or couples mooning to the sounds
of the "Moonlight Sonata") a great deal more can be done to
enhance television viewing.

    Nonprofit public television broadcasts almost all of what-
ever art-music viewing is available. Unfortunately for music
lovers, programs are few, variety is limited, and budgeting
is constrained. The Public Broadcasting Service tends to
feature famous musicians and musical organizations and the
best loved compositions. These are expected to draw a larger
audience than would be possible with unknown performers and
untested works. Nor has cable television developed into an

exciting alternative for music lovers. Several ambitious plans
for commercial cultural-cable television have failed to materialize, owing to unventuresome account executives and to advertisers whose narrow thinking let them pass by "an upscale
audience at bargain rates." A prime instance is furnished by
the demise of the CBS Cultural Cable in 1982. A couple of
small arts-cable networks (notably Arts & Entertainment, and
BRAVO) continue to operate, although they find it difficult
to turn a profit. BRAVO started as a modest pay-service
network operating on two nights a week, but gained only
60,000 subscribers. It later got satellite time and began to
broadcast seven nights a week. Advertising was avoided.
Robert Weisberg, the director of programming, said, in 1983,
that BRAVO produced 90 percent of its own TV shows, though
most of them were projects entailing minimal expense. There
was hope for turning the profit corner, as the number of subscribers grew. Interestingly, Weisberg said: "Our subscribers want music. We took a poll, and that's what they asked
for."[84] A continuing headache for cultural-cable networks is
the small mindedness of profit-hungry local cable transmitting
systems. For example, in order for a Bostonian to subscribe
to BRAVO, it must be bought from Cablevision of Boston, as
part of an expensive monthly package which includes rock-
music, sports, religious, stock market, "life style," and minority or foreign language channels.

A few motion pictures featuring art music have succeeded in attracting both the art-music and the movie-going
public. This was true for the Ingmar Bergman production
of the Mozart opera The Magic Flute, in 1974, which was shot
for Swedish TV and employed Swedish singers. To a lesser
degree, it was also true for Francesco Rosi's cinematically in-
ept production of Bizet's Carmen, in 1984, which featured
Julia Migenes Johnson and Plácido Domingo in the leading
roles. Contemporary with the Carmen picture was Amadeus,
a thoroughly enjoyable but fictional narration of Mozart's relationship to Salieri, which included a great deal of Mozart's
music. This motion picture drew huge audiences. The Amadeus soundtrack was a bestseller for months. What is more
significant, a large increase in the sale of recordings featuring Mozart's compositions was also noted.

An eighties development is the sudden immense growth
in the sale of home video cassette recorders and the availability of video cassettes for rental or purchase. The art-music

cassettes contain mostly operas (a majority by Verdi and Puccini), but they also include ballets, and concerts performed by internationally known singers, instrumentalists, and dancers. Not many such cassettes are available. In addition, the quality of the sound remains a major problem. Possibly video recordings with digital sound tracked by laser beam will correct the problem, provided the cost of these recordings is brought down to an affordable level. The number of customers for these video recordings might well increase dramatically.

Notes

1. Dorian, Commitment to Culture, pp. 464-465.
2. Suzi Gablik, Has Modernism Failed? (New York: Thames & Hudson, 1984), pp. 66-68.
3. Peter R. Kermani, in Symphony Magazine (October/November, 1982), pp. 11-12.
4. Leinsdorf, Cadenza, p. 118.
5. Ernest Fleischmann, "Who Runs Our Orchestras and Who Should?" High Fidelity (January 1969), p. 59. Also see, Robert L. Caulfield, "The Qualities of Leadership," Symphony Magazine (August/September 1982), p. 52.
6. Chapin, Musical Chairs, pp. 172-173.
7. See the Music Journal (July 1977), p. 54; Richard Dyer, "At Last--Druian's Boston 'Debut,'" Boston Globe, 17 January 1986, p. 42. Also see, Scott, The States and the Arts, p. 95; George Rochberg, "Contemporary Music in an Affluent Society," Music Journal (February 1968), p. 72; Cook, "Penderecki: The Polish Question--and Others!" Music Journal (February 1977), pp. 8-9.
8. The entire controversy is described by Theodore Price, in Musical America (January 1973), pp. 14-15, 28.
9. For example, see John Rockwell, in the New York Times, 18 November 1979, section 2, pp. 1, 23.
10. Howard Hanson, "A Plea for the Arts," Music Journal (November 1963), p. 25; Tassel, "Pros and Concerts," pp. 113-114; Ralph Black, in Symphony News (April 1979), p. 4; Ralph Black, "The Board Meeting: What's On the Agenda?" Symphony Magazine (June/July 1984), p. 120.
11. Toffler, The Culture Consumers, p. 63; Dickson, "Gentlemen, More Dolce Please!", p. 38. Later in the chapter, the cause célèbre of the spring of 1982, involving the board and management of the Boston Symphony Orchestra versus Vanessa Redgrave, will be discussed.

12. Edward Avian, "The San Diego Symphony Turn-around," Symphony Magazine (June/July 1984), p. 143.

13. Leinsdorf, Cadenza, p. 192; Margo Miller, "Marquee," Boston Globe, 5 January 1986, section B, p. 7.

14. Richard Dyer, "Bruce Crawford Knows He Can Manage the Met," Boston Globe, 28 October 1984, section A, p. 11.

15. Unsigned news item, New York Times, 28 October 1984, p. 20; Margo Miller, "BSO Official: Redgrave Juror Raised Safety Issue," Boston Globe, 3 November 1984, p. 21; Jerry Taylor, "Dershowitz, B'nai B'rith Hail Redgrave Decision," Boston Globe, 10 November 1984, p. 16; Margo Miller, "Redgrave Awarded $100,000 In Suit Against the BSO," Boston Globe, 10 November 1984, pp. 1, 16; "Arts and Politics," editorial, Boston Globe, 10 November 1984, p. 18; Margo Miller, "Jurors Say Her Politics Got Redgrave Fired," Boston Globe, 21 December 1984, p. 17.

16. Chasins, Music at the Crossroads, p. 115.

17. Hilde Somer, "The Market for Modern Music," Music Journal (January 1961), p. 32; Temianka, Facing the Music, pp. 214-215; Bernard Holland, "Let There Be Music--But Don't Forget the Fee," New York Times, 8 April 1984, section 2, pp. 1, 34.

18. Barbara Jepson, "How Musicians and Managers Coexist," New York Times, 18 July 1982, seciton 2, p. 17. Also see, Sills, Bubbles, pp. 71-72.

19. Alvin Toffler, "The Politics of the Impossible--Art and Society," in A Great Society?, ed. Bertram M. Gross (New York: Basic Books, 1968), pp. 254-256.

20. Ibid., p. 257. Five book giving insights into the psychology of music are Percy C. Buck, Psychology For Musicians (London: Oxford University Press, 1944); Paul R. Farnsworth, The Social Psychology fo Music (New York: Dryden, 1958); Robert W. Lundin, An Objective Psychology of Music, 2nd ed. (New York: Ronald, 1967); Hans and Shulamith Kreitler, Psychology of the Arts (Durham, N.C.: Duke University Press, 1972); John Booth Davies, The Psychology of Music (Stanford, Calif.: Stanford University Press, 1978).

21. Toffler, "The Politics of the Impossible," pp. 267-268.

22. Gary O. Larson, The Reluctant Patron: The United States Government and the Arts, 1943-1965 (Philadelphia: University of Pennsylvania Press, 1983), p. 6.

23. Baumol and Bowen, Performing Arts, pp. 3, 161, 144, 197-198; Herbert Roussel, The Houston Symphony Orchestra (Austin: University of Texas Press, 1972), p. 154; Netzer

The Susidized Muse, pp. 122-123; Frederick Winship, "45% of Nation's Opera Companies Report Red Ink," Boston Globe, 3 November 1984, p. 11.

24. Baumol and Bowen, Performing Arts, pp. 172, 175, 282; Ralph Black, in Symphony Magazine (February/March 1983), p. 34.

25. Linda K. Gallehugh, "Singing a New Song," Horizon (July/August 1983, pp. 49-50; Martin Bookspan, "Who Pays the Piper?" Ovations (February 1983), p. 36; Guido G. Salmaggi, "So You Want to be an Impressario?" Music Journal (March 1963), p. 48.

26. See, for instance, the reporting on such events in Ovation (July 1984), p. 7, and (October 1984), p. 10; also, the newsletter of the Boston Symphony Orchestra (Fall 1984).

27. The incident is described in Musical America (April 1953), p. 14.

28. Bernard Taper, The Arts in Boston (Cambridge: Harvard University Press, 1970), pp. 62-63.

29. Horizons (January/February 1982), p. 26; Baumol and Bowen, Performing Arts, pp. 308, 312.

30. Eugene Ormandy, in the Music Journal (April 1961), p. 12.

31. Robert K. Guthrie, "The Financial Crisis in Classical Music," Ovation (February 1982), p. 17; Sandra Salmans, "Big Business Tightens Its Arts Budget," New York Times, 20 February 1983, section 2, p. 27.

32. Waleson, "Paying the Piper," pp. 17, 19-21.

33. Salmans, "Big Business Tightens Its Arts Budget," pp. 7, 27.

34. Taper, The Arts in Boston, pp. 84-85.

35. Brustein, The Culture Watch, p. 162.

36. Bookspan, "Who Pays the Piper?", p. 19; Baumol and Bowen, Performing Arts, pp. 342-343.

37. See the Music Journal (January 1964), p. 4.

38. Goldin, The Music Merchants, pp. 201-202.

39. Bookspan, "Who Pays the Piper?", p. 19.

40. Unsigned news item, "Some Practical Aid for the Arts," New York Times, 31 July 1983, section 4, p. 7.

41. Quoted in Quaintance Eaton, "The Year on Legislation," Music Journal Annual (1963), p. 58.

42. Taper, The Arts in Boston, p. 16; Larson, The Reluctant Patron, p. 49.

43. Richard Hoggart, "Culture and Its Ministers," in Art, Politics, and Will, ed. Quentin Anderson, et al., (New York: Basic Books, 1977), pp. 191-212.

44. For information on the WPA Four Arts Project, please see Nicholas E. Tawa, Serenading the Reluctant Eagle: American Musical Life, 1925-1945 (New York: Schirmer, 1984), pp. 106-119.

45. Larson, The Reluctant Patron, pp. 1-3; also see, Netzer, The Subsidized Muse, p. 57.

46. Karen Monson, "The Anchorage Civic Opera," Musical America (March 1981), p. 36.

47. Netzer, The Subsidized Muse, p. 91.

48. Scott, The States and the Arts, pp. 14-15.

49. Charles B. Fowler, "On Education," Musical America (June 1979), pp. 14-15.

50. Nancy van de Vate, "The National Endowment: Playing Favorites," Musical America (April 1976), pp. 14-16.

51. Walter Goodman, "In Search of a Policy for Arts Funding," New York Times, 22 July 1984, section 2, p. 24.

52. Robert Pear, "Reagan's Arts Chairman," New York Times, 10 April 1983, section 2, p. 26.

53. Patrick J. Smith, "Music Book Publication--A Vicious Circle," Musical America (October 1968), p. 12.

54. Ibid., pp. 12-13.

55. Rudolph Tauhert, "Publishers Cater to Needs," Music Journal (September 1966), p. 33.

56. Dictionary of Contemporary Music, ed. John Vinton, s.v. "Publishing."

57. James Chute, "Publish or Perish?" Musical America (January 1982), p. 18.

58. Allan Kozinn, "The American Composers Orchestra," Symphony Magazine (June/July 1983), p. 24.

59. Gagne and Caras, Soundpieces, pp. 222-223.

60. Chute, "Publish or Perish?." p. 19.

61. Gagne and Caras, Soundpieces, p. 373.

62. Harold C. Schonberg, "A Critic Reflects on 44 Years in the Business," New York Times, 6 July 1980, section 2, p. 13.

63. Roy McMullen, Art, Affluence, and Alienation: The Fine Arts Today (New York: Praeger, 1968), p. 43.

64. Allan Kozinn, "Composers Recordings, Inc.-- Surprising Survivor," High Fidelity (September 1979), p. 79; Lipman, Music After Modernism, p. 213. Also see, Greckel, "Music Misses the Majority," p. 20; Furlong, "Season with Solti," p. 253.

65. "Orchestras and Recording: A Panel," Fanfare (January/February 1981), p. 34.

66. Allan Kozinn, "Record Quality 1978," Music Journal

(March 1978), pp. 9-10; Byron Belt, "For the Record," Music Journal (October 1976), p. 6; John Clark, "The Year in Records," Music Journal Annual (1962), p. 56.

67. "Orchestras and Recordings," pp. 24-25.

68. Dyer, "Keeping Times," p. 62.

69. David Sachs, "CRI at 30," Fanfare (September/ October 1984), p. 146; Kozinn, "Composers Recordings, Inc.," pp. 79-80; Joan La Barbara, "CRI's Historic Thirty Years," Musical America (September 1985), p. 17.

70. Richard Dyer, in the Boston Globe, 2 March 1983, p. 60.

71. David Moore, review of Serenus SRS 12092, in American Record Guide (January/February 1982), pp. 22-23.

72. Nicholas E. Tawa, Serenading the Reluctant Eagle: American Musical Life, 1925-1945, pp. 92-98, has more to say on this subject.

73. Per-Lee, Myra, "Broadcasting--Orchestras On the Air," Symphony News (June 1979), pp. 21-22. Also see p. 12, in the same issue.

74. Kozinn, "Composers Recordings, Inc.," p. 79; Cardiss Collins, letter in Symphony Magazine (December 1983), p. 12.

75. I am aware of all these practices in the Boston listening area; Nicholas Kenyon writes of them in the New York City area--see, "Musical Events: Puzzles," in the New Yorker, 15 February 1982, pp. 120-123.

76. A report on the conference, written by Joan La Barbara, is given in Musical America (November 1978), pp. 13, 40.

77. Linda Sanders, "When a Classical Station Goes Modern," New York Times, 13 February 1983, section 2, pp. 33, 41.

78. See, respectively, Harry J. Skornia, Television and Society (New York: McGraw-Hill, 1965), pp. 56-57; Charles A. Siepmann, in Pop Culture in America, ed. David Manning White, pp. 79-80.

79. Nathan Cobb, "Television Music," Boston Globe, 7 February 1986, pp. 71, 73.

80. Patricia Tregellas, "The Arts Are Polluted," Music Journal (October 1972), p. 23.

81. Skornia, Television and Society, pp. 57, 121, 137, 163.

82. "Orchestras and Recording," p. 26; John J. O'Connor, "Strike Up the Band (and other Chamber Group)," New

York Times, 25 April 1971, section 2, p. 15; Ed Seigel,
Adapting Stage Events to Television," Boston Globe, 24 April
1983, p. B 33; Netzer, The Subsidized Muse, p. 158.

    83. Donal Henahan, "Must Symphony Concerts and
Television Be Incompatible?" New York Times, 20 February
1983, section 2, p. 21.

    84. Jack Heimenz, "The Death of CBS Cable, and
Other Ills," Musical America (February 1983), pp. 11-12; also
see, Donald Pash, "What's Wrong with Public Broadcasting?"
Musical America (October 1977), p. 19.

Chapter 7

A SUMMING UP

The conditions that art music must face in the late
twentieth century are not the same as those of the earlier
decades. The roles, traditions, and sources of power of music associations have changed and are no longer as clearcut
as before. Issues like the rights of women and minorities
have demanded resolution and cast doubt on the ways of established cultural institutions. Prominent men and women of
wealth and education, and those with respectable scholarly or
artistic credentials no longer command the respect of yester-
year, when they speak about the superiority of high culture.
The old hierarchy of aesthetic values, the deference to wisdom dispensed by musical authorities on the artistic verities,
and the greater willingness to look outside one's self rather
than concentrate on the inner self for musical meaning are
things of the past.

As former certainties about the worth of art music have
crumbled, so also have the guidelines on the proper patterns
of behavior for audiences. There is every description of music lover today, whose taste may be narrow or cosmopolitan,
who may attend public music performances or stay home with
recordings, FM broadcasts, and cultural-television presentations. His or her role vis-a-vis music is one increasingly
carved out for oneself with no obeisance to tradition or the
strictures of "the wise and wellborn."

Symphony orchestras and opera companies find it more
difficult to win the uncritical backing of the men and women
who live in their communities and sit in their halls. Elitist
thinking is out, and with it the ability to browbeat the public. The public's freedom to select between musical alternatives without deference to any standard has also produced
some confusion, especially when a person feels the experience

is lacking to help reach decisions. Opting out of listening altogether is the solution of some; a magnetic musical personality to lead the way is the solution of others; continuously sampling now art, now rock or folk or ancient or contemporary is another solution. Many individuals, of course, decide to stay with the old certainties and continue along the trail blazed by previous generations of music lovers. Contrasting with them is the lesser number of American who seek radically new experiences in avant-garde idioms.

In short, there is endless variety in the American music scene. Since the 1970s, Americans have learned to recognize the legitimacy of diverse cultural expressions. They have also learned to abstain from a value system that measures "high art" against "popular art" and "folk art." The desire is to lower the barriers between different types of cultural expression. Indeed, art music thereby could benefit through an infusion of fresh ideas and a renewed vitality.

In previous pages, I have maintained that although art music plays a small role in America's total life, it has been granted serious consideration in the national scheme of things, if only because a minority numbering several millions of people, among them our more respected citizens, give it a major place in their lives. On the other hand, most Americans, rich or poor and formally educated or ignorant, have had little exposure to and demonstrate a negative reaction against it. This considerably limits cultural horizons, especially in a direction where some of the accumulated aesthetic insights of centuries reside. Beethoven's Ninth Symphony, Ives's "Concord" Sonata, and Barber's Knoxville, Summer of 1915 do have a place in American civilization.

A permanent aim of our democracy is the enhancement of the lives of its citizenry. To help accomplish this enhancement, art music must somehow become generally recognized as important to American society. This is not to be taken as meaning that the democratization of art music necessitates compromise in its integrity. It does, however, mean that the men and women who write music, perform it, and guide its fortunes must be sensitive to the workings of the American governmental system by providing an increase in viable cultural alternatives which are potentially of interest to every American. The many may continue to appreciate only what they already know. That is their right. But the effort is

worthwhile for the smaller number who discover aesthetic outlets which otherwise they might have been denied.

Still an art with few adherents in the total population,
the music of concert hall and opera house contends for a
place in the sun during a highly sophisticated technological
era that puts a premium on the efficient exploitation of the
greatest possible number of people and that denies recognition to "high art's" claim of qualitative supremacy. I do not
wish to argue that art music should supplant all other musics.
That argument cannot be sustained in a democracy. I do
suggest that art music is at least of equal value as other cultural expressions and does require help if the workings of
the marketplace act to wipe it out and if music lovers with
low incomes cannot afford to pay admission to hear it.

In the late-twentieth century, art music continues to
merit public and private support in order to afford people the
opportunity to decide between different modes of cultural expression in an American society that increasingly limits the
availability of varied cultural manifestations to its members--
whether owing to upbringing, educational default, high ticket
prices, inaccessible live performances, or, of most consequence,
the homogenizing action of an entertainment industry, which
tries to attract more and more people with less and less goods
of different character. We must be cautious, however, in
placing blame. This industry's prime objective cannot be to
propagate high culture, particularly if business losses result.

At the same time, the questions that William Truitt
raises have to be dealt with. "Indeed, he asks, "what is
democratic about our society?" He continues: "Production
and consumption? No. Access to the means of communication? No. Knowledge? No. Employment? No. Education?
No. Access to our shared cultural heritage? No."[1] We
should strive to make these Nos over to Yeses.

It is true that humans can lead satisfactory lives not
knowing a thing about art music. But surely this argument
is beside the point. Several respected European and American aestheticians, philosophers, psychologists, and cultural
historians have reached similar conclusions about the role of
music in human life. Throughout the history of mankind,
they have stated, music has been not only assiduously cultivated but also an effective means for achieving intellectual

and emotional balance within one's self and with one's environment. It has aided in resolving inner turmoil. It has
also been a favored medium for expressing the profound link-
age between the self and the outer world, thus fulfilling a
most basic need. In short, they have said, the proposition
is false that holds humans seek only music that diverts,
amuses, and offers escape. Art music does entertain, but it
is also meant to elevate and educate--that is to say, it means
to evoke our better selves and assist in our psychological and
aesthetic development.[2]

We must therefore show concern when conditions in the
United States threaten to produce a musical culture more
limited than what is expected from and required in a society
theoretically composed of free spirits. That culturally speaking America is less than what it might be has been a prominent
theme of all the chapters in this book.

The American is born neither a Hobbesian self-seeker
nor a Rousseauian straight shooter but circumstances make
them so. This is a central argument of our political system.
It follows that what Americans are as a people does stem in
large part from the circumstances shaping body and mind.
If a democratic nation sees in music nothing more than a passing diversion, it compromises its mandate and allows the individual to remain confined within the bounds set by circumstances. On the other hand, if a democratic nation shelters
an art-music world with narrow imagination and timid outreach,
or with scorn for and condescension toward the American public, it protracts an existence kept alive through artificial life-
support systems and not one that can join the mainstream of
American society. Such a nation nourishes an elitism unex-
plainable as the consequence of democratically determined
leadership, one redolent of European class distinctions and
snobbery, which have little to do with art or expressing what
should be the deepest aspirations of a liberated people.

Another theme of this book is that art music of the
past and in the present can touch far more men and women
than is now possible. Herbert Marcuse once wrote that this
sort of artistic expression is committed "to an emancipation of
sensibility [and] imagination." It "communicates truths not
communicable in any other language." It has universality
and "cannot be grounded in the world and world outlook of
a particular class, for art envisions concrete universal humanity

(<u>Menschlichkeit</u>), which no particular class can incorporate,"
that is to say, "the inexorable entanglement of joy and sorrow,
celebration and despair, Eros and Thanatos." Marcuse later
writes that an artistic composition intends to conjure up a
world "never and nowhere merely the given world of everyday reality, but neither is it a world of mere fantasy, illusion,
and so on. It contains nothing that does not also exist in the
given reality, the actions, thoughts, feelings, and dreams of
men and women, their potentialities and those of nature.
Nevertheless, the world of art is 'unreal' in the ordinary
sense of the word: it is a fictitious reality. But it is 'unreal' not because it is less, but because it is more as well as
qualitatively 'other' than the established reality. As fictitious
world, as illusion (<u>Schein</u>), "an artistic work can contain
"more truth than does everyday reality.... Only in the 'il-
lusory world' do things appear as what they are and what
they can be."[3]

In <u>The Necessity of Art</u>, Ernst Fischer states that although artistic functions may vary from one society and age
to another, there remains "an unchanging truth" in every
worthwhile artistic work, old and new. This enables listeners
of today to be moved by music from various past ages. What
matters, he says, is that a truly artistic composition is "a
<u>moment of humanity</u>" that has the "power to act beyond the
historical moment, to exercise an eternal fascination." Thinking along parallel lines, James De Priest, the Philadelphia-
born black conductor, speaks about the importance of art
music to American democracy and Afro-Americans living within
that democracy. He wants Afro-Americans to expand their
cultural horizons, and fears that the one-music-is-as-good-
as-another syndrome accepted by many modern Americans will
work to further ghettoize, not liberate, cultural expression
in his ethnic group. "Music," he states, "whether or not it
happens to be Western European, is for human beings. It
can be enlightening, enriching. It can be a meaningful encounter regardless of racial, ethnic, or national orientation.
But for Blacks in America, there is nothing that is alien in
classical music in terms of its essence. What one wants to
get in the soul of Beethoven is as easily perceived and is as
relevant to a Black human being as to a white human being
[sic]." He continues: "Because the <u>soul</u> of ... <u>any</u> composer
of <u>any</u> music speaks directly to the human heart. It pene-
trates through the layers of superficiality, all of the layers
of accumulated doctrine, all of the layers of acculturation....

The first experience is the human experience, which tran-
scends race, so that pain, happiness, depression, exultation--
all of the basic human emotions that have nothing to do with
race--are affected by music."[4]

I have already quoted many chroniclers of American
culture who warn that art music's place in American society
grows more and more ill defined, its approximate value to the
community less identifiable, and its contributions less appre-
ciated. Capitalist democracy, these writers say, has freed
the artist to be whatever he or she wants to be and enveloped
them in romantic loneliness, because it has come to regard
them as not important enough to be anything in particular
and something of an enpedestaled nuisance. They interact
more and more with institutions, not people, with institution-
alized precepts for identifying worthy musicians, precepts involving music per se and not its function in society. At the
same time, a majority of Americans regard the products they
offer as irrelevant luxuries that hardly any of them want to
buy.

This book has chronicled the despiritualization of the
nation owing to a faith in technocracy and business manage-
rialism. Political and economic leaders have promised and
sometimes we receive physical benefits for our faith. However, they do not promise and rarely do we receive spiritual
benefits. A pessimistic Suzi Gablik warns that because of
our profit-economy, and our scientific and technological orientation, we "cannot hope to produce art equal to that of
certain earlier forms of society--since capitalist production,
because it stresses the profit-making value of art and turns
it into a form of merchandise, is hostile to the spiritual production of art." Or, as Eric Hoffer states, capitalism can
produce abundance and release people's energies to strive in
the economic arena, but it "does not know how to cope with
people who are more interested in the quality of life than in
a high standard of living."[5] Nowhere does it establish the
criteria of knowledge and particular concerns that guide writers when they refer to the possible excellences of democratic
culture.

Earlier I said that equality means that possibility for
each American to achieve all of which he or she is capable,
the easing of the anomie and frustration that accompany an
awareness of personal limitations, and the nurturing of the

best in every individual so as to benefit him or her and so
society as a whole. If environment has diminished him or her
in mind and feeling, then an educational effort at identifica-
tional alteration is in order, one that encourages them to consider the goals and values of other reference groups. The
goal is cultural emergence through an exposure to the arts
where none had existed before and that seemed impossible
owing to one's background.

Repeated psychodramatic encounters to heighten sensitivity to organized sound and encouragement of visceral and
emotional response can aid in furthering subjective insight.
Mistaken is the presentation of music to novice listeners as
a language containing exact meanings of an intellectual sort.
Rather, they should be encouraged to sweep aside all ideas
of what they have been told art music is about. They should
be let loose to enjoy a work in any way they can. If enthus-
iastically and successfully conducted, such encounters do provide the escape velocity needed to break away from the gravi-
tational pull of ingrained and deadening habit.

A great majority of listeners, American and European,
never advance further in their appreciation of art music than
what has just been described. Nor need they go further.
I know this is heresy in music-education circles. Yet, I am
convinced, after speaking with many devoted music listeners,
that whether their love is Machaut, Vivaldi, Beethoven, Bartok, or Copland their understanding on the whole encompasses
this fundamentally instinctive stage of artistic meaning. Only
after the listener is won over and volunteers for further education should he or she proceed to contemplate the role of
repetition, variation, and contrast and their occurrence in
formal structural patterns.

Not enough educators work to lead people out of their
culturally circumscribed environments. No matter what the
stated public-policy positions about bettering students' spiritual condition, primary and secondary school actions point to
a different reality. Teaching staffs, whether they are conscious of it or not, encourage students to believe that education is primarily a ticket to better wages and more mate-
rially abundant lifestyles; music is a ticket to nowhere. Although there are some exceptions, a majority of colleges do
not do much better. James Reston, in 1985, wrote: "Since
high-school days they [young people] have been led to believe

that college is not a means to an understanding of the history
and poetry of life, but an employment agency, promising two
careers in every family and two cars in every garage." Economics and ways of making money are favorite academic subjects. He proclaims the late twentieth century to be "a period
of spiritual bewilderment" where, "in the name of religion"
Americans are encouraged "to confuse selfishness with self-
reliance" and "to concentrate on their own material well-being.
My kingdom come ... My will be done ... Hallowed be My
name...."6

Again and again, in the late eighties, we hear voices
warning Americans of their folly. We hear that the American
educational system graduates people who lack an awareness
of the rich variety of cultural works available to them. The
number of young people wishing education in the arts is down.
The graduates from our educational system do less reading,
less conversing, and have less patience for artistic compositions that do not immediately yield up their secrets.

As already pointed out in Chapter 3, if young people
are curious about art music, they often enroll in classes
granted meagre resources by administration, classes seen as
demanding little work or effort by faculty in other disciplines.
They may be conducted by music instructors some of whom
regard teaching as a boring task or an excuse for "hoopla,"
while others view worthwhile music education as only that
which leads to professionalism of some kind. However, the
professionalism espoused is not usually related to the world
outside the academe. When young people decide on entering
the music profession, too many educators continue to advise
them to think in terms of artistry and an artistic career as
soloists. Nevertheless, honesty demands that a warning be
attached to this advice, since less than a fifth of the graduates will ever become professional musicians, even on a part-
time basis--this in a decade that requires an increased investment of time, money, and effort in music study. At best educators give out muted cautions about genius being rare and
opportunity for professional advancement uncertain.

The close of the twentieth century has seen increased
bureaucratic interference with arts departments, not always
to their benefit. To save money, college administrators have
turned to hiring a host of part-time instructors, most of them
narrowly trained, to teach music. These teachers make difficul

a department's singleness of purpose. They hinder adoption
of a complete educational design defining objectives to be
reached. Administrators further bowdlerize instruction when
they employ student-enrollment figures and popularity, not
instructional integrity, quality, and soundness, as the primary basis for funding. Moreover, many administrative actions meant to benefit an entire institution can harm instruction in music. For example, in 1986, a New England university in the name of efficiency eliminated its separately housed
music library and record collection and dismissed its specially
trained arts librarians, instead mingling the music and arts
libraries with its general collection and putting both under
the supervision of general librarians. Most music scores and
some of the more important music books were deemed too expensive to lose and replace. Therefore their circulation was
restricted. Work-study students, not knowledgeable about
music but a source of cheap labor for the administration, were
in charge of finding and putting on recordings assigned for
class and general listening.

Educational mayhem has resulted. The university's music majors find that scores and books stored out of their sight
are difficult to take out of the general reading room. Non-
majors experience total frustration in requesting to hear recordings that are misplaced or misfiled. At best, they must
know the filing number and the title of the album, then reserve the recording a day beforehand in order to listen at
all (assuming it can be found). Membership in music classes
has dropped owing to the confusion.

Turning next to a closer look at our political situation,
the United States is a representative democracy. To function
properly, it requires enlightened elected leaders acting on
behalf of the entire electorate. It gives no legitimacy to self-
appointed or oligarchic leadership. People in power are expected to act in harmony with democratic principles. They
should remain sympathetic to the needs of their constituents
yet act for the good of the whole and outside the passions of
the moment. In order to insure the proper operation of a
representative democracy, these leaders must see to it that
no one sector, however dominant or convinced of its right-
ness, forces its taste on others. The alternative is cultural
totalitarianism.

There are politicians who speak of their worries over

the quality of American civilization and even vote some money
to the arts in order to sustain or improve that quality. However, they also stand ready to cut or eliminate appropriations.
Economizing in this fashion is most prevalent when the notion
prevails that the government should not intervene in the private lives of individuals and that acting in aid of the arts is
not within its province. Pruning the budget for the arts also
gains support in depressed economic times [but note the exception of the thirties and Roosevelt's New Deal], when the
jobless and hungry must draw succor from governmental agencies while tax receipts shrink.

Governmental actions are taken to regulate industry
when the citizen's bodily health and purchase of reliable material goods and services are involved. When one company
or small group of companies assume monopolistic positions
which stifle competition, reduce severely the variety of goods
or services offered for sale, and discourage a free exchange
of ideas, there is a history of federal and state governments
moving in to break up what is interpreted as a dominance
that acts contrary to the public good. Yet, the greatest circumspection attends the regulation of educational systems,
music industries, and public media that may adversely affect
the citizen's mental and spiritual health and restrict the availability of cultural goods and services.

For a start, public grants and tax-exemption for private
contributions to music associations should be contingent on
some democratization of boards of trustees and some accountability for music-programming decisions. Is there, for example,
an anti-American bias in the scheduling of music to be performed and in the hiring of orchestra directors? Such bias
has to be countered.

Moreover, if government truly cares about the public
good, it must also encourage greater diversity in what is sent
over the airwaves by means of meaningful regulations over
who deserve licenses. Situation comedies, crime stories, hos-
pital dramas, and music programs for adolescents are all right
so long as they are not the be-all and end-all of commercial
broadcasting. Art-music lovers do feel grateful to FM stations
specializing in "fine" music. But why is "fine" usually defined
as meaning works composed by Europeans before 1915? For
example, during one week of 1986, which I selected at random,
a Boston FM station that prides itself on the amount of art

music it broadcasts gave less than 3 percent of its radio time
to music by American composers (except during the two-hours
daily of "light" music), and less than 15 percent to music by
any 20th-century composers. Of the recordings heard, about
75 percent of them contained performances by European or Far
Eastern soloists and ensembles. Taped live performances by
two American opera companies, five American symphony orchestras, but no chamber groups were scheduled that week.
Not a single American or post-World War I composition was
played between them. One can legitimately ask: To what
extent did the featured American music associations and the
station manager have the well-being of American culture in
mind when they taped and he offered this limited fare?

Surveying the situation of American orchestras in 1986,
Erich Leinsdorf, an eminent orchestra conductor actively associated with several American symphony orchestras and opera
companies since 1937, writes of the dire necessity for reform
if art music is to survive. Repertory, he states, must expand
to include lesser works. Art-music groups cannot survive on
the continuous repetition of the best works by acknowledged
masters. Also, contemporary works should be selected for
performance that challenge and engage the interest of performers. The public will rarely get much from a work that musicians play politely and dutifully, or play while feeling bored
or alienated. The "star" system must be modified in order to
allow exposure to new native talent. A sophisticated publicity
effort must back performers and compositions unfamiliar to
the public.

Leinsdorf urges the appointment of directors of development who will advise on programs catering to diverse interests,
and who will devote thought to enlarging the perception and
increasing the curiosity of the general public. Such directors
need to link music to the other arts and to the various artistic styles, contemporary and historical. "Music," he points
out, "is not merely a sequence of sonorities. It is part of a
setting that has produced buildings, sculptures, paintings,
furniture, literature and more of considerable impact. The
musical repertory is an accumulation of several centuries from
several cultures. Fortunately, in this country our broad sympathies in music are in line with the whole concept of the
melting pot."

He ends by saying: "I place the need of a symphony

orchestra's repertory at 360 scores to be rotated over a three-
to five-year period. If, in a mindless quest for more listeners, the great popular symphonies of Tchaikovsky, Brahms,
and Beethoven are repeated to death, we can only expect a
situation already in evidence on TV, in which Beethoven's
'Für Elise' serves as background for selling Pizza Hut and a
shashlik-swinging conductorial caricature directs the final
page of the Ninth Symphony while some beef product is suggested for patronage."[7]

What Leinsdorf should have added is that a continuing
attempt must be made to determine as precisely as possible
people's attitudes toward art music and the art-music world.
Are educational efforts effective? Is there too much to-do
about "star" soloists, famous composers, and intellectual meaning in the writings about art music? I say this because few
music scholars and arts administrators take on the harder task
of studying music's functions within the American society.
What do ordinary people (not just the experts) say about music and why? What do they like or dislike in programming,
artistic personalities, performance procedures? What do they
suggest for strengthening cultural communication? Can associations do more to cultivate a broad constituency, not just
those who will give large sums of money but the greater number of music lovers who attend performances?

Men and women concerned over the situation of art music have to recognize that the way a music association programs and presents music determines and sets limits on the
nature of its constituency. Can reform in the former expand
and improve the quality of the latter? At times the deterrence
to attendance involves problems of parking, urban safety,
satellite dining establishments, and a miscellany of incidental
expenses. Is management on top of these problems? If a
subscriber fails to resubscribe, what attempt is made to learn
the real, not the surface, reason for this action? If an at-
tendee at a concert is not a subscriber, why did he or she
come, how did they react to the program, and why won't they
subscribe? If offered free tickets, a person refuses to go to
a performance, why the antagonism? Finding answers to these
questions is essential for art music's growth and development.
In those areas involving decisions of an artistic nature, the
inputs should have more the character of advisories than
commands.

Certainly, boards of trustees, especially as presently

constituted, and managements of orchestras and opera companies should not operate as they do now in making artistic decisions about the hiring of conductors and instrumental and vocal soloists. If a musician is to be engaged because, as they claim, he or she excels in matters of artistry, then the hidden agenda of popularity and money-draw should not be dominant considerations. For example, since superior artistic ability is the desideratum in selecting an orchestral director, then the position should be made open to all, including native Americans--who are now so often slighted. Whatever the criteria for selection, the process should allow at the beginning for a peer group of respected musicians to judge the relative merits of candidates by means of incognito taped performances. In particular, this procedure is meant to insure fairness for American conductors, who for so long now have been given short shrift by the major American performing ensembles. Furthermore, no conductor should be given the appointment unless willing to make a major commitment to the music organization, agreeing to devote full-time attention to its nurturing. Given the realities of contemporary American life, this includes not only socializing with high-society figures but also important but less glamorous activities like talking to concertgoers, visiting local schools and colleges, sitting down to political breakfasts, attending meetings of the city council and the state legislature, and sharing in community-group dinners. The conductor meets others to explain, listen, understand, ask what the music association can do for the community, and discover how the music association and its community can work together for a common cultural cause. Here, the native born and reared candidate has an obvious advantage over the foreign born and reared counterpart.

What one comes down to is art music's ability to maintain a capacity to grow and develop in an American environment. Can it further establish its legitimacy through connection with democratic concepts? Can its proponents demonstrate that its expressive forms and institutions are indeed true manifestations of their society--not because a few people say so but because most people see it to be so? Finally, can we produce political and business leaders infused with a sense of accountability for the state of culture in the United States? Will they help realize a richer democracy, one characterized by a greater cultural sophistication, refinement, and urbanity?

At the end, how many of us can say, as does Henry

James, in a letter sent to H. G. Wells in 1915: "I live, live intensely and am fed by life, and my value, whatever it may be, is my own kind of expression of that.   Art <u>makes</u> life, makes interest, makes importance ... and I know of no substitute whatever for the force and beauty of its process." The condition of art music in American society hinges on our reply.

Notes

1.   Willis H. Truitt, "Art for the People," in <u>The Arts in a Democratic Society</u>, ed. Alan Mann (Bowling Green, Ohio: Popular Press, 1977), p. 62.

2.   See, for example, Ernst Fischer, <u>The Necessity of Art</u>, trans. Anna Bostock (London: Penguin, 1978), pp. 7-8.

3.   Herbert Marcuse, <u>The Aesthetic Dimension</u> (Boston: Beacon, 1978), pp. 9-10, 16, 54.

4.   Ibid., p. 11; Abdul, <u>Blacks in Classical Music</u>, pp. 204-205.

5.   Gablik, <u>Has Modernism Failed?</u>, p. 29; Eric Hoffer, <u>In Our Time</u> (New York: Morrow Quill, 1977), p. 40.

6.   James Reston, "The Class of 1985," <u>New York Times</u>, 19 May 1985, section 4, p. 21.

7.   Erich Leinsdorf, "One Conductor's Prescription for Musical Survival," <u>New York Times</u>, 16 March 1986, section 2, pp. 1, 6.

SELECTIVE BIBLIOGRAPHY OF WORKS CONSULTED

Abdul, Raoul. Blacks in Classical Music. New York: Dodd, Mead, 1977.

Abraham, Gerald. The Tradition of Western Music. Berkeley: University of California Press, 1974.

Ames, Amyas. "The Political Power of the Arts." Music Journal, September 1970, pp. 36-37.

Ardoin, John. "The American Composer: Underdog of American Orchestras." Musical America, June 1961, pp. 12-13, 58-59.

Arian, Edward. "The San Diego Symphony Turnaround." Symphony Magazine, June/July 1984, pp. 60-63, 143.

The Arts in a Democratic Society, see Mann, Dennis Alan, ed.

The Arts on Campus, see Mahoney, Margaret, ed.

Barri, Richard. "1969: The Year of the Edifice Complex." Music Journal Annual, (1969): pp. 45-46.

_____. "Opera for the People." Music Journal, October 1972, pp. 16-17, 72.

Barzun, Jacques. Critical Questions. Edited by Bea Friedland. Chicago: University of Chicago Press, 1982.

_____. Human Freedom, rev. ed. Philadelphia: Lippincott, 1964.

_____. "Scholarship Versus Culture." Atlantic, November 1984, pp. 93-104.

Bass, Judy. "Keys to Success." Boston, August 1983, pp. 84-87.

Baumol, William J., and Bowen, William G. Performing Arts--The Economic Dilemma. New York: Twentieth Century Fund, 1966.

Baxter, Robert. "Sergiu Celibidache at Curtis." Symphony Magazine, June/July 1984, pp. 77-80.

Becker, Ernest. Escape from Evil. New York: Free Press, 1975.

Becker, Howard S. Art Worlds. Berkeley: University of California Press, 1982.

Belt, Byron. "For the Record." Music Journal, October 1976, pp. 6, 49.

Bennett, Myron. "Music as Furniture." High Fidelity, February 1972, pp. 64-66.

Berger, Bennett M. Looking for America. Englewood Cliffs, N.J.: Prentice-Hall, 1971.

Berman, Ronald. America in the Sixties. New York: Free Press, 1968.

Bing, Rudolf. 5000 Nights at the Opera. Garden City, N.Y.: Doubleday, 1972.

Bly, Robert. "In Search of an American Muse." New York Times Book Review, 22 January 1984, pp. 1, 29.

Bond, Victoria. "New Music's Scholarly Friend: A Talk with Joan Peyser." Symphony Magazine, February/March 1983, pp. 28-29, 65-66.

Bookspan, Martin. "Who Pays the Piper?" Ovations, February 1983, pp. 19, 36.

Bookspan, Martin, and Yockey, Ross. Zubin. New York: Harper & Row, 1978.

Bowen, Jean. "Women in Music." Musical America, August 1974, p. 20.

Brown, Ina Corinne. Understanding Other Cultures. Englewood Cliffs, N.J.: Prentice-Hall, 1963.

Brustein, Robert. The Culture Watch: Essays on Theater and Society, 1969-1974. New York: Knopf, 1975.

_____. Revolution as Theater. New York: Liveright, 1971.

Buck, Percy C. Psychology for Musicians. London: Oxford University Press, 1944.

Burton, Bob. "Serious Music--U.S.A." Music Journal, January 1965, p. 76.

Carr, Jay. "Tragedy Doesn't Fit Us--We've Become Too Small." Boston Globe, 4 March 1984, section B, pp. 1, 9.

Carrington, Mark. "6 Orchestras Adopt a Composer." Symphony Magazine, February/March 1983, pp. 224-26, 62-63.

Caulfield, Robert L. "The Qualities of Leadership." Symphony Magazine, August/September 1982, pp. 51-53.

Chancellor, John. "Melodic Lines and Bottom Lines." Symphony Magazine, August/September 1983, pp. 19-22.

Chapin, Schuyler. Musical Chairs. New York: Putnam, 1977.

Chasins, Abram. "Making It in Music." Musical America, April 1981, pp. 22-23.

_____. Music at the Crossroads. New York: Macmillan, 1972.

Chute, James. "Publish or Perish?" Musical America, January 1982, pp. 18-21.

Cobb, Nathan. "Television Music." Boston Globe, 7 February 1986, pp. 71, 73.

Connor, Frank Hayden. "The Publisher Serves Education." Music Journal, September 1966, p. 64.

Cook, Eugene. "Penderecki: The Polish Question--and Others." Music Journal, February 1977, pp. 8-10, 42.

Corleonis, Adrian. "Ferruccio Busoni." Fanfare, January/February 1984, pp. 90-116.

Crawford, Richard. American Studies and American Musicology. I.S.A.M. Monographs: Number 4. Brooklyn: Institute for Studies in American Music, 1975.

Crozier, Michel. The Trouble with America. Translated by Peter Heinegg. Berkeley: University of California Press, 1984.

Crutchfield, Will. "Orchestras in the Age of Jet-Set Sound." New York Times, 6 January 1985, section 2, pp. 1, 19.

Culture for the Millions?, see Jacobs, Norman, ed.

Cumming, Robert. "Total War." Music Journal Annual (1962), pp. 9, 74-75.

Cunningham, Carl. "How Black Is Black?" Musical America, January 1975, pp. 24-26.

Curtin, Phyllis. "Pioneering for New Music." Music Journal, October 1961, pp. 55-53, 86-87.

Dahlhaus, Carl. Analysis and Value Judgment. Translated by Siegmund Levarie. New York: Pendragon, 1983. Originally published
in 1970, as Analyse und Werturteil.

Davies, John Booth. The Psychology of Music. Stanford, Calif.:
Stanford University Press, 1978.

Davis, Clive, with Willwerth, James. Clife: Inside the Record Business. New York: Morrow, 1975.

DeMott, Benjamin. Surviving the 70's. New York: Dutton, 1971.

Dettmer, Roger. "The State of U.S. Conductors." Fanfare, Septem-
ber/October 1982, pp. 85-96, 506-507.

Dickson, Harry Ellis. "Gentlemen, More Dolce Please!." Boston:
Beacon, 1969.

Dickstein, Morris. Gates of Eden: American Culture in the Sixties.
New York: Basic Books, 1977.

Dorian, Frederick. Commitment to Culture. Pittsburgh: University
of Pittsburgh Press, 1964.

Dreyfus, Laurence. "Early Music Defended Against Its Devotees."
Musical Quarterly 69 (1983): pp. 297-322.

Dyer, Richard. "Bruce Crawford Knows He Can Manage the Met."
Boston Globe, 28 October 1984, section A, p. 11.

_____. "Curtin Call." Boston Globe Magazine, 18 March 1984,
pp. 9, 18-22, 27-30, 35-36.

_____. "For Free-Lance Musicians, Boston Is On and Off Key."
Boston Globe, 27 March 1983, section A, pp. 1, 8.

_____. "Keeping Time." Boston Globe Magazine, 22 May 1983,
pp. 10, 50, 54-64.

Eaton, Quaintance. "The Year on Legislation." Music Journal Annual (1963), pp. 58, 60.

_____. "Women Come Into Their Own in Our Orchestras." Mus-
ical America, 15 February 1955, pp. 30, 179, 183.

Edelman, Ricahrd. "New Directions for Opera." Music Journal,
June 1966, pp. 29-30, 56.

Ehle, Robert C. "The Evolution of Musical Style." American Music
Teacher, January 1983, pp. 20, 22-23.

English, John W. Criticizing the Critics. New York: Hastings
    House, 1979.

Farnsworth, Paul R. The Social Psychology of Music. New York:
    Dryden, 1958.

Fawcett, Edmund, and Thomas, Tony. The American Condition. New
    York: Harper & Row, 1982.

Finn, Jr., Chester E. "Colleges Must Heal Themselves." Boston
    Globe, 19 February 1985, p. 15.

Fischer, Ernst. The Necessity of Art. Translated by Anna Bostock.
    London: Penguin, 1978. [Originally published in 1959.]

Fisher, Charles M. "The Performing Arts in Akademia." Music Jour-
    nal, April 1968, pp. 36-37, 66-67.

Fleischmann, Ernest. "Who Runs Our Orchestras and Who Should?"
    High Fidelity, January 1969, pp. 59-62.

Fleming, Shirley. "The Case of the Disappearing Strings." High
    Fidelity, September 1964, pp. 43-46.

Ford, Thomas R., ed. The Revolutionary Theme in Contemporary
    America. Lexington: University of Kentucky Press, 1965.

Fowler, Charles B. "The Arts in Our High Schools: New Data."
    Musical America, January 1985, pp. 2, 35-37.

_____. "ARTS Program Supports Young Talent." Musical America,
    May 1983, pp. 11-13, 38-39.

_____. "Classical Music Is Singing the Blues." Musical America,
    June 1985, pp. 12-46.

_____. "Deciding What to Teach." Musical America, October
    1983, pp. 12-13.

_____. "Musical Achievement--Good News and Bad." Musical
    America, May 1982, pp. 12, 24.

_____. "Reaching the Kids: How Symphonies Do It." Musical
    America, February 1985, pp. 11-13, 15.

Francis, John W. "Classical Video: 2. Opera." Fanfare, September/
    October 1984, pp. 98-102.

Frank, Mortimer H. "Conversations with Lorin Maazel." Fanfare,
    January/February 1985, pp. 109-115.

Freedman, Samuel G. "New Fund for the Arts Gets a Tryout in Boston." New York Times, 4 August 1985, p. 52.

Fretwell, Dorrie S. "Let the Ladies Do It." Musical America, September 1975, pp. 14-16.

Fromm, Erich. To Have or To Be?. New York: Bantam, 1981.

Furlong, William Barry. Season with Solti. New York: Macmillan, 1974.

Gablik, Suzi. Has Modernism Failed?. New York: Thames & Hudson, 1984.

Gagne, Cole, and Caras, Tracy. Soundpieces: Interviews with American Composers. Metuchen, N.J.: Scarecrow, 1982.

Gallehugh, Linda K. "Singing a New Song." Horizons, July/August 1983, pp. 49-51.

Giannini, Vera. "Sherrill Milnes." Ovation, February 1982, pp. 13-15.

Gilson, Etienne. Painting and Reality. Cleveland: World, 1959.

Glueck, Grace. "Soap Opera, Yes, But Not Without Its Appeal." New York Times, 12 February 1984, section 2, pp. 33, 35.

Gold, Gerald. "Classics Head for a Mass Market." New York Times, 1 May 1983, section 2, pp. 23-24.

Goldberg, Joe. "To Be Young and a Concert Pianist." New York Times Magazine, 18 October 1981, pp. 82-91.

Goldin, Milton. The Music Merchants. Toronto: Macmillan, 1969.

Goodman, Walter. "In Search of a Policy for Arts Funding." New York Times, 22 July 1984, section 2, p. 24.

Gordon, Suzanne. Lonely in America. New York: Simon & Schuster, 1976.

Gottfried, Martin. A Theater Divided. Boston: Little, Brown, 1969.

Greckel, W. C. "Music Misses the Majority." Music Journal, December 1972, pp. 20-21, 32, 51-55, 67, 70-72.

Green, Harris. "That Subscription Crowd Must Go!" New York Times, 7 June 1970, section 2, p. 13.

Gross, Bertram M., ed. A Great Society? New York: Basic, 1968.

Guinn, John. "Crisis in Detroit." Musical America, January 1982, pp. 32-35.

Gunzenhauser, Stephen. "Are American Conductors Really Victims of Discrimination?" Ovation, May 1982, pp. 7, 36.

Guthrie, Robert K. "The Financial Crisis in Classical Music." Ovation, February 1982, pp. 17-20.

Hall, Barbara. "Rockefeller Speaks Out for Arts Education." Boston Globe, 15 January 1984, pp. 52-53.

Hanson, Howard. "Cultural Challenge." Music Journal, January 1961, pp. 4-5, 69.

_____. "A Plea for the Arts." Music Journal, November 1963, pp. 25, 58-61.

Harris, Dale. "100 Years at the Metropolitan Opera." Ovation, September 1983, pp. 14-18.

Harris, Marvin. America Now: The Anthropology of a Changing Culture. New York: Simon & Schuster, 1981.

Hart, Philip. "Art Surveys: To See Ourselves." Musical America, August 1974, pp. 15-17.

_____. Conductors. New York: Scribner's Sons, 1979.

_____. Orpheus in the New World. New York: Norton, 1973.

_____. "The Symphonic Strike Season." Saturday Review, 26 September 1970, pp. 47-49, 55.

Haskell, Harry. "A Symphony Orchestra Dies at 50." Musical America, December 1982, pp. 26-28.

Heckscher, August. "Government and the Arts." Music Journal, March 1963, pp. 17, 82-83.

Hecsh, Herbert. "The Year of the Edifice Complex." Music Journal, September 1965, pp. 48, 60, 95.

Henahan, Donal. "How Should Conductors Be Judged?" New York Times, section 2, pp. 1, 19.

_____. "Must Symphony Concerts and Television Be Incompatible?" New York Times, 20 February 1983, section 2, pp. 21, 24.

_____. "One Tiresome Extreme May Breed Another." New York Times, 21 January 1984, section 2, p. 19.

Hendrickson, Walter B. "Speak Up for the Amateur!" Music Journal, April 1968, pp. 34, 65-66.

Heylbut, Rose. "Brainwash or Back Talk?" Music Journal Annual (1967), pp. 36, 37, 58, 62, 65.

Heimenz, Jack. "The Death of CBS Cable, and Other Ills." Musical America, February 1983, pp. 11-12.

Hodgson, Godfrey. America in Our Time. New York: Random House, 1976.

Hoffa, Harlan. "On Education." Musical America, September 1974, pp. 14-15, 27, 40.

Hoffer, Eric. In Our Time. New York: Morrow Quill, 1977.

Holland, Bernard. "In Praise of Early Music." New York Times Magazine, 22 May 1983, pp. 64-65, 79, 82, 92.

_____. "It Takes More Than Talent to Build a Musical Career." New York Times, 19 February 1984, section 2, pp. 1, 19.

_____. "Let There Be Music--But Don't Forget the Fee." New York Times, 8 April 1984, section 2, pp. 1, 34.

Horne, Marilyn, with Scovell, Jane. Marilyn Horne: My Life. New York: Atheneum, 1983.

Hughes, Robert. "On Art and Money." New York Review of Books, 6 December 1984, pp. 20-27.

Hume, Paul. "A Tale of Two Cities' Opera Companies." Ovation, September 1984, pp. 8-9, 29-30, 62.

Jackson, C.D. "The Quality of Life in This Technological Age." Music Journal, January 1964, pp. 11-12, 86.

Jacob, Norman, ed. Culture for the Millions? Boston: Beacon, 1964.

Jepson, Barbara. "After the Pulitzer, Then What?" New York Times, 28 October 1984, section 2, pp. 23-24.

_____. "How Musicians and Managers Coexist." New York Times, 18 July 1982, section 2, pp. 17, 20.

_____. "You've Come a Long Way: Women in Symphony Orchestras." Music Journal, December 1977, pp. 13-16.

Johnston, Edgar G., ed. Preserving Human Values in an Age of Technology. Detroit: Wayne State University Press, 1961.

Kaplan, Max. "Music and Mass Culture." Music Journal, March 1960,
pp. 20-21, 150.

_____. "Sociology of the Musical Audience." Music Journal, Jan-
uary 1961, pp. 60-61, 110.

Kerr, Walter. The Decline of Pleasure. New York: Simon & Schuster, 1962.

Keyes, Ralph. We, the Lonely People. New York: Harper & Row,
1973.

Khrennikov, Tikhon, and Shostakovich, Dmitri. "Impressions of
American Music." Music Journal, March 1960, pp. 10-11, 90.

Koplewitz, Laura. "From Pen to Podium with New Music." Symphony
Magazine, February/March 1982, pp. 9-13, 64-65.

_____. "Joan Tower: Building Bridges for New Music." Sym-
phony Magazine, June/July 1983, pp. 36-40.

Kouwenhoven, John A. The Arts in Modern American Civilization.
New York: Norton, 1967.

_____. Half a Truth Is Better Than None. Chicago: University
of Chicago Press, 1982.

Kozinn, Allan. "The American Composers Orchestra." Symphony
Magazine, June/July 1983, pp. 23-27.

_____. "Record Quality 1978." Music Journal, March 1978, pp.
9-13.

Kozma, Tibor. "Music vs The Majority." Music Journal, March 1963,
pp. 50, 86, 101.

Kramer, Hilton. "A Yearning for 'Normalcy'--The Current Backlash
in the Arts." New York Times, 23 May 1976, section 2, pp. 1,
25.

Kreitler, Hans, and Kreitler, Shulamith. Psychology of the Arts.
Durham, N.C.: Duke University Press, 1972.

Kupferberg, Herbert. Those Fabulous Philadelphians. New York:
Scribner's Sons, 1969.

La Barbara, Joan. "CRI's Historic Thirty Years." Musical America,
September 1985, pp. 16-17.

Larson, Gary O. The Reluctant Patron: The United States Government and The Arts, 1943-1965. Philadelphia: University of Pennsylvania Press, 1983.

Lasch, Christopher. The Culture of Narcissism. New York: Warner, 1979.

Lees, Gene. "The Dotage of American Radio." High Fidelity, January 1978, pp. 12, 16, 29.

Lehmann, Phyllis. "Women in Orchestras." Symphony Magazine,
December 1982, pp. 11-15, 56-57, 60.

Leinsdorf, Erich. Cadenza. Boston: Houghton Mifflin, 1976.

_____. "The Confused Status of Music." Music Journal, April
1965, pp. 37, 76-78.

_____. "My Life with the Boston Symphony." Musical America,
May 1976, pp. 12-13.

_____. "One Conductor's Prescription for Musical Survival."
New York Times, 16 March 1986, section 2, pp. 1, 6.

Levine, Joseph. "The Vanishing Musician." Music Journal, March
1962, pp. 38-40, 76.

Lipman, Samuel. The House of Music. Boston: Godine, 1984.

_____. Music After Modernism. New York: Basic Books, 1979.

_____. "U.S. Orchestras Have Problems at the Podium." Boston
Globe, 10 July 1983, section A, pp. 31, 38.

Lippard, Lucy R. Overlay. New York: Pantheon, 1983.

Lloyd, David. "A Singer's Opera Company." Music Journal, June
1966, pp. 17, 50-51.

Lowens, Irving. "Kennedy Center: The First Five Years." Musical
America, February 1977, pp. 16-17.

Lowery, W. McNeil. "The Foundation and the Arts." Music Journal,
February 1964, pp. 48-51, 92-93.

_____. "Music and the Ford Foundation." Music Journal, April
1961, pp. 50-52.

Lundin, Robert W. An Objective Psychology of Music, 2nd ed. New
York: Ronald, 1967.

Maazel, Lorin. "Homogenized Art Is Tasteless." Music Journal, October 1962, pp. 36, 78.

McCathren, Don. "Programming Is An Art." Music Journal, March
1963, pp. 55, 68, 98.

McMullen, Roy. Art, Affluence, and Alienation: The Fine Arts To-
    day. New York: Praeger, 1968.

Mahoney, Margaret, ed. The Arts on Campus: The Necessity for
    Change. Greenwich, Conn.: Graphic Society, 1970.

Mann, Dennis Alan, ed. The Arts in a Democratic Society. Bowling
    Green, Ohio: Bowling Green University Popular Press, 1977.

Marcuse, Herbert. The Aesthetic Dimension. Boston: Beacon, 1978.

Martin, B. F. "Elmar Oliviera." Ovation, October 1984, pp. 22-25.

Mayer, Martin. "The Strikes and the Future." Musical America,
    May 1974, pp. 18-21.

Meyer, Leonard B. Music, The Arts, and Ideas. Chicago: Univer-
    sity of Chicago Press, 1967.

Miller, Douglas T., and Nowak, Marion. The Fifties. Garden City,
    N.Y.: Doubleday, 1977.

Miller, Margo. "Redgrave Awarded $100,000 in Suit Against the
    BSO." Boston Globe, 10 November 1984, pp. 1, 16.

Monson, Karen. "The Anchorage Civic Opera." Musical America,
    March 1981, pp. 36-37.

_____. "Emanuel Ax." Ovation, April 1955, pp. 8-12.

Montagu, Ashley, and Matson, Floyd. The Dehumanization of Man.
    New York: McGraw-Hill, 1983.

Mooney, Michael M. The Ministry of Culture. New York: Wyndham,
    1980.

Moor, Paul. "Our Operatic Expatriates." High Fidelity, November
    1960, pp. 50-52.

_____. "What Became of Joyce Flissler?" Musical America, May
1979, pp. 23-24.

Morgan, Robert P. "The New Pluralism." High Fidelity, March 1981,
    pp. 56-60.

Moriarty, John. "A Boon for Opera: The Santa Fe Apprentice."
    Music Journal, October 1964, pp. 28-29, 66-67.

Neil, J. Meredith. Toward a National Taste. Honolulu: University
    Press of Hawaii, 1975.

Netzer, Dick. The Subsidized Muse: Public Support for the Arts
in the United States. Cambridge, England: Cambridge University Press, 1978.

O'Connor, John J. "Strike Up the Band (and the Chamber Group)."
New York Times, 25 April 1971, section 2, p. 15.

"Orchestras and Recording: A Panel." Fanfare, January/February
1981, pp. 22-37, 251-252.

Osborne, Conrad L. "Does Opera Have a Future?" High Fidelity,
March 1970, pp. 60-65, 101.

Page, Tim. "For Some Gifted Musicians Freelancing Offers Career."
New York Times, 15 January 1984, p. 36.

Pash, Donald. "What's Wrong with Public Broadcasting." Musical
America, October 1977, pp. 19-21.

The Performing Arts: Problems and Prospects. Rockefeller Panel
Report on the Future of Theatre, Dance, Music in America. New
York: McGraw-Hill, 1965.

Per-Lee, Myra. "Broadcasting--Orchestras on the Air." Symphony
News, June 1979, pp. 21-24, 90.

Phillips, Harvey E. "The American Composers Orchestra." Musical
America, February 1981, pp. 32-33.

Plaskin, Glenn. Horowitz. New York: Morrow, 1983.

Porter, Andrew. A Musical Season. New York: Viking, 1974.

Reeves, Richard. American Journey. New York: Simon & Schuster,
1982.

Rich, Alan. "The Training of Conductors." Horizon, January 1980,
pp. 58-62.

Risenhoover, Morris, and Blackburn, Robert T. Artists As Professors. Urbana: University of Illinois Press, 1976.

Rizzo, Sheila. "An Interview with Eve Queler." Fanfare, January/
February 1983, pp. 86-88.

Rochberg, George. "Contemporary Music in an Affluent Society."
Music Journal, February 1968, pp. 54, 71-72.

Rockefeller, 3rd., John D. "The Arts and the Community." Music
Journal, September 1963, pp. 27, 86-88.

Rockwell, John. All American Music. New York: Knopf, 1983.

_____. "At 25, Lincoln Center Makes Plans for a Lively Future."
New York Times, 21 October 1984, section 2, pp. 1, 19.

_____. "Busy Activity on the 'Early Music' Front." New York
Times, 16 November 1980, section 2, pp. 17, 24.

_____. "City Opera Tries a Bold New Tack." New York Times,
4 March 1984, section 2, pp. 1, 19.

Roos, Jim. "Music at Michigan State--Are the Students with It?"
Musical America, August 1968, pp. 6-7, 32.

Rosenberg, Bernard, and White, David Manning, eds. Mass Culture
Revisited. New York: Van Nostrand Reinhold, 1971.

Rothstein, Edward. "How Important Is the Music Debut?" New York
Times, 2 January 1983, section 2, pp. 1, 23.

Roussel, Hubert. The Houston Symphony Orchestra, 1913-1971.
Austin: University of Texas Press, 1972.

Sachs, David. "CRI at 30." Fanfare, September/October 1984, pp.
146-150.

Salmaggi, Guido G. "So You Want to Be an Impressario?" Music
Journal, March 1963, pp. 46, 48.

Salmans, Sandra. "Big Business Tightens Its Arts Budget." New
York Times, 20 February 1983, section 2, pp. 1, 27.

Sanders, Linda. "When a Classical Station Goes Modern." New York
Times, 13 February 1983, section 2, pp. 33, 41.

Schickel, Richard. Intimate Strangers: The Culture of Celebrity.
Garden City, N.Y.: Doubleday, 1985.

Schmid, Paul B. "Conducting an Amateur Orchestra." Symphony
Magazine, June/July 1984, p. 10.

Schonberg, Harold C. "Audiences Hot, Audiences Cold." New York
Times, 11 February 1968, section 2, p. 15.

_____. "Can Composers Regain Their Audiences?" New York
Times, 4 December 1977, section 2, pp. 1, 15.

_____. "A Critic Reflects on 44 Years in the Business." New
York Times, 6 July 1980, section 2, pp. 13-14.

_____. "Earl Wild's 'Defiantly Kitsch' Celebration." New York
Times, 25 October 1981, section 2, pp. 21, 24.

_____. Facing the Music. New York: Summit, 1981.

_____. "Have Cultural Centers Benefited the Arts?" New York Times, 11 July 1983, section 2, pp. 1, 26.

Schuman, William. "The Malady Lingers On." Music Journal Annual (1968), pp. 30-32, 99-101.

Scott, Mel. The States and the Arts. Berkeley: University of California Institute of Governmental Studies, 1971.

Seltzer, George. The Professional Symphony Orchestra in the United States. Metuchen, N.J.: Scarecrow, 1975.

Sennett, Richard. The Fall of Public Man. New York: Vintage, 1978.

Shanet, Howard. Philharmonic: A History of New York's Orchestra. Garden City, N.Y.: Doubleday, 1975.

Siegel, Ed. "Adapting Stage Events to Television." Boston Globe, 24 April 1983, section B, pp. 33, 45.

Sills, Beverly. Bubbles. New York: Grosset & Dunlap, 1981.

Skornia, Harry J. Television and Society. New York: McGraw-Hill, 1965.

Small, Christopher. Music, Society, Education. London: Calder, 1977.

Smith, Patrick J. "Music Book Publication--A Vicious Circle." Musical Review, October 1968, pp. 12-13.

Smothers, Ronald. "His 'Maestro' Was Hard Won." New York Times, 5 November 1976, p. 22.

Snyder, Louis. Community of Sound: The Boston Symphony and Its World of Players. Boston: Beacon, 1979.

Somer, Hilder. "The Market for Modern Music." Music Journal, January 1961, pp. 32, 115.

Southern, Eileen. The Music of Black Americans. New York: Norton, 1971.

Stevens, Nancy. "Young Audiences Is Twenty-Five." Musical America, February 1977, pp. 12-15.

Taper, Bernard. The Arts in Boston. Cambridge: Harvard University Press, 1970.

Tassel, Jane. "Gunther Schuller." Ovation, November 1985, pp. 23-26.

_____. "Pros and Concerts." Boston Magazine, October 1983, pp. 113-119.

Tauhert, Rudolph. "Publishers Cater to Needs." Music Journal, September 1966, pp. 33, 83.

Tawa, Nicholas E. Serenading the Reluctant Eagle. New York: Schirmer, 1984.

Taylor, Fannie. "Audiences--What's Happened to Them?" Musical America, December 1970, pp. 10-12, 31.

Taylor, Jerry. "Dershowitz, B'nai B'rith Hail Redgrave Decision." Boston Globe, 10 November 1984, p. 16.

Temianka, Henri. Facing the Music. New York: McKay, 1973.

Tingsten, Herbert. The Problem of Democracy. Totowa, N.J.: Bedminster, 1965.

Toffler, Alvin. The Culture Consumers. New York: Random House, 1973.

_____. Future Shock. New York: Random House, 1970.

Tregellas, Patricia. "The Arts Are Polluted." Music Journal, October 1972, pp. 22-23.

Trilling, Lionel. The Last Decade. Edited by Diana Trilling. New York: Harcourt Brace Jovanovich, 1979.

Vate, Nancy Van de. "The National Endowment Playing Favorites?" Musical America, April 1976, pp. 14, 16.

Waleson, Heidi. "Orchestra Conducting Was What She Always Wanted." New York Times, 20 February 1983, section 2, pp. 21, 32.

_____. "Paying the Piper: Orchestras on the Road." Symphony Magazine, June/July 1984, pp. 17-22.

Weber, William. Music and the Middle Class. New York: Holmes & Meier, 1975.

Wechsler, Bert. "America's Own State Radio." Music Journal, April 1981, pp. 16-17.

Weiss, Allen. "Coming to You Alive." Music Journal, May 1976, pp. 20-21, 40-41.

Williams, Jr., Robin M. American Society, 3rd ed. New York: Knopf, 1970.

Williamson, Alix. "The Problematic Art of the Musical Publicist." Music Journal, January 1965, pp. 78-85.

Winship, Frederick. "45% of Nation's Opera Companies Report Red Ink." Boston Globe, 3 November 1984, p. 11.

Wiser, John D. "IBR Makes Things Happen." Fanfare, May/June 1983, pp. 67-68, 315.

Yankelovich, Daniel. New Rules. New York: Bantam, 1982.

Zakariasen, Bill. "Marilyn Horne." Ovation, July 1983, pp. 12-15, 44.

Zinar, Ruth. "Musical Taste of Adolescents." Music Journal, January 1973, pp. 10-11, 44-45, 53.

Zoll, Donald Atwell. The Twentieth Century Mind. Baton Rouge: Louisiana State University Press, 1967.

INDEX

271